Cisco Certified Support Technician (CCST) IT Support 100-140 Official Cert Guide

Companion Website and Pearson Test Prep Access Code

Access interactive study tools on this book's companion website, including practice test software, review exercises, Key Term flash card application, a study planner, and more!

To access the companion website, simply follow these steps:

1. Go to www.ciscopress.com/register.

2. Enter the print book ISBN: **9780135403921**.

3. Answer the security question to validate your purchase.

4. Go to your account page.

5. Click on the **Registered Products** tab.

6. Under the book listing, click on the **Access Bonus Content** link.

Note that you must register your book by December 31, 2028 to access the available bonus content.

When you register your book, your Pearson Test Prep practice test access code will automatically be populated with the book listing under the Registered Products tab. You will need this code to access the practice test that comes with this book. You can redeem the code at **PearsonTestPrep.com**. Simply choose Pearson IT Certification as your product group and log into the site with the same credentials you used to register your book. Click the **Activate New Product** button and enter the access code. More detailed instructions on how to redeem your access code for both the online and desktop versions can be found on the companion website.

If you have any issues accessing the companion website or obtaining your Pearson Test Prep practice test access code, you can contact our support team by going to **pearsonitp.echelp.org**.

T0355834

Cisco Certified Support Technician (CCST) IT Support

100-140

Official Cert Guide

MARK SMITH

DAVID BAYNE

JOHN PICKARD

Cisco Press

iv   Cisco Certified Support Technician (CCST) IT Support 100-140 Official Cert Guide

Cisco Certified Support Technician (CCST) IT Support 100-140 Official Cert Guide

Mark Smith, David Bayne, and John Pickard

Copyright © 2025 Cisco Systems, Inc.

Published by:
Cisco Press
Hoboken, New Jersey

All rights reserved. This publication is protected by copyright, and permission must be obtained from the publisher prior to any prohibited reproduction, storage in a retrieval system, or transmission in any form or by any means, electronic, mechanical, photocopying, recording, or likewise. For information regarding permissions, request forms, and the appropriate contacts within the Pearson Education Global Rights & Permissions Department, please visit https://www.pearson.com/global-permission-granting.html.

No patent liability is assumed with respect to the use of the information contained herein. Although every precaution has been taken in the preparation of this book, the publisher and author assume no responsibility for errors or omissions. Nor is any liability assumed for damages resulting from the use of the information contained herein.

1 2024

Library of Congress Control Number is on file.

ISBN-13: 978-0-13-540392-1

ISBN-10: 0-13-540392-8

Warning and Disclaimer

This book is designed to provide information about the Cisco Certified Support Technician (CCST) IT Support 100-140 exam. Every effort has been made to make this book as complete and as accurate as possible, but no warranty or fitness is implied.

The information is provided on an "as is" basis. The authors, Cisco Press, and Cisco Systems, Inc. shall have neither liability nor responsibility to any person or entity with respect to any loss or damages arising from the information contained in this book or from the use of the discs or programs that may accompany it.

The opinions expressed in this book belong to the author and are not necessarily those of Cisco Systems, Inc.

Please contact us with concerns about any potential bias at https://www.pearson.com/report-bias.html.

Trademark Acknowledgments

All terms mentioned in this book that are known to be trademarks or service marks have been appropriately capitalized. Cisco Press or Cisco Systems, Inc., cannot attest to the accuracy of this information. Use of a term in this book should not be regarded as affecting the validity of any trademark or service mark.

All terms mentioned in this book that are known to be trademarks or service marks have been appropriately capitalized. Cisco Press cannot attest to the accuracy of this information. Use of a term in this book should not be regarded as affecting the validity of any trademark or service mark.

Microsoft and/or its respective suppliers make no representations about the suitability of the information contained in the documents and related graphics published as part of the services for any purpose. All such documents and related graphics are provided "as is" without warranty of any kind. Microsoft and/or its respective suppliers hereby disclaim all warranties and conditions with regard to this information, including all warranties and conditions of merchantability, whether express, implied or statutory, fitness for a particular purpose, title and non-infringement. In no event shall Microsoft and/or its respective suppliers be liable for any special, indirect or consequential damages or any damages whatsoever resulting from loss of use, data or profits, whether in an action of contract, negligence or other tortious action, arising out of or in connection with the use or performance of information available from the services.

The documents and related graphics contained herein could include technical inaccuracies or typographical errors. Changes are periodically added to the information herein. Microsoft and/or its respective suppliers may make improvements and/or changes in the product(s) and/or the program(s) described herein at any time. Partial screenshots may be viewed in full within the software version specified.

Microsoft® and Windows® are registered trademarks of the Microsoft Corporation in the U.S.A. and other countries. Screenshots and icons reprinted with permission from the Microsoft Corporation. This book is not sponsored or endorsed by or affiliated with the Microsoft Corporation.

Feedback Information

At Cisco Press, our goal is to create in-depth technical books of the highest quality and value. Each book is crafted with care and precision, undergoing rigorous development that involves the unique expertise of members from the professional technical community.

Readers' feedback is a natural continuation of this process. If you have any comments regarding how we could improve the quality of this book, or otherwise alter it to better suit your needs, you can contact us through email at feedback@ciscopress.com. Please make sure to include the book title and ISBN in your message.

We greatly appreciate your assistance.

GM K12, Early Career and Professional Learning: Soo Kang

Alliances Manager, Cisco Press: Caroline Antonio

Director, ITP Product Management: Brett Bartow

Executive Editor: James Manly

Managing Editor: Sandra Schroeder

Development Editor: Ellie Bru

Senior Project Editor: Tonya Simpson

Copy Editor: Chuck Hutchinson

Technical Editor: Scott Stephenson

Editorial Assistant: Cindy Teeters

Cover Designer: Chuti Prasertsith

Composition: codeMantra

Indexer: Timothy Wright

Proofreader: Donna E. Mulder

Americas Headquarters	Asia Pacific Headquarters	Europe Headquarters
Cisco Systems, Inc.	Cisco Systems (USA) Pte. Ltd.	Cisco Systems International BV
San Jose, CA	Singapore	Amsterdam, The Netherlands

Cisco has more than 200 offices worldwide. Addresses, phone numbers, and fax numbers are listed on the Cisco Website at www.cisco.com/go/offices.

CCDE, CCENT, Cisco Eos, Cisco HealthPresence, the Cisco logo, Cisco Lumin, Cisco Nexus, Cisco StadiumVision, Cisco TelePresence, Cisco WebEx, DCE, and Welcome to the Human Network are trademarks; Changing the Way We Work, Live, Play, and Learn and Cisco Store are service marks; and Access Registrar, Aironet, AsyncOS, Bringing the Meeting To You, Catalyst, CCDA, CCDP, CCIE, CCIP, CCNA, CCNP, CCSP, CCVP, Cisco, the Cisco Certified Internetwork Expert logo, Cisco IOS, Cisco Press, Cisco Systems, Cisco Systems Capital, the Cisco Systems logo, Cisco Unity, Collaboration Without Limitation, EtherFast, EtherSwitch, Event Center, Fast Step, Follow Me Browsing, FormShare, GigaDrive, HomeLink, Internet Quotient, IOS, iPhone, iQuick Study, IronPort, the IronPort logo, LightStream, Linksys, MediaTone, MeetingPlace, MeetingPlace Chime Sound, MGX, Networkers, Networking Academy, Network Registrar, PCNow, PIX, PowerPanels, ProConnect, ScriptShare, SenderBase, SMARTnet, Spectrum Expert, StackWise, The Fastest Way to Increase Your Internet Quotient, TransPath, WebEx, and the WebEx logo are registered trademarks of Cisco Systems, Inc. and/or its affiliates in the United States and certain other countries.

All other trademarks mentioned in this document or website are the property of their respective owners. The use of the word partner does not imply a partnership relationship between Cisco and any other company. (0812R)

About the Authors

Mark Smith has been teaching for the past 23 years. Ten years ago, at the high school in his district, he started a Cisco Academy, which has grown into a full-fledged CTE program offering Python programming, IT Essentials, CCNA 1, and CCNA 2. In addition, he runs a top-ranked regional cybersecurity club. He is an adjunct at a local community college as well. Mark earned his master's in instructional technology and has CompTIA ITF+, CompTIA A+, CompTIA Network+, CCST: IT Support, CCST: Networking, and CCST: Cybersecurity certifications.

David Bayne has spent years teaching IT, both at the high school and community college levels, and has prepared hundreds of students for careers in IT. He holds CCNA and CompTIA A+ certifications, as well as a master's degree in educational technology. He currently teaches Internet of Things, drone programming, and inventing design courses. When David is not teaching, he reads (mostly mysteries and sci-fi) and spends time with family. He lives near Sacramento, California, with his wife and daughters and their three cats.

John Pickard is an associate professor at East Carolina University in the College of Engineering and Technology, with more than 20 years of experience teaching information and cybersecurity technology. He also works as a subject matter expert and content developer in support of the Cisco Networking Academy.

Throughout his career he has held various IT certifications, including Cisco Certified Network Professional, Cisco Certified Network Associate, Microsoft Certified Professional, EMC Information Storage and Management, IPv6 Forum Certified Engineer (Gold), IPv6 Forum Certified Trainer (Gold), CompTIA Network+, and CompTIA A+. John is also a Cisco Certified Academy Instructor.

John received his PhD in technology management at Indiana State University, an MBA from Wayland Baptist University, and a bachelor of science in professional aeronautics from Embry-Riddle University.

His research interests include IPv6, IPv6 adoption, wireless sensor networks, Internet of Things (IoT), and industry-academia partnerships.

About the Technical Reviewer

Scott Stephenson was born and raised in Texas, where he has spent his entire career as a public education teacher. He has taught for the Cisco Networking Academy for 25 years and has been an instructor trainer for the past 11 years. He was recognized by the Cisco Academy as the National Instructor of the Year in 2007. He holds a bachelor's degree in music education and a master's degree in management information systems and a master's degree in educational leadership. He holds 27 technology certifications and 7 teaching certifications. He has worked on projects from the National Science Foundation and the Department of Labor as an information and communication technology curriculum writer. He retired in 2016 after 30 years in public education but continues to lecture, teach, and work with instructors to help inspire and enrich the lives of young people. He now spends time traveling the world and teaching for several Cisco Networking Academy Instructor Training Centers.

Dedications

Mark Smith: I'd like to dedicate this book to my wife, my partner, my friend, Michelle. You have been a huge support for me in both my professional and personal endeavors. Thank you.

I would also like to dedicate this book to my three incredible children: Cheyenne, Sage, and Skyler. I am immensely proud of the incredible humans you have all become! I love you and thank you for being who you are. Now call and visit more often!

David Bayne: I'd like to dedicate this book to my mom, who was a great supporter of me broadening my horizons to even write the book but who unfortunately didn't make it to see the book in print. To my aunt Elaine, who has been an unwavering supporter throughout my teaching career, and to my wife, Karen, who put up with my being away for long hours writing and editing. Thanks for all the support!

John Pickard: This book is dedicated to my beloved wife, Lisa, whose unwavering patience and support carried me through the long hours of work over many years. Her understanding and love have been my foundation. I also dedicate this to my father, whose enduring belief in the power of persistence inspired me to push beyond my limits. Your guidance and encouragement have shaped me into who I am today.

Acknowledgments

Mark Smith:

Thank you to James, Ellie, Scott, Chuck, Tonya, and everyone else at Cisco Press for helping to bring this book to life. It was a wild, fascinating ride to be a part of.

A huge thank you to Karen at WASTC/Cisco Networking Academy for believing in me and pushing me to write this book. You have been an incredible advocate of my program. Thank you!

David and John, I couldn't think of better writing partners. Thank you for the opportunity to collaborate with both of you. David, a special thank you for letting me bounce so many ideas off you!

Finally, thank you to all my students over the past 23 years. You have made me a better instructor, even if some of you might have contributed to my early male pattern baldness.

David Bayne:

Thanks to Karen at the Cisco Networking Academy, who thought of me as a possible writer and put me in touch with James to even start writing, and to James and Ellie and everyone at Cisco Press who have guided me through this process. As Ellie said, "All writers have a first time!" and I've taken that to heart. Thanks to my brother Richard, who lent me his house where I could work in a quiet place without the distractions of pets and other things. And thanks to John and Mark, who were a great collaborative writing team!

John Pickard:

I would like to express my deepest gratitude to my colleagues and mentors in the Air Force, Unicon, and at East Carolina University, whose guidance and support have been instrumental throughout this journey. Your insights and encouragement have been invaluable. Special thanks to my students, who constantly challenge and inspire me to grow. I am also thankful to my friends and family for their unwavering support; your love and understanding have been my greatest strength, especially during the most demanding times. Finally, I extend my heartfelt appreciation to James, Ellie, and everyone at Cisco Press for their expertise and dedication in bringing this book to life.

Contents at a Glance

Contents

Icons Used in This Book

Router

Wireless Router

Wireless Bridge

Server

File Server

PC/Terminal

Router with
Firewall

Database

Switch

Command Syntax Conventions

The conventions used to present command syntax in this book are the same conventions used in the IOS Command Reference. The Command Reference describes these conventions as follows:

- **Boldface** indicates commands and keywords that are entered literally as shown. In actual configuration examples and output (not general command syntax), boldface indicates commands that are manually input by the user (such as a **show** command).

- *Italic* indicates arguments for which you supply actual values.

- Vertical bars (|) separate alternative, mutually exclusive elements.

- Square brackets ([ ]) indicate an optional element.

- Braces ({ }) indicate a required choice.

- Braces within brackets ([{ }]) indicate a required choice within an optional element.

Introduction

Congratulations! If you are reading this introduction, then you have probably decided that a career as an IT support technician is an important first step for your future success, and obtaining the CCST IT Support certification will prove that you have a solid understanding of help desk–related topics and concepts.

Professional certifications have been an important part of the computing industry for many years and will continue to be important for years to come. Many reasons exist for these certifications, but the most popular cited reason is credibility. All other considerations held equal, a certified employee/consultant/job candidate is considered more valuable than one who is not certified.

This book was written to help up-and-coming IT professionals build a solid foundational understanding of what it takes to be an IT support technician. It is structured specifically to prepare candidates for the Cisco Certified Support Technician (CCST) IT Support 100-140 exam but aims to equip you with knowledge that will stay useful long after you earn the certification.

Goals and Methods

The most important and somewhat obvious goal of this book is to help you pass the CCST IT Support (100-140) exam. While this book has more than enough questions to help you prepare for the actual exam, the goal isn't to have you simply memorize as many questions and answers as you possibly can.

One key methodology used in this book is to help you discover the exam topics that you need to review in more depth, to help you fully understand and remember those details, and to help you prove to yourself that you have retained your knowledge of those topics. This book does not try to help you pass by memorization but helps you truly learn and understand the topics. The knowledge the CCST IT Support exam covers is vital for any IT support professional. This book would do you a disservice if it didn't attempt to help you learn the material. To that end, the book will help you pass the CCST IT Support exam by using the following methods:

- Helping you discover which test topics you have not mastered

- Providing explanations and information to fill in your knowledge gaps

- Providing practice exercises on the topics and the testing process

Who Should Read This Book?

This book is geared toward new IT professionals and those with an interest in becoming IT support technicians; however, veteran IT professionals just getting into the help desk or needing to obtain the certification will benefit as well. Although other objectives can be achieved from using this book, the book is written with one goal in mind: to help you pass the exam.

So why should you want to pass the CCST IT Support exam? Earning the certification validates your understanding of core IT support concepts and techniques. Furthermore, the CCST IT Support certification will serve as a springboard to more advanced certifications down the road. Many of the concepts and themes we introduce here are practically universal in IT Support exams.

Strategies for Exam Preparation

The strategy you use for CCST IT Support might be slightly different than strategies used by other readers, mainly based on the skills, knowledge, and experience you already have obtained. For instance, if you already have familiarity with help desk and other IT Support concepts and techniques, your approach will likely differ from someone who's brand new and does not have any prior knowledge.

Regardless of the strategy you use or the background you have, the book is designed to help you get to the point where you can pass the exam with the least amount of time required. For instance, there is no need for you to practice or read about IPv6 addresses or Active Directory if you fully understand it already. However, many people like to make sure that they truly know a topic and thus read over material that they already know. Several book features will help you gain the confidence that you need to be convinced that you know some material already, and to also help you know what topics you need to study more.

How This Book Is Organized

Although this book could be read cover-to-cover, it is designed to be flexible and allow you to easily move between chapters and sections of chapters to cover just the material that you need more work with. Chapters 1 through 8 are the core chapters and can be covered in any order. If you do intend to read them all, the order in the book is an excellent sequence to use.

The core chapters, Chapters 1 through 8, cover the following topics:

- **Chapter 1, "Help Desk":** This chapter covers the essential functions and skills required in a modern IT help desk, starting by examining the IT support technician's roles and responsibilities. Key customer service communication skills are discussed, highlighting the importance of clear interactions. The chapter covers time management and explores queue management techniques, including triage processes and technologies. It also details the role of service-level agreements (SLAs) in maintaining standards, key performance indicators (KPIs) for measuring success, and the functionality of ticketing systems. Best practices for documentation and an eight-step problem-solving process are also introduced.

- **Chapter 2, "Hardware":** This chapter discusses IT safety; computer ports and interfaces; how to identify, install, and upgrade computer components; and common hardware/peripheral issues.

- **Chapter 3, "Networking and Network Connectivity":** This chapter discusses networking, where students locate basic network information, basic end-to-end network connectivity and testing, and authentication to secure network connection.

- **Chapter 4, "Windows OS":** This chapter covers common Windows operating system issues and how to resolve them. It covers the installation and repair of collaboration and productivity software. It also discusses Windows system and security tools, including Active Directory. Finally, it goes over how to map drives in Windows to simplify management.

- **Chapter 5, "macOS":** This chapter discusses macOS. It covers important system tools as well as built-in security tools and provides a brief history of how macOS came to be.

- **Chapter 6, "Virtualization, Cloud, and Remote Access":** This chapter explores the critical roles of virtualization, cloud computing, and remote access in modern IT environments. It covers the basics of cloud computing, its benefits, and major providers. The chapter also explains cloud service models (SaaS, PaaS, IaaS) and deployment options (public, private, hybrid, community), comparing cloud computing to on-premise data centers. Virtualization is introduced, detailing hypervisors and virtual machines, and how it integrates with software-defined networking (SDN). Finally, the chapter covers remote access tools.

- **Chapter 7, "Security":** This chapter introduces fundamental cybersecurity concepts. This includes security threats and security threat mitigation. The chapter looks at who is behind security threats and the common types of threats that the IT professional will often encounter.

- **Chapter 8, "The IT Professional":** IT support technicians need to practice professionalism, follow company policies, and support confidentiality. They also must be able to use remote access tools while troubleshooting. In addition, they must be able to research issues their users are seeing and document the solutions they implement. Finally, in this chapter, we revisit the troubleshooting process.

How to Access the Companion Website

To access the companion website, which gives you access to the electronic content with this book, start by establishing a login at www.ciscopress.com and registering your book by December 31, 2028. To do so, simply go to www.ciscopress.com/register and enter the ISBN of the print book: **9780135403921**. After you have registered your book, go to your account page and click the **Registered Products** tab. From there, click the **Access Bonus Content** link to get access to the book's companion website.

Note that if you buy the *Premium Edition eBook and Practice Test* version of this book from Cisco Press, your book will automatically be registered on your account page. Simply go to your account page, click the **Registered Products** tab, and select **Access Bonus Content** to access the book's companion website.

How to Access the Pearson Test Prep (PTP) App

You have two options for installing and using the Pearson Test Prep application: a web app and a desktop app. To use the Pearson Test Prep application, start by finding the registration code that comes with the book. You can find the code in these ways:

- You can get your access code by registering the print ISBN 9780135403921 on ciscopress.com/register. Make sure to use the print book ISBN, regardless of whether you purchased an eBook or the print book. After you register the book, your access code will be populated on your account page under the Registered Products tab. Instructions for how to redeem the code are available on the book's companion website by clicking the Access Bonus Content link.

- If you purchase the Premium Edition eBook and Practice Test directly from the Cisco Press website, the code will be populated on your account page after purchase. Just log in at ciscopress.com, click **Account** to see details of your account, and click the digital purchases tab.

NOTE   After you register your book, your code can always be found in your account under the Registered Products tab.

Once you have the access code, to find instructions about both the PTP web app and the desktop app, follow these steps:

Step 1.   Open this book's companion website as shown earlier in this Introduction under the heading, "How to Access the Companion Website."

Step 2.   Click the **Practice Exams** button.

Step 3.   Follow the instructions listed there for both installing the desktop app and using the web app.

Note that if you want to use the web app only at this point, just navigate to pearsontestprep.com, log in using the same credentials used to register your book or purchase the Premium Edition, and register this book's practice tests using the registration code you just found. The process should take only a couple of minutes.

Figure Credits

Figure 1-1: Bojan Milinkov/Shutterstock

Figure 1-3: Gorodenkoff/Shutterstock

Figure 1-4: fizkes/Shutterstock

Figure 1-6: James Steidl/Shutterstock

Figure 1-7: Ralf Kleemann/Shutterstock

Figure 1-8: NicoElNino/Shutterstock

Figure 1-9: Miha Creative/Shutterstock

Figure 1-10: maigi/Shutterstock

Figure 2-2: Chii Chobits/Shutterstock

Figure 2-3: Dmitry Melnikov/Shutterstock

Figure 2-4: normaals/123RF

Figure 2-5: Kabardins photo/Shutterstock

Figure 2-6: Kilroy79/Shutterstock

Figure 2-7: Coleman Yuen/Pearson Education Asia Ltd

Figure 2-8: Ruslan Kudrin/Shutterstock

Figure 2-9: Coleman Yuen/Pearson Education Asia Ltd

Figure 2-10: BaYaoPix/Shutterstock

Figure 2-11: Gooly/Shutterstock

Figure 2-12: adrianhancu/123RF

Figure 2-13: Mikael Damkier/Shutterstock

Figure 2-14: Zakhar Mar/Shutterstock

Figure 2-15: Robert Babczynski/Shutterstock

Figure 2-16: Topolszczak/Shutterstock

Figure 2-17: RMIKKA/Shutterstock

Figure 2-18: mycola/123RF

Figure 2-19: Aleksei Lazukov/Shutterstock

Figure 2-20: Peter Galleghan/Shutterstock

Figure 2-21: MaxkyTH/Shutterstock

Figure 2-22: kvinoz/Shutterstock

Figure 2-23: © 2024, Microsoft

Figure 3-1: S.john/Shutterstock

Figure 3-2: marigranula/123RF

Figure 3-3: MyPro/Shutterstock

Figure 3-4, Figure 3-5, Figure 3-8, Figure 3-9, Figure 3-17, Figure 3-18, Figure 3-19, Figure 3-20, Figure 3-21: © 2024, Microsoft

Figure 3-6: © 2024, Apple Inc.

Figure 3-7, Figure 3-22, Figure 3-23: © 2024, The Linux Foundation

Figure 3-14: Magnetic Mcc/Shutterstock

Figure 3-15: Trong Nguyen/Shutterstock

Figure 3-25: lucadp/123RF

Figure 4-1, Figure 4-2, Figure 4-3, Figure 4-4, Figure 4-5, Figure 4-7, Figure 4-8, Figure 4-11, Figure 4-13, Figure 4-14, Figure 4-15, Figure 4-17, Figure 4-18, Figure 4-19, Figure 4-20, Figure 4-21, Figure 4-22, Figure 4-23, Figure 4-24, Figure 4-25, Figure 4-26, Figure 4-27, Figure 4-28, Figure 4-29, Figure 4-30, Figure 4-31, Figure 4-34, Figure 4-35, Figure 4-36, Figure 4-37, Figure 4-38, Figure 4-39, Figure 4-40, Figure 4-41, Figure 4-42, Figure 4-43, Figure 4-44, Figure 4-45, Figure 4-49: © 2024, Microsoft

Figure 4-6: StarGraphic/Shutterstock

Figure 4-9, Figure 4-12, Figure 4-46, Figure 4-49a: Alphabet Inc.,

Figure 4-10, Figure 4-32: © 2024, Adobe

Figure 4-16, Figure 4-47: © Dropbox

Figure 4-33: Raspberry Pi

Figure 4-48: © 2007–2024, Cloudwards.net

Figure 4-49b: © 1996–2024, Amazon.com, Inc.

Figure 5-1, Figure 5-2, Figure 5-3, Figure 5-4, Figure 5-5, Figure 5-6, Figure 5-7, Figure 5-8, Figure 5-9, Figure 5-10: © 2024, Apple Inc.

Figure 6-4: monticello/Shutterstock

Figure 6-1: phonlamaiphoto/123RF

Figure 6-2: KsanderDN/Shutterstock

Figure 6-3: photo_gonzo/Shutterstock

Figure 6-5: DANIEL CONSTANTE/Shutterstock

Figure 6-10: Funtap/Shutterstock

Figure 6-11: tete_escape/Shutterstock

Figure 7-1: cylonphoto/123RF

Figure 8-1, Figure 8-2: © 2024, Alphabet Inc.,

Figure 8-3, Figure 8-4: © 2024, Microsoft

Figure 8-5: Tech support forum

Figure 8-6: AlexHliv/Shutterstock

Figure 8-7: Willyam Bradberry/Shutterstock

Figure 8-8: DedMityay/Shutterstock

Figure 8-9: Nuttapong punna/Shutterstock

CHAPTER 1

Help Desk

This chapter covers the following topics:

- **The IT Support Technician:** This section explores the role of the IT support technician in the organization.

- **Customer Service Communication Skills:** This section describes various key customer service communication skills for IT support technicians.

- **Time Management:** This section details the importance of effective time management in help desk operations.

- **Help Desk Queue Management:** This section describes the benefits and steps of the queue management triage process and common queue management technologies.

- **Service-Level Agreement:** This section describes key service-level agreements used in the help desk.

- **Key Performance Indicators:** This section describes key performance indicators for the help desk.

- **Ticketing Systems:** This section explores key functionalities of help desk ticketing systems.

- **Documentation:** This section describes best practices for effective documentation.

- **The Problem-Solving Process:** This section describes an eight-step problem-solving process.

The chapter covers information related to the following Cisco Certified Support Technician (CCST) IT Support exam objectives:

- 1.1 Define key help desk concepts.

- 1.2 Prepare documentation to summarize a customer interaction.

- 1.3 Describe the problem solving process.

"Do I Know This Already?" Quiz

The "Do I Know This Already?" quiz allows you to assess whether you should read this entire chapter thoroughly or jump to the "Exam Preparation Tasks" section. If you are in doubt about your answers to these questions or your own assessment of your knowledge of the topics, read the entire chapter. Table 1-1 lists the major headings in this chapter and their corresponding "Do I Know This Already?" quiz questions. You can find the answers in Appendix A, "Answers to the 'Do I Know This Already?' Quizzes."

Table 1-1 "Do I Know This Already?" Section-to-Question Mapping

Foundation Topics Section	Questions
The IT Support Technician	1, 2
Customer Service Communication Skills	3
Time Management	4
Help Desk Queue Management	5
Service-Level Agreements	6, 7
Key Performance Indicators	8
Ticketing Systems	9
The Problem-Solving Process	10–12
Documentation	13

CAUTION The goal of self-assessment is to gauge your mastery of the topics in this chapter. If you do not know the answer to a question or are only partially sure of the answer, you should mark that question as wrong for purposes of the self-assessment. Giving yourself credit for an answer you correctly guess skews your self-assessment results and might provide you with a false sense of security.

1. What is the highest level or tier of support provided by an organization's IT help desk?

   a. Tier 1

   b. Tier 2

   c. Tier 3

   d. Tier 4

2. At what point in the trouble ticket process is the ticket created?

   a. After a technician has validated the user request

   b. After a technician has determined whether the issue can be resolved

   c. After a technician has resolved the issue

   d. After a technician has escalated the issue

3. An IT support technician showing they are engaged and understand the user's concern is an example of which important communication skill?

   a. Active listening

   b. Empathy

   c. Assertiveness

   d. Conflict resolution

4. Why is time management important for IT support technicians?

   a. It helps them avoid handling multiple support requests.

   b. It allows them to prioritize tasks based on urgency and importance, minimizing response times and improving customer satisfaction.

   c. It ensures that they work only on critical issues, bypassing the less significant problems.

   d. It eliminates the need for tracking time spent on tasks and projects.

5. Which of the following describes the correct sequence of actions in help desk queue triaging?

   a. Allocate resources first, then evaluate incoming requests based on severity and impact, prioritize the requests, escalate as needed, and finally document the process.

   b. Evaluate incoming requests based on severity and impact, categorize and prioritize them, allocate appropriate resources, decide if escalation is necessary, and document the process.

   c. Document the process first, then evaluate incoming requests, categorize and prioritize them, allocate resources, and decide if escalation is needed.

   d. Categorize and prioritize requests first, allocate resources, document the process, evaluate incoming requests based on severity and impact, and then decide if escalation is necessary.

6. Which of the following elements are commonly included in a help desk service-level agreement (SLA)? (Choose all that apply.)

   a. Service Scope

   b. Performance Metrics

   c. User Feedback Surveys

   d. Responsibilities and Expectations

   e. Marketing Strategies

   f. Escalation Procedures

7. What is the typical next step when an issue cannot be resolved within the initial SLA resolution timeframe?

   a. The issue is escalated to a senior technician or specialist.

   b. The SLA is immediately revised to extend the resolution time.

   c. The SLA is terminated due to noncompliance.

   d. The user is required to resolve the issue independently.

8. Which of the following key performance indicators (KPIs) would best help an IT help desk assess its efficiency in resolving user issues?

   a. First call resolution (FCR) rate

   b. Ticket volume

   c. Customer satisfaction (CSAT) score

   d. Average resolution time

1

9. An IT support technician receives a call from a user reporting an issue with their email. After gathering all necessary details, the technician logs the problem into the company's ticketing system and assigns it a priority level based on the urgency of the issue. Later in the day, another user reports a similar issue. The technician checks the ticketing system and notices an open ticket for the same problem, so they update the existing ticket instead of creating a new one. What is the main advantage of the technician's approach in this scenario?

    a. It enables the technician to resolve both issues without updating the system.

    b. It prevents duplication of work by consolidating related issues into a single ticket.

    c. It enables the technician to skip documenting the issue and focus on fixing it.

    d. It eliminates the need to assign priority levels to incoming issues.

10. What is the first step in the eight-step problem-solving process for IT support technicians?

    a. Gather detailed information.

    b. Define the problem.

    c. Identify a probable cause of the failure.

    d. Document the changes made to resolve the problem.

11. In the problem-solving process, what should be done if the problem persists after implementing the initial solution?

    a. Skip further steps and accept the initial solution as sufficient.

    b. Document the changes made and conclude the process.

    c. Reassess the problem, gather additional information, reevaluate possible causes, and develop a new plan.

    d. Immediately escalate the issue to a higher level without further investigation.

12. Which of the following actions is part of the "Gather detailed information" step in the problem-solving process? (Choose all that apply.)

    a. Collect logs and error messages from affected systems.

    b. Interview users and stakeholders to understand the problem.

    c. Analyze network traffic to detect potential anomalies.

    d. Review system and application configurations for recent changes.

13. A technician who regularly assesses and revises documentation to ensure it incorporates the latest changes is following which documentation best practice?

    a. Keep it up-to-date.

    b. Make it accessible.

    c. Be clear and concise.

    d. Organize logically.

Foundation Topics

Introduction

Figure 1-1   *The IT Help Desk Is Vital for Resolving Technical Issues, Ensuring Productivity, and Maintaining Smooth Operations*

An IT **help desk** is a vital part of any organization, acting as the primary contact point for employees or customers who need assistance with technical issues, have inquiries, or require support. Organizations typically provide several tools for users to request help, such as online reporting applications, live chat, telephone, or email.

The help desk assists employees with a wide range of hardware and software problems. For example, they handle password resets, help with using company resources like printers and laptops, and solve more complex issues such as network problems.

It's important to understand the difference between a help desk and a call center. While both serve support functions, they focus on different areas. A call center mainly handles large volumes of calls related to customer service, telemarketing, sales, and general inquiries, often dealing with nontechnical issues like account information and billing questions. Staff in call centers are trained in customer service, and their performance is measured by metrics such as call volume and customer satisfaction.

In contrast, a help desk specializes in technical support for IT-related issues, such as software errors, hardware failures, and network problems. Help desk staff have specialized technical knowledge, and their performance is evaluated based on the time taken to resolve issues and the number of support tickets they handle.

The size of an IT help desk in an organization can vary widely depending on several factors, including the organization's size, industry, geographic distribution, and specific IT needs. This size can range from one to just a few individuals in small organizations to large organizations that have many technicians providing multiple tiers, or levels, of support. The right size for an organization depends on factors such as the volume of support requests, how demanding the service-level agreements (SLAs) are, and the use of automated systems such as chatbots and service management tools.

IT support technicians often resolve user issues quickly. For example, if an organization's Internet network fails, users might contact the help desk to find out why they can't access external sites. The technician would inform them of the network outage and provide an estimated time for resolution. They might also offer temporary solutions to minimize disruption until the issue is fully resolved.

When a support request is valid, the technician creates a **trouble ticket** using specialized software to manage requests and incidents. These tickets help track the progress of the issue, ensuring it is addressed promptly, and provide a record for future reference. Users can initiate tickets through a system dashboard, which IT support technicians then validate.

To gather additional information about the request, the IT support technician uses effective questioning techniques and listens carefully to the user's responses. This approach involves asking open-ended questions to fully understand the issue and taking detailed notes. The technician may also need to investigate the device physically or connect remotely to replicate the problem, execute commands, and check configurations. This thorough approach helps in accurately diagnosing and resolving the issue, ensuring minimal downtime for the user.

Once the technician has collected and analyzed the information, they will either solve the problem and close the trouble ticket or escalate the ticket to a higher-tier technician for further assistance.

An example of a typical help desk trouble ticketing process is shown in the flow chart shown in Figure 1-2.

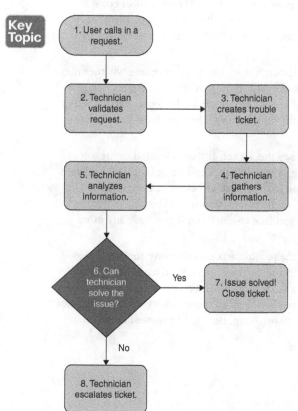

Figure 1-2 *Steps of a Trouble Ticketing Process*

1. **User Calls in a Request.** The process begins when a user contacts the help desk via phone, email, or a ticketing system. They explain their issue or request assistance with a particular problem. For example, a user may call the help desk and say, "I can't access my email. It keeps giving me a 'server not found' error."

2. **Technician Validates Request.** Now the technician listens to the user's request, confirming the issue and ensuring it is within the help desk's scope. They may ask clarifying questions to understand the problem better. For example, the technician can ask some simple questions to better understand the issue like, "Can you tell me if you're receiving this error on your laptop or phone? Also, are you connected to the Internet?"

3. **Technician Creates Trouble Ticket.** Once the request is validated, the technician creates a trouble ticket in the ticketing system. This ticket includes important details such as the user's contact information, the issue reported, and any relevant notes from the conversation. In this example the technician creates a ticket titled "Email Access Issue," assigning it a priority level based on the severity of the problem.

4. **Technician Gathers Information.** Next, the technician collects additional information about the user's environment and the problem. This information may include device specifications, error messages, recent changes, or steps the user has already tried. The technician asks, "What email client are you using? Have you made any recent changes to your network settings?"

5. **Technician Analyzes Information.** The technician reviews the gathered information, looking for patterns, common issues, or possible solutions. They may also consult knowledge bases or documentation. The technician recalls a previous incident where similar issues arose due to DNS settings and checks whether the user's settings are correct.

6. **Can Technician Solve the Issue?** At this point, the technician determines whether they have enough information to solve the issue or if it requires further assistance. They will consider their expertise and available resources. For example, the technician finds that the user's DNS settings are indeed incorrect and believes they can fix it based on this information.

7. **Yes, Issue Is Solved and Technician Closes the Ticket.** If the technician can resolve the issue, they will guide the user through the solution, confirming that the problem is fixed. They then document the resolution in the ticket and close it. For example: The technician says, "I've adjusted your DNS settings, and you should be able to access your email now. I'll close the ticket, but feel free to reach out if you have any more issues."

8. **No, Technician Escalates the Ticket.** If the technician cannot resolve the issue, they will escalate the ticket to a higher-level technician or a specialized team. They provide all the details collected so far to ensure a smooth handoff. For example: The technician realizes the problem is related to a server-side issue that requires network administrator access. They escalate the ticket to the network team, noting all troubleshooting steps taken.

This structured process helps ensure that user issues are addressed efficiently and effectively, leading to higher satisfaction and quicker resolutions.

In summary, help desks can offer a combination of human assistance, automated replies, and access to various tools and documents. However, there are no specific rules mandating what they must include. As a result, each help desk is unique, providing a customized set of resources to meet the specific needs of its organization and users.

The IT Support Technician

Figure 1-3   *The IT Help Desk Is Fast-Paced, Requiring Quick Problem-Solving and Multitasking to Support Users Efficiently*

In the fast-paced world of IT support, IT support technicians are the frontline workers, combining technical know-how with excellent customer service to quickly solve user problems and keep business operations running smoothly. Success in this role requires a mix of technical skills and strong interpersonal abilities.

Key technical skills required of these technicians include troubleshooting various hardware and software issues, clearly explaining complex technical solutions, and effectively solving problems under pressure. Additionally, being good at time management, multitasking, adapting to new technologies, and committing to ongoing learning enhance their ability to provide high-quality user support and maintain smooth IT operations.

Help desk IT technicians must be able to

- Show technical skills in different operating systems, software, and hardware to quickly diagnose and fix issues.

- Excel in customer service by clearly communicating technical solutions and empathetically addressing user concerns, building trust and satisfaction.

- Manage time effectively and multitask to prioritize and resolve tickets promptly, ensuring consistent adherence to service-level agreements.

- Handle queue management efficiently and use ticketing systems to track and resolve user issues.

- Monitor and achieve key performance indicators (KPIs) to measure and improve service delivery.

- Use problem-solving skills to analyze issues, find root causes, and creatively implement solutions using available resources.

A help desk operates in an organized, professional setting, and usually structured around levels, or **support tiers**, for addressing user problems and issues. Customers request help with specific tech issues via calls or emails to the help desk. The support tier levels are

- **Tier 0 support:** Tier 0 refers to self-service support options that allow users to resolve issues independently without contacting IT support staff. This tier includes resources like FAQs, knowledge bases, troubleshooting guides, and online forums. Users can search these resources for solutions to common problems, helping to reduce the overall volume of support tickets. Tier 0 is designed to empower users to solve simple issues on their own, such as password resets or software installation guides, before escalating to higher tiers of support.

- **Tier 1 support:** Tier 1 technicians respond to these requests in the order they arrive. They are tasked with gathering relevant information from customers and accurately entering it into a ticket or work order. If it is a simple problem to resolve, the technician will handle the problem themselves; otherwise, they will escalate it to a Tier 2 technician who will have more knowledge and experience.

- **Tier 2 support:** When escalating the ticket, the Tier 1 technician must clearly describe the problem and any actions they have taken to resolve the issue for the Tier 2 technician. This clear description helps others understand the situation without needing to ask the customer the same questions. The Tier 2 technician then contacts the customer to gather additional information to resolve the issue or problem. If no solution is available, Tier 2 technicians escalate the problem to Tier 3.

- **Tier 3 support:** Tier 3 technicians are specialists and are typically the most highly skilled product specialists. They deal with the most difficult and technical problems that Tier 1 and Tier 2 technicians can't solve. They have expert knowledge in specific areas of technology and are responsible for fixing complex issues, finding advanced solutions, and offering top-level support. They often work with developers and engineers to address deep-rooted system problems, create updates, and improve IT systems. Their job also includes investigating problems thoroughly, spotting patterns to prevent future issues. They document new fixes for use by the Tier 1 and Tier 2 technicians.

- **Tier 4 support:** Tier 4 is typically the final escalation level, where support issues are referred to external vendors, partners, or manufacturers for resolution. These technicians have the expertise and access to proprietary tools or knowledge that internal IT teams do not possess. They handle issues related to specialized hardware, software, or systems that require assistance from the original provider. Tier 4 technicians work closely with the internal IT team to provide updates and ensure the issue is resolved, often involving product replacements, patches, or system upgrades.

Table 1-2 summarizes the levels of IT help desk support within an organization. In some organizations the tiers may be collapsed together so that Tier 1 and Tier 2 issues are handled by the same personnel, or Tier 2 and Tier 3 are combined.

Key Topic

Table 1-2   The Five Tiers of IT Support

IT Support Level	Function	Description
Tier 0	Self-help and self-support by the user	Using information from the web, FAQs, blogs, manuals, apps, and so on, users attempt to resolve simple issues themselves. If users cannot resolve their issues, they submit a request to the help desk for support.
Tier 1	Basic help desk resolution and service	Tier 1 technicians are trained to solve known problems and to follow scripts for fulfilling service requests. They escalate issues they cannot resolve to Tier 2 technicians.
Tier 2	In-depth technical support	Tier 2 technicians have deep product knowledge. They handle problems beyond the scope of Tier 1 technicians. They escalate to Tier 3 if no solution is found.
Tier 3	Expert product support and service	Tier 3 technicians provide the highest level of support inside the organization. They are the most highly skilled specialists, architects, or engineers. They document new fixes for use by Tier 1 and Tier 2 technicians.
Tier 4	Contracted external support	Tier 4 is outside support for problems with assets or software not serviced by the organization. A good example is copier or printer support.

NOTE   Help desk IT technicians must provide support according to the customer's service-level agreement. SLAs are discussed in detail later in the chapter.

Customer Service Communication Skills

Figure 1-4   *Good Communication Skills Help Technicians Effectively Resolve Issues and Understand User Concerns, Ensuring Efficient Support*

Effective communication is essential for providing outstanding IT help desk service. Technicians must use various skills to understand and solve user problems, ensuring a positive experience and quick resolution. Here are some important customer service skills every IT support technician should have:

- **Active Listening:** Paying full attention to users, understanding their problems, and responding thoughtfully. For example, if a user describes an issue with their printer, the technician might say, "So you're saying your printer is showing an error and won't print, right?" This shows the technician is engaged and understands the user's concern.

- **Empathy:** Understanding and sharing the feelings of users to connect with them and show that their concerns matter. For example, in response to a user having trouble accessing a file, the technician would respond with "I'm really sorry to hear that you're having trouble accessing your report, especially with your important meeting coming up. I can imagine how stressful this must be. Let's get this sorted out as quickly as possible." This response shows the technician is engaged and understands the user's concern.

- **Clarity and Simplicity:** Explaining technical concepts in easy-to-understand terms, avoiding confusing jargon. Instead of saying, "You need to clear your DNS cache," the technician could say, "Let's refresh your Internet connection by clearing some temporary files. I'll walk you through the steps."

- **Patience:** Taking the time to explain things thoroughly without showing frustration, especially when users are confused or upset. For example, if a user struggles to follow instructions, the technician might say, "That's okay! Let's take it step by step. Take your time and let me know when you're ready for the next part."

- **Positive Language:** Using encouraging words to create a supportive environment and make users feel more comfortable. Instead of saying, "I can't fix this right now," the technician might say, "I'll need a little time to research this. Let's work together to find the best solution."

- **Assertiveness:** Confidently and respectfully expressing thoughts and needs, especially when setting expectations or explaining policies. A technician might say, "I can help you with this issue, but I'll need some time to investigate it. I'll follow up with you within the next hour."

- **Follow-up Skills:** Checking in with users after resolving an issue to ensure their satisfaction and build trust. In this situation, after fixing an issue, the technician could send an email saying, "I wanted to check in and see if your printer is working well now. Please let me know if you need any more help."

- **Conflict Resolution:** Managing difficult situations and calming upset users to resolve issues effectively. For example, if a user is angry about a long wait time, the technician might say, "I understand your frustration. I'm here to help you now. Let's focus on getting your issue resolved as quickly as we can."

- **Documentation Skills:** Clearly recording user interactions and solutions for future reference and knowledge sharing. It is very important that after solving a user's problem, the technician records the issue and the steps taken in the ticketing system, using clear language so that anyone reviewing the ticket can quickly understand the situation.

Mastering these customer service communication skills is crucial for IT support technicians to excel in their roles. By actively listening, demonstrating empathy, and communicating with clarity, technicians can accurately comprehend and address user concerns. Patience and the use of positive language foster a supportive environment, while assertiveness ensures that expectations are clearly defined and respected. Following up with users builds trust, adaptability allows for tailored communication approaches, and conflict resolution skills enable the effective management of challenging situations. Lastly, robust documentation skills ensure that knowledge is meticulously recorded and readily accessible for future reference.

Time Management

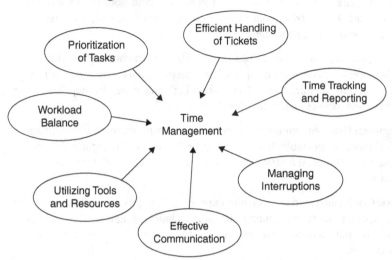

Figure 1-5 *There Are Many Components to Effective Time Management*

Time management is a crucial skill for IT support technicians, because they often juggle multiple tasks and priorities while striving to provide timely and effective support to users. In a fast-paced and dynamic work environment, the ability to manage time efficiently can significantly impact a technician's productivity, job performance, and overall success.

One of the primary reasons that time management is essential for IT support technicians is the need to handle a high volume of support requests within a limited timeframe. Technicians must be able to prioritize tasks based on urgency and importance, ensuring that critical issues are addressed promptly without neglecting less pressing but still significant concerns. By effectively managing their time, technicians can minimize response times, reduce downtime for users, and maintain a high level of customer satisfaction.

Moreover, time management skills enable IT support technicians to allocate their resources and energy efficiently. This involves setting realistic goals, breaking down complex tasks into manageable subtasks, and focusing on one task at a time to avoid multitasking-related inefficiencies. By planning and organizing their workload, technicians can minimize distractions, reduce stress, and maintain a clear focus on their objectives.

Effective time management also allows IT support technicians to continuously improve their skills and knowledge. In the rapidly evolving world of technology, staying up-to-date with the latest tools, techniques, and best practices is essential. By allocating time for learning and professional development, technicians can enhance their problem-solving abilities, expand their expertise, and provide higher-quality support to users.

Furthermore, strong time management skills contribute to a positive work-life balance for IT support technicians. By efficiently managing their time at work, technicians can ensure that they complete their tasks within designated hours, reducing the need for overtime or work-related stress outside of office hours. This balance is vital for maintaining motivation, preventing burnout, and fostering a healthy and productive work environment.

Help Desk Queue Management

Figure 1-6 *Congested Queues Lead to Inefficiency and Delays*

Queue management is another important responsibility of a help desk IT technician. It involves efficiently handling incoming user queries and requests, maintaining service levels, prioritizing tasks, and providing timely solutions.

Triaging

A key part of queue management is effective **triaging**, which means assessing and categorizing incoming requests to determine their urgency and nature. This assessment helps assign requests to the right queue or escalate them to the appropriate support personnel.

Effective triaging offers several benefits, including

- **Improved Efficiency:** By prioritizing and categorizing requests, help desk teams can work more efficiently, reducing wait times and increasing the speed of resolution.

- **Enhanced User Satisfaction:** Prompt and appropriate responses to critical issues lead to higher user satisfaction and trust in the help desk services.

- **Better Resource Management:** Efficient triaging helps allocate resources where they are needed most, optimizing the use of skilled technicians and reducing bottlenecks.

- **Reduced Downtime:** By addressing critical issues promptly, effective triaging minimizes downtime and its associated costs, ensuring business continuity.

Modern help desk management systems often have automated triaging features that assess and categorize requests based on predefined criteria. Machine learning algorithms can further enhance this process by predicting the urgency and complexity of issues based on historical data. Automated triaging reduces the manual workload on technicians.

Regardless of the method used, effective triaging follows a systematic process:

1. The first step involves evaluating incoming requests. An IT support technician will look at each request based on several factors, such as how severe the issue is, how many users are affected, and the potential impact on business operations. Requests are then categorized by urgency, typically ranging from critical (needing immediate attention) to low priority (which can wait).

2. Once categorized, requests are prioritized to ensure that the most important issues are resolved first. This prioritization is crucial for maintaining service levels and making sure that key business functions are not disrupted. High-priority issues might include system outages, security breaches, or major software problems, while lower-priority issues might involve routine maintenance or minor user questions.

3. Next, appropriate resources are allocated. Effective triaging helps use resources more efficiently. By identifying which requests need immediate attention and which can wait, help desk managers can assign the right personnel to the right tasks. This approach ensures that skilled technicians handle complex problems, while less experienced staff address simpler issues.

4. Part of triaging is deciding when an issue needs to be escalated to higher-level support. Some problems may be too complex for the Tier 1 help desk IT technician. Clear escalation protocols ensure that issues are resolved by the most qualified personnel, reducing resolution times and improving overall service quality.

5. Last is documentation. Effective triaging also involves clear communication with users and accurate documentation. Keeping users informed about the status of their requests, estimated resolution times, and any actions taken is essential for managing expectations and maintaining trust. Proper documentation of each triaging decision helps in tracking the progress of requests and provides valuable data for analyzing trends and improving future triaging processes.

Queue Management Technologies

Help desk management systems can track, categorize, and prioritize tickets efficiently. Knowledge bases and expert systems offer quick solutions to common problems, speeding up resolution times. Remote diagnostic tools allow technicians to troubleshoot issues without needing physical access to systems. Integrating various systems through application programming interfaces (APIs) can improve data flow and provide a comprehensive view of the support landscape. Proper use of technology by help desk IT technicians significantly enhances the speed and quality of support.

Help desk management systems, also known as ticketing systems, are software platforms designed to manage and track user requests and issues. Some popular examples of help desk management systems include

■ **Jira Service Management:** Jira is a tool for tracking and managing IT service requests and incidents.

■ **Zendesk:** Zendesk is a comprehensive support ticketing system that offers features for tracking, managing, and resolving customer support tickets.

- **ServiceNow:** ServiceNow is an IT service management platform that provides tools for managing incidents, requests, problems, and changes.

- **Zoho Desk:** The Zoho help desk software integrates well with other Zoho products, offering automation, multichannel support, and reporting capabilities.

- **Salesforce Service Cloud:** This robust system integrates seamlessly with Salesforce's CRM features, making it ideal for companies already using Salesforce.

Knowledge bases are repositories of information that IT support technicians and users can access to find solutions to common problems. Expert systems use artificial intelligence (AI) to provide more accurate and efficient answers. Popular tools include

- **Confluence:** Confluence is a collaboration tool that allows teams to create, share, and organize knowledge.

- **Freshdesk:** Freshdesk is an online help desk software with a built-in knowledge base to assist in resolving issues quickly.

- **Zendesk Guide:** Zendesk Guide is an intelligent knowledge base solution that integrates seamlessly with Zendesk's support ticketing system, allowing businesses to create, organize, and share help articles and FAQs.

Remote diagnostic tools allow technicians to troubleshoot and fix issues without needing physical access to the user's device. Examples include

- **Microsoft Remote Desktop:** RDS provides remote access to Windows computers and servers. It is commonly used in enterprise environments and integrates well with other Microsoft services.

- **VNC Connect:** VNC Connect is a remote access and control tool that offers secure and reliable remote desktop access. It supports multiple platforms and provides features such as file transfer, chat, and encryption.

- **Parallels Access:** Parallels Access provides remote access to computers and applications from mobile devices. It offers a user-friendly interface, high performance, and support for Windows and Mac systems.

API integrations allow different software systems to communicate and share data, improving the flow of information and providing a comprehensive view of the support landscape. Examples include

- **Zapier:** This tool connects different apps and automates workflows by creating integrations. It supports thousands of apps, including Google Workspace, Slack, and Salesforce.

- **MuleSoft:** This integration platform is used for connecting applications, data, and devices.

- **TIBCO:** TIBCO provides an integration and analytics platform that connects applications, data, and devices across cloud and on-premises environments.

Queue Levels

IT support technicians also monitor queue levels and identify bottlenecks to adjust resource allocation for optimal service delivery. This ensures that each request is promptly addressed and efficiently resolved. Regular communication with users, providing updates on their requests, and documenting all actions taken are essential aspects of queue management.

By examining queue data, help desk IT technicians can spot bottlenecks where requests accumulate or take longer to resolve than anticipated. These bottlenecks often occur due to a high volume of requests that can overwhelm the support team, complex issues that need more time or specialized knowledge to resolve, and resource constraints when there aren't enough skilled technicians available to handle the workload efficiently. Identifying these problems allows the help desk to take proactive measures to improve response times and service quality.

Effective queue management ensures that each support request is addressed promptly and resolved efficiently. This process involves prioritizing requests so that high-priority issues are tackled first while less critical problems are scheduled for later. Automation plays a key role by handling repetitive tasks and simple queries, allowing technicians to focus on more complex issues. Additionally, regular follow-ups are essential to continuously check the status of unresolved issues, preventing them from being overlooked.

SLAs and KPIs

Queue management also involves implementing service-kevel agreements and key performance indicators. Both SLAs and KPIs are discussed in more detail in the following sections.

Service-Level Agreements

Figure 1-7 *Service-Level Agreements Define Expected Service Standards*

Service-level agreements (SLAs) are formal contracts between IT service providers and their customers or employees, outlining the expected level of service. They define the expected response and resolution times for different requests, ensuring the help desk meets its commitments. SLAs also specify the services provided, performance metrics, and response and resolution times, ensuring everyone knows what to expect. By defining these elements, the SLA ensures accountability and consistency, helping help desk staff prioritize and address issues efficiently. It also includes steps for escalating unresolved problems and outlines penalties and solutions for not meeting the standards.

For example, an IT help desk SLA might require that critical issues, like a network outage affecting all employees, be acknowledged within 15 minutes and resolved within 2 hours. This means that if the network goes down, the help desk needs to start working on fixing the problem within 15 minutes of it being reported and should have it resolved within 2 hours.

Another example is an SLA that defines how issues are escalated. The SLA may require that issues should be resolved within 2 hours. If the resolution cannot be achieved within this timeframe, the incident must be escalated to a senior technician or specialist. If the issue remains unresolved after an additional 2 hours (4 hours total), it is escalated to the IT manager or a higher-level support team for further action. If the problem still persists after 6 hours, it is escalated to the external vendor or a dedicated crisis management team for immediate intervention.

SLAs with **five nines** (99.999 percent) availability are more expensive than those with lower uptime guarantees (such as 99.9 percent or 99 percent). The term *five nines* refers to a high level of system availability or uptime, which is commonly used in SLAs for critical services like cloud computing, telecommunications, or data centers. Achieving five nines means that a service is available 99.999 percent of the time, which allows for only about 5.26 minutes of downtime per year. Achieving this level of availability requires significant investments in redundancy, fault-tolerant systems, continuous monitoring, and robust disaster recovery plans. These additional technical requirements increase the cost of infrastructure and maintenance.

Some of the key SLAs in an IT help desk environment include

- **Service Scope:** Details the range of services covered, such as technical support, troubleshooting, software updates, and maintenance.

- **Performance Metrics:** Criteria used to measure the help desk's effectiveness and efficiency. Common metrics include response time (time to acknowledge a request), resolution time (time to resolve an issue), and first-call resolution rate (percentage of issues resolved on the first contact).

- **Responsibilities and Expectations:** Outline the duties of both the help desk and users. The help desk must provide timely support, maintain communication, and ensure quality service. Users must provide detailed information about issues, follow procedures for requesting help, and cooperate with help desk personnel.

- **Escalation Procedures:** Define the process for escalating issues that cannot be resolved within the agreed timeframes or require higher-level intervention. This ensures that unresolved issues get the appropriate attention and resources.

- **Penalties and Remedies:** Enforce compliance with the SLA and may include penalties for failing to meet service levels and remedies or compensation for affected users.

- **Review and Revision:** SLAs are reviewed and updated periodically to reflect changes in technology, user needs, and organizational goals. Regular reviews ensure the SLA remains relevant and effective.

By setting clear expectations and measurable standards, SLAs help ensure that the IT help desk delivers consistent and reliable service, enhancing user satisfaction and organizational efficiency.

Key Performance Indicators

Figure 1-8 *Key Performance Indicators Are Measurable Values for How Effectively the Help Desk Is Achieving Its Goals*

Key performance indicators (KPIs) are measurable values that show how well an organization, team, or individual is meeting key business goals. In an IT help desk, KPIs track and evaluate the performance of help desk operations to ensure they meet the organization's objectives. Effective KPIs are specific, measurable, achievable, relevant, and time-bound (SMART).

KPIs, such as average response time, first-call resolution rate, and customer satisfaction scores, measure the effectiveness of the queue management process and highlight areas for improvement. Regular reporting and analysis of these metrics enable help desk managers to make informed decisions, optimize resources, and continuously enhance service quality.

Common key KPIs for an IT help desk include

- **First Call Resolution (FCR) Rate:** Measures the percentage of issues resolved on the first contact with the help desk. A high FCR rate indicates effective problem-solving and user satisfaction.

- **Average Response Time:** Tracks the average time taken for the help desk to respond to a user's request. Shorter response times generally reflect a more efficient and attentive help desk.

- **Average Resolution Time:** Measures the average time taken to resolve an issue from the moment it is reported. This helps assess the help desk's efficiency in handling and resolving issues.

- **Ticket Volume:** Tracks the number of support requests or tickets received over a specific period. Analyzing ticket volume can identify trends and areas for improvement in help desk operations.

- **Customer Satisfaction (CSAT) Score:** Gauges user satisfaction with help desk services, typically measured through post-interaction surveys where users rate their experience.

- **Backlog of Tickets:** Tracks the number of unresolved or open tickets at any given time. A high backlog can indicate issues with workload management or resource allocation.

- **Ticket Escalation Rate:** Measures the percentage of tickets escalated to higher-level support. A high escalation rate might indicate that front-line support cannot resolve many issues, suggesting a need for additional training or resources.

- **Cost per Ticket:** Measures the average cost incurred to resolve a single support ticket, helping understand the financial efficiency of help desk operations.

- **Service-Level Agreement (SLA) Compliance:** Measures the percentage of tickets resolved within the agreed-upon SLA timeframes. High compliance rates indicate that the help desk is meeting its service commitments.

By monitoring these KPIs, an organization's IT help desk can identify strengths and weaknesses in its operations, make data-driven decisions, and continuously improve its service delivery to better meet users' needs.

Ticketing Systems

Help desk ticketing systems help organizations manage user problems or requests. Ticketing software is specifically designed to ensure that corporate users or clients receive support in a timely and systematic manner. They also ensure that all tickets get noticed and addressed.

Ticketing systems vary depending on the need of the organization. For example, there are ticketing systems designed for the needs of internal corporate users and other systems to support service providers or external customers.

Ticketing software is specifically designed to track, prioritize, and resolve user issues. When a user reports a problem or makes a request, a ticket is created in the system. This ticket is then assigned a unique identifier and categorized based on the nature of the issue.

The system enables IT support technicians to monitor the status of each ticket, ensuring that all reported issues are acknowledged and addressed.

Key functionalities of help desk ticketing systems include

- **Centralized Management:** All user issues and requests are consolidated into a single platform, making it easier to track and manage them efficiently.

- **Prioritization and Categorization:** Tickets can be categorized based on their type (e.g., technical issues, service requests) and prioritized based on their urgency and impact. This ensures that critical issues are addressed promptly.

- **Automated Workflows:** Many ticketing systems include automation features that streamline the ticket handling process. For example, they can automatically route tickets to the appropriate technician or department based on predefined criteria.

- **Communication and Collaboration:** These systems facilitate communication between users and help desk staff. Users can track the status of their tickets, while technicians can update tickets with progress notes and resolutions. Some systems also support collaboration among technicians, enabling them to share knowledge and resources.

- **Reporting and Analytics:** Ticketing systems provide detailed reports and analytics on help desk performance. Metrics such as ticket volume, resolution time, and customer satisfaction can be tracked to identify trends and areas for improvement.

A help desk ticket typically includes the following information:

- **Ticket ID:** A unique identifier for the ticket to track and reference it.

- **Date and Time:** When the ticket was created and any subsequent updates.

- **Requester Information:** Details about the user who reported the issue, including their name, contact information, and sometimes their department or role.

- **Issue Description:** A detailed description of the problem or request, including any error messages, symptoms, or context.

- **Priority Level:** The urgency of the issue, often categorized as low, medium, high, or critical.

- **Category/Type:** Classification of the issue, such as hardware, software, network, or user account problems.

- **Status:** The current state of the ticket, such as open, in progress, on hold, or resolved.

- **Assigned Technician:** The person or team responsible for handling the ticket.

- **Resolution Details:** Information about how the issue was resolved or the actions taken to address it.

- **Resolution Date and Time:** When the issue was resolved.

- **Comments and Notes:** Additional information or updates related to the ticket, including any communication with the requester or other relevant details.

- **Attachments:** Any files or screenshots related to the issue, such as error logs or configuration settings.

- **Follow-Up Actions:** Any steps required after resolution, such as user confirmation or additional checks.

This information helps ensure that issues are tracked, managed efficiently, and resolved in a timely manner.

Documentation

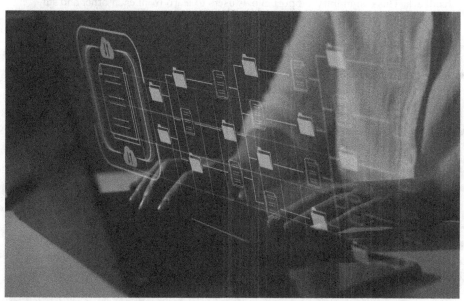

Figure 1-9 *Good Documentation Ensures Knowledge Sharing, Streamlines Troubleshooting, and Improves Service Quality Over Time*

Help desk documentation is essential because it gives users the information they need to solve problems and use technology effectively, even when live support isn't available. Quality **documentation** includes documents, knowledge articles, videos, and forums that guide users through troubleshooting and procedures. It ensures consistency, reduces errors, saves time, and helps both new and experienced users by making information easily accessible and clear. Regular updates keep the documentation relevant and useful, enhancing overall efficiency and user satisfaction.

- **Documents:** Written materials that are essential for using products and services. These materials include guides with step-by-step instructions, technical references like API documentation, practical examples for common problems, version histories that track product changes, and source code documentation for developers. Automated tools can assist in efficiently creating and updating these documents.

- **Knowledge Articles:** Articles that focus on specific tasks or issues, offering solutions to common problems, detailed troubleshooting tips, and instructions. They also provide advice on software and hardware compatibility and optimization, helping users quickly resolve issues with targeted, easy-to-follow information.

- **Videos:** Visual resources that explain complex topics. Tutorial videos provide step-by-step instructions, demonstration videos show how products or features work, and explanatory videos simplify difficult concepts with visuals and narration. These videos help users understand and follow along more easily.

- **Forums:** Interactive platforms where users can ask questions, share ideas, and collaborate. Users can post questions, receive answers, suggest improvements, and provide feedback. This community support allows users to learn from each other and stay connected while solving issues.

Here are some best practices for effective documentation:

- **Keep It Up-to-Date:** Regularly review and update documentation to reflect the latest changes. For example, if a software update introduces new features, update the user guide accordingly. Quarterly checks can help keep documents current.

- **Make It Accessible:** Ensure documentation is easy to find and access. Use a centralized system like a knowledge base or intranet, and make sure it's accessible from various devices, such as computers and smartphones.

- **Be Clear and Concise:** Use straightforward language and avoid jargon. For example, replace "Initialize the device" with "Turn on the device." Clear instructions in a simple, step-by-step format help users follow along without confusion.

- **Organize Logically:** Structure documentation with a clear hierarchy and logical organization. Group information into categories like "Installation" and "Troubleshooting," and use headings, subheadings, and an index or table of contents for easy navigation. Tagging documents with relevant keywords improves searchability.

- **Incorporate User Feedback:** Gather and use feedback from users and technicians to improve documentation. For example, if users find a section confusing, rewrite it for clarity. A system for user comments and suggestions helps keep the content relevant and user-friendly.

- **Use Visual Aids:** Enhance understanding with visual aids like screenshots, diagrams, and videos. For instance, a video tutorial can be more effective than written instructions alone. Diagrams and screenshots can illustrate complex processes, making the instructions easier to follow.

The Problem-Solving Process

Figure 1-10 *A Structured Problem-Solving Process Ensures Consistent, Efficient Solutions, Minimizing Downtime and User Frustration*

Troubleshooting involves a methodical approach to solving problems with computers and other tech components. Issues can come up during regular maintenance or when a customer reports a problem. Using a logical approach helps you narrow down possible causes in a systematic way. By asking the right questions, testing the correct hardware, and analyzing relevant data, you can better understand the issue and develop a solution. Troubleshooting is a skill that improves with experience. Each time you solve a problem, you learn how to adjust the process, combine or skip steps, and find solutions more efficiently. The troubleshooting process is a flexible guide that you adapt to suit each situation.

A systematic problem-solving process is essential for an IT help desk for several reasons. It ensures consistency and reliability in service delivery by standardizing issue-handling approaches, which helps maintain quality across different team members and shifts. This structured approach enhances efficiency and speed by minimizing redundant efforts and reducing downtime. It also improves accuracy by thoroughly analyzing potential causes, with documentation aiding future problem-solving. A systematic process supports knowledge management by creating a knowledge base and identifying patterns for continuous improvement. It boosts customer satisfaction through clear communication and progress tracking, and makes scalability easier by simplifying training and handling increased issues. Additionally, it aids in root cause analysis, compliance, and reporting, and optimizes resource management by effectively using human and technical resources.

The problem-solving process is a structured approach to tackling issues systematically and effectively. It begins with clearly defining the problem to understand what needs to be addressed. Next, detailed information is gathered to better grasp the situation. Identifying the probable cause of the problem helps in formulating a plan to resolve it. Once a plan is devised, changes are made based on that plan, and their results are observed. If the problem persists, the process is repeated to find a solution. Finally, documenting the changes and outcomes ensures that future issues can be resolved more efficiently. This methodical approach helps in solving problems thoroughly and improving overall problem-solving skills.

Figure 1-11 shows an eight-step **problem-solving process**.

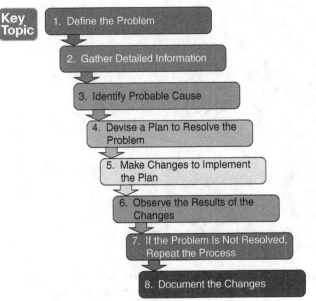

Figure 1-11   *The Eight-Step Problem-Solving Process*

Step 1: Define the Problem

The first step in solving a problem is to define it clearly. This means pinpointing exactly what the issue is and describing it in detail. It's important to be specific about the nature and scope of the problem. Doing so includes identifying symptoms, such as error messages or unusual system behavior, determining how many users or systems are affected, and understanding the impact on productivity and user experience. Gathering contextual information, like hardware and software details or recent changes, also helps. Finally, create a clear problem statement that summarizes the symptoms, scope, and impact to guide the next steps in the problem-solving process.

Common steps to define the problem:

- **Identify the Symptoms:** Describe what's happening, including error messages and user reports.

- **Determine the Scope:** Find out how many users or systems are affected and if the issue is localized or widespread.

- **Clarify the Impact:** Assess how the problem affects operations, productivity, data integrity, and user experience.

- **Gather Contextual Information:** Collect details about the hardware, software, network configurations, and recent updates.

- **Formulate a Clear Problem Statement:** Write a specific description of the problem, summarizing the symptoms, scope, and impact.

Step 2: Gather Detailed Information

In this step, you need to collect as much relevant information as possible about the problem. This step includes gathering logs, user reports, error messages, and any other important data. The goal is to get a full understanding of the issue's context, such as when it began, how often it occurs, and any recent changes that might have caused it.

Common steps to gathering detailed information:

- **Collect Logs and Error Messages:** Gather logs from affected systems, applications, and network devices, and document any error messages. These logs can offer clues about the cause of the problem.

- **Interview Users and Stakeholders:** Speak with users experiencing the issue to understand the context, frequency, and any patterns. Their insights can provide details that technical data might miss.

- **Review System and Application Configurations:** Check the settings and configurations of the involved systems and applications, noting any recent changes or updates that could be linked to the problem.

- **Analyze Network Traffic:** If the issue involves the network, use monitoring tools to examine traffic patterns, identify bottlenecks, or detect anomalies that may point to network-related causes.

- **Examine Performance Metrics:** Look at performance data for the affected systems and applications to identify any deviations from normal behavior that might coincide with the start of the problem.

Step 3: Identify a Probable Cause of the Failure

Once you have gathered all the relevant information, the next step is to figure out what might be causing the problem. This step involves analyzing the data to spot patterns or unusual behaviors that could point to the root cause. You may also need to consult with experts or review past similar issues to identify likely causes.

Common steps to identifying a probable cause of the failure:

- **Analyze Collected Data:** Review logs, error messages, user interviews, configurations, network traffic, and performance metrics to spot patterns, correlations, and anomalies that could point to the root cause.

- **Consult Documentation and Knowledge Bases:** Look through existing documentation, user manuals, and knowledge bases for similar issues and their solutions, as past incidents can offer clues to the cause.

- **Re-create the Issue:** If possible, reproduce the problem in a controlled environment to isolate the conditions that trigger it and confirm potential causes.

- **Evaluate Recent Changes:** Investigate any recent changes to systems, software, or hardware, because new problems are often linked to recent updates or modifications.

- **Engage Subject Matter Experts:** Consult with colleagues or external experts who have specialized knowledge of the systems involved to help identify less obvious causes.

Step 4: Devise a Plan to Resolve the Problem

Once you have identified a probable cause, the next step is to create a detailed plan to fix the problem. This plan should clearly outline the steps needed to resolve the issue, including specific actions, required resources, and a timeline for implementation. It should also consider potential risks and how to address them.

Common steps to devise a plan to resolve the problem:

- **Brainstorm Potential Solutions:** Collaborate with your team to generate a list of possible solutions based on the identified cause, leveraging collective expertise to explore various approaches.

- **Evaluate Feasibility and Risks:** Assess each solution for practicality, considering resources, time constraints, and impact on operations. Identify and weigh the risks or unintended consequences of each option.

- **Select the Best Solution:** Choose the most effective solution with minimal risk and disruption, ensuring it aligns with organizational goals and policies.

- **Develop an Implementation Plan:** Create a detailed plan outlining the steps to implement the chosen solution, including required resources, roles, responsibilities, timeline, and any necessary approvals.

- **Plan for Contingencies:** Prepare for potential challenges by developing backup plans, identifying alternative actions if the primary plan encounters issues or doesn't fully resolve the problem.

Step 5: Make Necessary Changes to Implement the Plan

With the plan ready, the next step is to put it into action. This means performing the tasks outlined in the plan, like applying updates, reconfiguring systems, or replacing faulty parts. It's crucial to follow the plan closely and document each step for future reference.

Common steps to make necessary changes to implement the plan:

- **Communicate the Plan:** Inform team members, management, and users about the planned changes, timeline, and any operational impacts. Clear communication ensures everyone is prepared and knows their role.

- **Gather Required Resources:** Ensure all necessary tools, equipment, software, and personnel are ready for implementation, with access permissions and backup systems in place.

- **Execute the Plan:** Carefully follow and document each step of the plan, maintaining accurate records and tracking progress.

- **Monitor the Process:** Watch the implementation closely to catch any issues early, using monitoring tools and real-time feedback from your team.

- **Adjust as Needed:** Be prepared to modify the plan if unexpected issues arise, using contingency plans and keeping everyone updated to stay on track and resolve the problem effectively.

Step 6: Observe the Results of the Changes

After you make the changes, it's important to closely monitor the results to see if they are effective. This means checking if the problem has been fixed and if the systems are working properly. Both automated tools and manual checks should be used to ensure thorough monitoring.

Common steps to observe the results of the changes:

- **Monitor System Performance:** Track the system's performance to ensure the changes are effective, using monitoring tools to follow KPIs and other key metrics.

- **Collect User Feedback:** Gather input from affected users through surveys or interviews to identify any ongoing issues.

- **Verify Problem Resolution:** Confirm the problem is fixed by comparing current performance and user experience with the initial data.

- **Document Observations:** Record performance data, user feedback, and any remaining issues or unexpected outcomes.

- **Conduct a Post-Implementation Review:** Meet with the team to review the results, discuss lessons learned, and determine if further actions are needed.

Step 7: If the Problem Is Not Resolved, Repeat the Process

If the problem continues after making the initial changes, you need to start the process over. This means going back to reassess the problem and gathering more information if needed. It's important to update your understanding of the issue and explore different causes and solutions until the problem is completely resolved.

Common steps if the problem is not resolved:

- **Reassess the Problem Definition:** Review and update the original problem description to ensure all symptoms, scope, and impacts are accurately noted. Consider any new developments or additional factors.

- **Gather Additional Information:** Collect more detailed data if needed, such as further log analysis, extra user feedback, additional performance metrics, or a broader system review. Look for any missed details.

- **Reevaluate Possible Causes:** Reconsider potential causes of the problem, exploring alternative explanations or root causes. Consult with experts again for fresh insights.

- **Formulate a New Plan:** Develop a revised plan based on new information and reevaluation. This may involve different or more comprehensive actions than the original plan.

- **Implement Revised Changes:** Execute the new plan, making the necessary changes systematically, and ensure all actions are documented and monitored.

- **Monitor and Observe:** After implementing the revised changes, closely watch the results and compare them with expected outcomes to see if the problem is resolved. Gather user feedback and performance data.

- **Document the Process:** Record all new findings, actions taken, and results, adding this information to the existing records for a complete account of the problem-solving process.

- **Review and Reflect:** If the problem persists, conduct a thorough review to understand why previous attempts failed, identify weaknesses in the approach, and consider more extensive measures if needed.

Step 8: Document the Changes Made to Resolve the Problem

After you fix the problem, it's essential to document all changes made during the resolution. This documentation should include a detailed account of the problem, the gathered information, the suspected cause, the plan, the actions taken, and the outcomes. Proper documentation serves as a reference for the future, helps train new staff, identifies patterns for recurring issues, and supports continuous improvement. When this knowledge is preserved, future issues can be resolved more quickly.

When the repair is done, finish the troubleshooting process with the customer by explaining the problem and solution both verbally and in writing. Confirm the solution with the customer, demonstrating how the problem was fixed and allowing them to test it. Once the customer is satisfied, complete the repair documentation.

Common steps to document changes made to resolve the problem:

- **Problem Definition:** Clearly document the original problem, including symptoms, scope, impact, and context.

- **Information Gathered:** Record details such as logs, error messages, user reports, and system configurations.

- **Identified Cause:** Document the analysis and the identified cause, including considered hypotheses.

- **Solution Plan:** Describe the plan to resolve the problem, including the brainstorming process and chosen solution.

- **Implementation Process:** Document each step of implementation, including adjustments and challenges.

- **Results Verification:** Include the outcomes, supported by data and user feedback, confirming if the problem was resolved.

- **Post-Implementation Review:** Reflect on the outcomes, note lessons learned, and offer recommendations for the future.

- **Store Documentation:** Ensure all documentation is stored in an organized and accessible fashion.

Exam Preparation Tasks

As mentioned in the Introduction, you can customize your strategy for exam preparation. Suggested tasks include the exercises here, Chapter 9, "Final Preparation," and the exam simulation questions on the companion website.

Review All Key Topics

Review the most important topics in this chapter, noted with the Key Topic icon in the outer margin of the page. Table 1-3 lists a reference of these key topics and the page numbers on which each is found.

Table 1-3   Key Topics for Chapter 1

Key Topic Element	Description	Page Number
Figure 1-2	Steps of a Trouble Ticketing Process	7
Table 1-2	The Five Tiers of IT Support	11
List	Effective communication skills	12
List	The triage process	16
List	Key SLAs in an IT help desk environment	19
List	Common KPIs for an IT help desk	21
List	Key functionalities of help desk ticketing systems	22
List	Documentation best practices	24
Figure 1-11	The Eight-Step Problem-Solving Process	26

Define Key Terms

Define the following key terms from this chapter and check your answers in the glossary:

help desk, trouble ticket, support tiers, active listening, empathy, conflict resolution, time management, triaging, queue management, service-level agreements (SLAs), five nines, key performance indicators (KPIs), documentation, problem-solving process

CHAPTER 2

Hardware

This chapter covers the following topics:

- **Safety:** This section explores physical and environmental safety of hardware as well as individual safety.

- **Ports and Interfaces:** The section describes various ports and interfaces used for video as well as data communication.

- **Identifying, Installing, and Upgrading Computer Components:** This section explores key computer components, their functions, as well as basic installation tips and upgrading guidelines.

- **Hardware and Peripheral Issues:** This section details some common troubleshooting tips and issues you might encounter with hardware and peripheral devices.

This chapter covers the basics of computer hardware and topics related to computer hardware. Safety, ports and interfaces, computer components, and common hardware/peripheral issues are all covered in this chapter. While it would take an entire book to cover the breadth of computer hardware, this chapter will help give you an overview as well as prepare you for certification.

The chapter covers information related to the following Cisco Certified Support Technician (CCST) IT Support exam objectives:

- 2.1 Demonstrate how to follow basic safety procedures.

- 2.3 Assist end users in locating, identifying, and understanding the characteristics of various ports and cables.

- 2.4 Identify, install and upgrade various components in a desktop computer.

- 2.5 Investigate commonly encountered hardware issues.

- 3.2 Troubleshoot commonly encountered connectivity issues with peripherals.

"Do I Know This Already?" Quiz

The "Do I Know This Already?" quiz allows you to assess whether you should read this entire chapter thoroughly or jump to the "Exam Preparation Tasks" section. If you are in doubt about your answers to these questions or your own assessment of your knowledge of the topics, read the entire chapter. Table 2-1 lists the major headings in this chapter and their corresponding "Do I Know This Already?" quiz questions. You can find the answers in Appendix A, "Answers to the 'Do I Know This Already?' Quizzes."

Table 2-1 "Do I Know This Already?" Section-to-Question Mapping

Foundation Topics Section	Questions
Safety	1–3
Ports and Interfaces	4–6
Identifying, Installing, and Upgrading Computer Components	7–9
Hardware and Peripheral Issues	10

CAUTION The goal of self-assessment is to gauge your mastery of the topics in this chapter. If you do not know the answer to a question or are only partially sure of the answer, you should mark that question as wrong for purposes of the self-assessment. Giving yourself credit for an answer you correctly guess skews your self-assessment results and might provide you with a false sense of security.

1. What is the minimum number of volts of static electricity that can harm computer components?
   a. 30 volts
   b. 100 volts
   c. 3,000 volts
   d. 5,000 volts

2. What is the acronym to help you remember how to use a fire extinguisher?
   a. P.A.S.T.
   b. A.I.M.M.
   c. P.A.S.S.
   d. C.L.E.A.R.

3. What is the study of engineering and designing of products and systems to help people called?
   a. Kinesiology
   b. Applied biomechanics
   c. Physiology
   d. Ergonomics

4. What video port is not considered high definition and carries only an analog port?
   a. VGA
   b. DVI-D
   c. HDMI
   d. DisplayPort

5. What USB form factor is capable of carrying audio, video, and power?
   a. USB-A
   b. USB-B

      c. USB-C

      d. Micro-USB

  6. What is the most common connector for an Ethernet cable?

      a. RJ-11

      b. RJ-45

      c. BNC

      d. LC-ST

  7. What computer component is known as the brain of the computer?

      a. Processor

      b. Chipset

      c. Motherboard

      d. RAM

  8. What storage device doesn't need external power and data cables?

      a. Hard drive

      b. SSD

      c. Optical drive

      d. M.2

  9. What three computer components must be compatible with each other?

      a. CPU, motherboard, storage device

      b. CPU, motherboard, RAM

      c. Motherboard, power supply, chipset

      d. Motherboard, RAM, storage device

  10. If a certain piece of software is not installing, what could be a probable cause?

      a. The software is 64-bit and trying to be installed on a 32-bit operating system.

      b. The software is incompatible with the storage device.

      c. The computer has too much RAM for the software to function properly.

      d. The computer is lacking an optical drive.

Foundation Topics

Safety

Lots of jobs require safety training and require their employees to be mindful of best safety practices. For instance, a mechanic should know the dangers of working on an engine. Likewise, an electrician should know the dangers of working with electricity. This is true with the IT support technician as well. Safety to the individual as well as safety to the parts you work on is vital to understand.

Electrical Shock

Electrical shock occurs when uncontrolled electricity flows through your body. This electrical flow can range from the tingle of a 9-volt battery on your tongue—an old, not advisable way people would test 9-volt batteries to see if they were still good—to severe injury and even death. There is an adage that states, "amps kill, not volts."

NOTE This is an overly simplistic deduction of Ohm's law because you can't have amps without volts, but it does help answer why touching a plasma globe doesn't instantly kill you (higher volts and lower amps).

As shown in Figure 2-1, **Ohm's law** states W = VA or Watts = Volts × Amps.

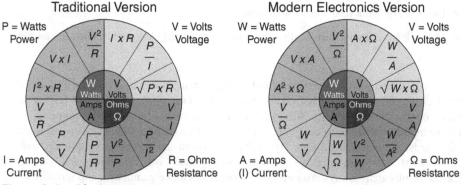

Figure 2-1 *Ohm's Law*

In a reductionist method of describing electricity, the water hose analogy is often used. **Amps**, or current, is often described as the volume of water moving through the water hose, and **volts**, or voltage, is the water pressure. Notice, you can't have one without the other. However, this analogy helps you have a basic understanding that amps are the amount of electricity and consequently what can cause serious harm. You don't need a degree in electrical engineering to be an IT support technician, but it is a good idea to have a basic understanding of electricity so as not to harm yourself.

There is one component that an IT support technician needs to be especially careful around: this is a computer's power supply unit, or **PSU**. Unless specifically trained, you should never open a PSU to fix it. A damaged PSU should be sent back to the factory for repair because they have capacitors in them that hold lethal electrical charge—even after unplugged! This holds true with monitors as well. Never open a monitor for the same reason.

You should be aware of these specific electrical shock hazards when working in IT:

- **Damaged cords and equipment:** Exposed or frayed wires on cords or inside equipment can be a shock hazard.

- **Improperly grounded equipment:** Most surge protectors will help with this, but you should make sure the grounded light is illuminated. Equipment plugged directly into the wall should have the third grounding pin utilized if applicable in your country, as well as the receptacle unless using a two-prong "double insulated" type.

- **Working on live equipment:** For the most part, don't do this unless you know there is zero risk of electrical shock.

- **Liquids:** Water conducts electricity, so keep liquids away from electrical components that are not waterproofed.

Safety tips to minimize electrical shock:

- Do inspect cords and equipment for damage.

- Don't overload power strips/surge protectors and don't daisy-chain them either (plugging one into another one).

- Don't work on electrical equipment while it's plugged in or on.

- Don't eat or drink near electrical equipment.

- Do look around your surroundings to look for potential electrical hazards; be aware.

ESD

Remember shuffling your feet on carpet and touching your friends to give them a shock of static electricity? You were, in fact, giving them electrostatic discharge, or **ESD**. ESD is the releasing of that static electricity. What might seem as harmless fun between two people can be extremely damaging to computer components. Hard drives, solid-state drives, RAM, graphic cards, and motherboards are especially sensitive to static electricity. Basically, any component that has electronic chips and/or memory modules is susceptible to ESD damage. While the results aren't always instantaneous damage, it can be cumulative and ultimately destroy the device.

To go back to the example of "shocking" your friend, it takes over 3,000 volts for a regular person to feel ESD. Ever hear or see the spark of static electricity when, say, touching a doorknob? That's over 5,000+ volts! As previously covered in this chapter, the reason it doesn't kill us is that the amps are very low. Unfortunately, computer components can be damaged with as little as 30 volts. If you're working on sensitive computer components—say, replacing a motherboard—and you feel ESD, there's a good chance you have already done irreversible damage to that part. There are many videos circulating online that try to refute the claim that ESD can cause damage to computer components. It can.

ESD prevention tips:

- Don't work on computer components while standing on carpet (or rugs) unless the carpet/rug has been specifically treated for ESD.

- Don't work on computer components under blowing air from an HVAC system or similar because it can increase static electricity.

- Don't wear wool or synthetic fabrics that can conduct static electricity.

- Don't wear metal jewelry when working on computer components.

- Do adjust the humidity in your room if at all possible—under 40 percent humidity increases static electricity while over 55 percent can cause moisture damage, so try to aim between 45 and 55 percent humidity if at all possible.

- Do store sensitive computer components in antistatic bags (remember the inside of the bag helps reduce static electricity, not the outside; so don't place your motherboard on top of that antistatic bag to work on it).

- Do use an antistatic mat to place your parts on.

- Do wear an antistatic wrist strap.

A note on antistatic wrist straps: these are invaluable tools for the IT support technician. One connects the wrist strap to one hand—usually your nondominant hand so it doesn't cross in front of your work path as often—and the other end, usually with an alligator clip, to the metal chassis of the computer case if you're working on that. There is a misnomer that this process "grounds" you. That is not really the case. Rather, it's important to remember that electricity flows between positive and negative or negative and positive. The antistatic wrist strap equalizes the charge between you and the component you're working on, thus eliminating the flow or discharge of the static electricity. This is why it is important to place the alligator clip to something, ideally metal, near the component you're working on—to help dissipate the electrostatic charge. It is not advisable to clip on to the power supply, because if the alligator clip were to inadvertently touch any of the internal components of the power supply, it could send a dangerous volt to you.

Fire Safety

Fire safety is important in every industry and should be important to every individual as well. Far too many people have had their kitchens burned down from a fire on the stove. Unfortunately, that scenario often goes like this: John heats up a pan of oil to make some fries. The pan catches on fire from the oil heating up too much. Panicked, John sees his kitchen faucet nearby and rushes the flaming pan under the water to put out the fire. Oil and water do not mix. The water displaces the flaming oil and sends shooting, flaming oil all over his kitchen. Don't be John; learn fire types and the proper ways to stop those fire types.

Figure 2-2 depicts the common classes of fires.

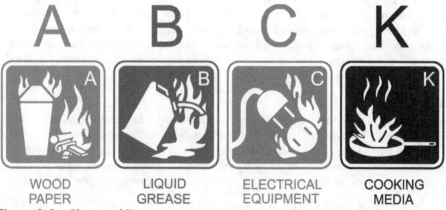

Figure 2-2 *Classes of Fire*

Every home and business should have at least one ABC fire extinguisher within easy access—more than one if in a larger area. An ABC fire extinguisher will put out type A, B, and C classes of fires listed in Figure 2-2. If you're working in a specialty industry, such as a restaurant, then a Class K, specifically for grease/oil fires, would be beneficial as well. In IT, you might deal with a wood or paper fire, which a Class A fire extinguisher would work on, but you might also deal with an electrical fire. Again, water is conductive, so you would not want to put out an electrical fire with water. Instead, a typical ABC fire extinguisher, because of the Class C in particular, will be able to put out most electrical fires.

A note on fire extinguishers: fire extinguishers do not last forever. The propellant inside of them dissipates over time. This is why it is critical to have them checked annually (or sooner) or replaced. While most fire extinguishers have a gauge that reads green for good and red for bad, it is not recommended to rely on this gauge alone. Fire extinguishers should be serviced by a reputable company. It is good advice to contact your local fire agency to see if there is an opportunity to learn fire safety and use a fire extinguisher before an emergency.

To use a fire extinguisher, remember the acronym **P.A.S.S.**:

- **P** is for pull the pin on the fire extinguisher. While this might seem obvious, in the heat of the moment, people often forget.

- **A** is for aim. Aim the nozzle to the base of the fire to smother it. It is human nature to aim at the top of the flames because that is what you see. Resist that urge and aim at the base to smother the source/fuel of the fire.

- **S** is for squeeze. Squeeze the trigger slowly and evenly so as to not use all of the extinguishing agents too quickly.

- **S** is for sweep. Whiling aiming at the base of the fire, sweep the nozzle from side to side to make sure to cover as much of the base of the flames as possible.

If applicable, call your local emergency services before the fire is too large for you to put out or after if you are afraid there might still be hot spots.

Prevention of fires is of utmost importance to the IT support technician. The first step is to reduce fire hazards in your workplace. Keep your workplace free of clutter: don't stockpile papers, wires, and other combustible material to reduce the risks of something catching fire. Regularly inspect equipment for damaged cords, overheating components, and overloaded power strips/surge protectors. Have a fire safety plan in your workplace and schedule regular checks of your fire alarms to make sure they are working.

Personal Safety

While the standard IT support technician might not be breathing in dangerous chemicals or working with highly explosive materials in normal working conditions, that doesn't mean there aren't personal safety issues to consider. One major threat to IT technicians is online safety. Often, it is the IT staff who are targeted by **threat actors** to gain access to a network/ computer system. However, that topic will be covered in more depth in Chapter 7, "Security."

Another often-overlooked risk to the IT support technician is physical safety. One area of focus in recent decades has been on repetitive strain injuries, or **RSI**s. You will often be working long hours at a desk typing on your keyboard and clicking away with your mouse. Carpal tunnel syndrome is a very real condition that affects many office workers and involves pinching the nerve in your wrist. It is a condition that often causes pain in the hand and wrist. This condition occurs because of the repetitive motion of typing and using your mouse. To help prevent carpal tunnel, take breaks from your computer when at all possible— stand up, stretch, hydrate, and move your body. Another prevention technique is the use of ergonomic devices.

Ergonomics is the study of engineering and designing of products and systems to help people. This can be as simple as chairs to help promote better posture when sitting at a desk, the rise of adjustable desks to allow for standing and working, mouse pads with wrist guards to help the posturing of your hand, and even keyboards to help your hands be in a more natural position when typing.

Figure 2-3 shows an example of an ergonomic keyboard.

Figure 2-3 *Ergonomic Keyboard*

In addition to RSIs, injuring yourself lifting is also a possible safety risk. You might often be tasked with moving around heavy pieces of equipment. Even lighter equipment can pose a risk of injury if not carried or placed correctly. Use a dolly or moving cart when at all possible. If you must lift an object, use your legs and don't pull up with your back muscles. Ask for help if a piece of equipment needs more than one person to move it.

In addition to injuring yourself physically through moving a heavy object or getting an RSI, you also need to be careful not to be the target of a physical attack. You will often be working alone or late at night. You might be transporting valuable IT equipment from one office to another. This makes you a target for a would-be thief. Be aware of your surroundings and communicate with your colleagues about when and where you're at if it could be a risky situation.

Finally, maintain a healthy lifestyle. Drink plenty of water, eat a balanced diet, take breaks from the computer (in accordance with your company policy), use blue light filters on your monitor to help prevent eyestrain (most operating systems, including phones, have a "night light" feature to help reduce harmful blue light), and get sleep.

"An ounce of prevention is worth a pound of cure."—Benjamin Franklin

Ports and Interfaces

One commonly confused concept in IT is the difference between an interface and a port. You will often hear these terms used interchangeably, but there is a difference. An **interface** is how a device communicates. For example, a mouse is a hardware interface. In particular, it is an input interface. The mouse lets the user send x and y coordinates to the operating system to move the cursor around the screen. Consequently, the mouse is a hardware interface that is also an input interface. How it connects to the computer is through a port.

> **NOTE** You will often hear terms like an *input* or *output device*. You need to think of it from the perspective of the computer itself. If the information is going into the computer, it is an input device. If the information is going out of the computer, it is an output device. Common input devices are mice, keyboards, scanners, and the like. Common output devices are monitors, speakers, printers, and so forth. If you have an all-in-one printer, then you have an **input/output device**. The printer is an output device, but the scanner is an input device.

The mouse also communicates with a software interface called a driver. The **driver** is software that translates the raw input from the hardware to the operating system. It can also translate output from the operating system to the hardware (think of an image being displayed on your monitor).

A **port** is often the physical connection to the computer. Most mice in the past decade are USB. The USB is the port that the mouse uses to connect to the computer. The physical port is what transfers the electrical signals back and forth. To clarify, the mouse is a hardware input interface that sends x and y coordinates to the operating system through the software interface of a driver so that the operating system can understand the data being fed to it. The mouse itself is plugged into a USB port. The USB port itself is capable of inputting and outputting data—think of a flash drive—but is only inputting data from the mouse.

> **NOTE** When talking about hardware, we usually speak of physical ports—an actual electrical part you can touch. However, there are virtual ports as well. For example, when you go on the Web and search a vital question like what music artist said what to whom, you are often using Hypertext Transfer Protocol Secure, or https, which uses port 443. Port 443 is a virtual port for https communication. You can't physically touch the port.
>
> A wireless card, or wireless NIC, is a physical port, not a virtual port. While you don't plug anything into it, you could touch the actual chip that is sending and receiving radio waves to communicate.

Video Ports

Video ports are just what they sound like—ports that output video. Before we delve into the various video ports every IT technician should know, it is important to know the difference between analog and digital video signals. An analog video signal is presented in a waveform, whereas a digital video signal is discrete binary bits of 0 or 1 (see Figure 2-4).

Binary is how computers function and dates back to early circuits. A circuit was either open, or off (0), or it was closed, or on (1). If you look on a PSU, you will see a switch with a 0 and a 1. Zero means off, and one means on. Early video ports were analog, so if the monitor received analog signals, the computer would have to convert from binary to analog for the monitor to understand it. Today, most monitors are digital, so the move from analog to digital makes sense.

ANALOG VS DIGITAL SIGNAL

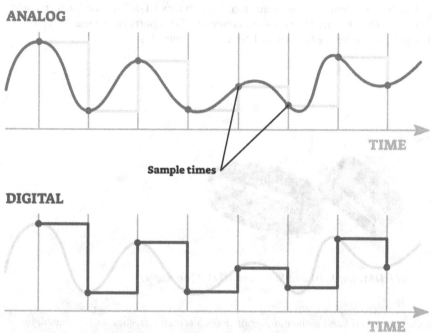

Figure 2-4 *Analog vs. Digital Signal*

NOTE   Consumers have been inundated with various technical/marketing terms for their televisions for the past two decades. Terms such as *HD*, *Full HD*, *UHD*, and now *8k*—not to mention *QLED*, *OLED*, and so forth—have saturated the marketplace. While the latter is beyond the scope of this certification, you should know the former. *HD* stands for high definition and is 1280×720 pixels. A **pixel** is merely a single dot of color on a screen. So, HD is 1280 pixels horizontally and 720 pixels vertically. Interestingly, display resolutions for HD and FHD are often referred to as the vertical pixels rather than the horizontal pixels; hence, HD is often called *720(p)*. The p stands for progressive because it allows the television to display all lines at once rather than interlaced, which writes odd lines on the first pass and even lines on the second pass. *Full HD* is 1920×1080, 1080(p), or (i); *UHD* is 3840×2160, or 4k; and now we're seeing 7680×4320, or 8k! While these resolutions are more specific to televisions, you will see them marketed in computer monitors as well. One more common monitor resolution that never really came to television is 2k, or 2560×1440, and often called *1440p*. This does not mean all computer monitors follow these resolutions. In fact, many laptops have a 4:3 aspect ratio—making it more square than rectangular—and will have very different resolutions. Today, most of these HD resolutions are digital in port communication, with the one major exception of the aging component port, which is an analog port that is capable of HD resolution.

HDMI

High-Definition Multimedia Interface, or **HDMI**, ports are one of the most common video ports for both televisions and monitors. It is a digital port consisting of 19 pins that can transmit both audio *and* video. With the introduction of the HDMI 2.1 standard, an HDMI 2.1 port can support 4k, 5k, 8k, and 10k at 120 Hz and 48 gigabits per second (Gbps) of bandwidth/data. This is a huge improvement from the previous HDMI standard, which could only support up to 4k at 60 Hz. The two most common HDMI ports are standard (Type A) and Mini (Type C, not to be confused with USB C). See Figure 2-5.

Figure 2-5   *Mini HDMI (on Left) and Standard HDMI (on Right)*

NOTE *Hz* stands for hertz and is the number of times a screen refreshes, or is redrawn, in one second. The official 4k standard for television is 4k at 60 Hz. Gamers will often speak about achieving the maximum frames per second, or fps, when playing video games. This is a direct relation to how often the graphics card can refresh the screen and thereby has a correlation to the hertz of the monitor. For example, if a gamer is receiving stats from the game stating they are playing at 120 fps, but they are using an older HDMI port that is capable of displaying only 60 Hz, then they are only seeing 60 fps on their monitor even if their video card is capable of displaying more. This is why many "gaming" monitors sold use Display-Ports because it is capable of displaying more hertz.

DisplayPort

DisplayPort is a popular digital, 20-pin, video port that many gamers prefer over HDMI. It supports both video and audio like HDMI. While it has never really gained traction in the television space, it is fairly common on modern video cards and monitors. It can output, on the high end, 8k at 240 Hz with 77.37 Gbps of bandwidth/data! For some, it is easy to confuse a DisplayPort and an HDMI port because one side looks identical to the other. However, a DisplayPort has a flat end on one side. There is also a mini DisplayPort that looks quite different. See Figure 2-6.

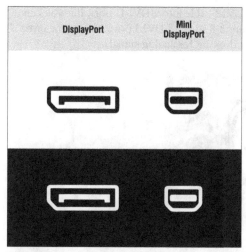

Figure 2-6 *DisplayPort and Mini DisplayPort Illustration*

DVI

A **DVI** is an older 24-pin port that can be both digital and analog and carries only video and *not* audio. Unfortunately, marketing of this port made it more confusing for consumers. There are several variations of DVI: DVI-D Single Link, DVI-D Dual Link, DVI-I Single Link, DVI-I Dual Link, and DVI-A. DVI-A was pure analog and is not used anymore. However, you will still see DVI-D and DVI-I in some older computers. DVI-D is a pure digital connection. It is capable of a max resolution of 3840×2400 at 30 Hz in Dual Link. You will still see people use DVI-D today because it can display 1080p at 144 Hz, but you would have to have a separate audio cable. See Figure 2-7 to see what a DVI-D looks like.

Figure 2-7 *DVI-D Cable*

DVI-I is another port you might still see. It is capable of carrying an analog and a digital signal on separate pins. It does not convert digital to analog signals or vice versa. Rather, it can pass through analog signals on certain pins and digital signals on other pins. This is important because you can't plug a DVI-A or DVI-I cable into a DVI-D port, but you can plug a DVI-D cable into a DVI-I port. See Figure 2-8 to see a DVI-I port. Notice the cross formation with four dots around it. Those four dots are for analog signals.

Figure 2-8   *DVI-I Port*

VGA

A **VGA** cable is a 15-pin analog port. It does not carry audio signals much like DVI. VGA is one of the original video ports. While it can display up to 2048×1536 at 85 Hz, it is *not* considered a high-definition port. This means you can display 1920×1080 at 60 Hz, but it will be an analog signal and HD is a digital signal. Component ports are the only analog ports that are capable of being called HD because they still carry a digital signal over the analog communication. VGA would have to convert the digital signal to analog and, consequently, is not labeled as true HD. In fact, if you were to compare an HDMI display at 1920×1080 to a VGA display at 1920×1080, you would notice that the VGA display is fuzzier and not as crisp. VGA cables are often blue (see Figure 2-9) but can come in other colors.

Figure 2-9   *Traditional Blue VGA Cable*

USB-C

USB-C can carry audio and video. However, it can do more than that. USB-C, while a port, is also a form factor. This means that it's one of the more complicated concepts for consumers. See the subsection "USB-C" later for more information.

USB

Universal Serial Bus, or **USB**, is a common port type found in most computers today. By design, it can transmit both power and data. The *serial* in its name is an important distinction because it is an evolution of the original 9-pin **serial port**, also called an RS-232 port. While serial ports have all but disappeared from modern computers, they are still in use in industrial control systems and commercial routers and switches. While serial ports are slow in data transfer and do not support power over their wires like USB, they are reliable and easily programmed. Luckily, while most modern computers do not include serial ports anymore, there are many serial-to-USB adapters on the market to communicate with serial port devices. Some people confuse serial ports with VGA ports because of the similar external design, but there are two ways to identify them easily. First, serial ports have only 9 pins, whereas VGA ports have 15 pins. Also, most serial ports are male (pins sticking out), whereas most VGA ports are female (holes for the male pins on the cable to plug in to). In other words, serial ports are male and their cables are female, whereas VGA ports are female and their cables are male. See Figure 2-10 to see a serial port next to a VGA port on the rear input/output panel of a motherboard.

Figure 2-10 *Directly Below the Large Pink Parallel Port Is a Serial Port (Left) and a Blue VGA Port (Right)*

USB speeds have dramatically improved over the years. The first USB version, USB 1.0, was capable of 1.5 megabits per second (Mbps); USB 1.1, 12 Mbps; USB 2.0, 480 Mbps; USB 3.0, 5 gigabits per second (Gbps); USB 3.1, 10 Gbps; USB 3.2, 20 Gbps; USB 4, 40 Gbps; and USB 4 2.0, 80 Gbps.

USB Form Factors

In addition to the different USB versions, which primarily affect speed, there are also different **USB form factors**. Consequently, USBs can look different from each other. Traditionally, when most consumers think USB, they are thinking of USB-A. This is the original rectangular port that has a singular orientation, which means you can only plug it in one way. USB-B is more square and has been traditionally used to connect to printers and is now a popular connection to 3D printers. Mini-USB was a popular standard for phones and portable electronic devices for some time before micro-USB replaced it. Both are singular orientation, and the plug can only be plugged in one way. The newer form factor that has been gaining rapid momentum is USB-C. USB-C is not singular orientation and can be plugged in right side up or upside down. It is now becoming common on most electronic devices, including phones. In addition to the ease of plugging in, there are a multitude of other benefits to USB-C. See the following section for more information. Figure 2-11 helps you visualize the different USB form factors.

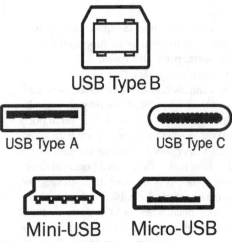

Figure 2-11   *USB Form Factors*

USB-C

USB-C is fast becoming the most ubiquitous of USB form factors. It is also one of the more complicated form factors. By definition, USB-C can carry data and power like the original USB standard. It is now being used as the favored port to power many laptops out there. However, it is also capable of carrying video and audio. Its bidirectional method of plugging in—so you don't have to worry about which side is up—and smaller footprint have made this a prolific form factor. However, the capabilities of USB-C vary wildly and depend on the actual interface technology being used behind the form factor.

USB 3.0, capable of 5 Gbps, can be a USB Type A or USB Type C form factor. USB 3.1, capable of 10 Gbps, can also be Type A or C. However, USB 3.2 is almost exclusively USB Type C, which is capable of 20 Gbps. How do you know which USB type your USB-C port is? Read the documentation for the specific electronic component that has the USB-C connection.

To add to the complexity, USB 4 is often called **Thunderbolt**, but technically Thunderbolt 3/4 is one **proprietary** implementation of USB 3.1/4 capable of 40 Gbps. Non-Thunderbolt USB 4 is only capable of 20 Gbps. Thunderbolt 5 uses USB-C as well and is capable of 80 Gbps. So, all Thunderbolt 3/4/5 interfaces are USB-C ports, but not all USB-C ports are Thunderbolt. Again, how do you know if you have a regular USB-C port or a Thunderbolt USB-C port? Read the documentation or look for the proprietary lightning bolt icon next to the port. See Figure 2-12.

Ethernet Ports

The most common interface for an Ethernet port is an **RJ-45** connector (see Figure 2-13) plugged into a network interface card (NIC). The Ethernet port on the NIC is what you would use to physically connect the Ethernet cable to the Internet or local network. If you connect wirelessly, you use a wireless NIC, and no physical cable is needed. There are also fiber connections to connect to networks, but they are typically not found as direct connections to consumer devices at this time.

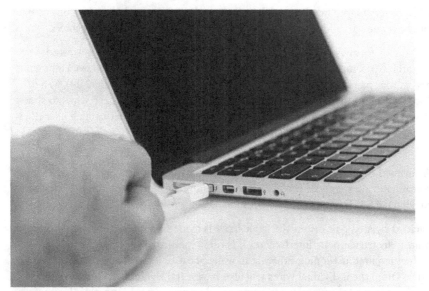

Figure 2-12 *Thunderbolt USB-C Port (Look for a Lightning Bolt by the Port)*

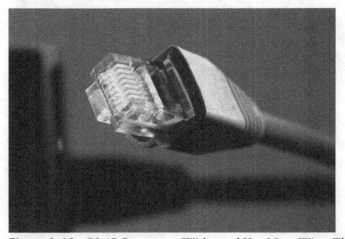

Figure 2-13 *RJ-45 Connector (Wider and Has More Wires Than the Older Telephone Connector, Which Was an RJ-11)*

An Ethernet cable to connect to a network might be called a CAT 5e, UTP, 1000BASE-T cable with an RJ-45 connector. Let's break this down:

- An Ethernet cable is often categorized as a CAT cable, with *CAT* abbreviated from Category. There are currently eight categories of Ethernet cables: CAT 1–5 are rarely used anymore; CAT 5e and 6/6a are commonly used, and CAT 7/8 are used for short runs in data centers. The higher the category, the faster the Ethernet cables can transfer the data. This explanation is a tad oversimplistic but helps in the general overview. CAT 5e is still used in many places and is capable of delivering 1 Gbps of data. CAT 6a can deliver 10 Gbps of data. Both CAT 5e and CAT 6 are capable of sending data 100 meters before needing a signal repeater. CAT 7/8 can deliver 40 Gbps of data but only between 10 and 30 meters and are typically used only in data centers.

- The *TP* stands for twisted pair. Starting with CAT 3, electrical engineers started twisting the wires together to reduce electrical interference. Now, we have eight wires twisted in four pairs to reduce interference and gain speed (see Figure 2-14). When cutting your own Ethernet wiring, you must untwist the ends of these wires to slide them into an RJ-45 connector. In addition to TP, which all Ethernet cabling uses now, you can also purchase **STP** or **UTP**. Both are twisted pair, but *U* stands for unshielded and *S* stands for shielded.

  - Unshielded is what it sounds like. The cable is unshielded from any sort of electromagnetic interference. The cables are generally cheaper and more flexible than shielded cables. For most smaller runs inside a home or office, UTP is acceptable.

  - Shielded twisted pair means the cable itself is made of a material to help protect against electromagnetic interference. It is often made of PVC or plenum. Plenum is often required if running Ethernet in walls because it has flame-retardant properties. Often the individual wires will also have a foil shielding to protect against interference. STP is often used in commercial projects or for long runs. However, STP is usually more expensive than STP and not as flexible.

Figure 2-14   *Twisted Pairs in Ethernet*

- *PVC* is polyvinyl chloride, which can produce toxic fumes and should be used in open-air situations.

- Plenum cables have a fire-resistant jacket and should be used inside walls, drop ceilings, or under raised floors.

- The 1000BASE-T part means that there is 1000 Mbps of bandwidth. You will also see this written as 1GBASE as well. The *G* stands for gigabit, which is equal to 1000 megabits. The *BASE* merely refers to baseband signaling, which means only Ethernet signals are carried on it. The *T* stands for twisted pair. Yes, this is redundant because the *T* in UTP and STP also stands for twisted pair.

> **NOTE**   Another term you will hear with Ethernet is *PoE*, which stands for Power over Ethernet. Normally, Ethernet is for data. However, if the switch supports it or you use an externally powered POE injector, you can deliver up to 95 watts of power to the end device with the newest standards. However, it is more typical to deliver 15–30 watts on most devices. PoE is used to power IP telephones, IP cameras, and more. This means the IP phone could have only one Ethernet cable plugged in to deliver data and power to run the phone! While the consumer space has not really started seeing an adoption of PoE, the commercial space has been using it for some time. You must use a CAT 5e or greater cable to use POE.

Common Power Cables (Desktop, Laptop, Mobile)

Most desktop computers use a C13 power cord on one end and a country-specific plug on the other end. This cord then connects to the computer's PSU. This common cable allows for easy shipping to many countries because the C13 is a universal standard and readily matched with the correct country-specific plug on the other end (see Figure 2-15). Some computer manufacturers use a proprietary power adapter, but it is rare in the desktop marketplace. The power cable will go from the wall directly to the PSU the majority of the time. The PSU will then convert the AC electricity from the wall outlet to DC electricity for the computer to run.

Figure 2-15   *Typical Desktop Power Cable with C13 Plug (Left) and Country-Specific Plug (Right)*

Unfortunately, for many decades, laptops have used proprietary power adapters. There are dozens of proprietary charging tips/types for different manufacturers. Even the same manufacturer often has different charging tips/types for different models. To make it even more confusing, even if two laptops have the same charging tip, that doesn't mean you can use one charging cable on the other because often it has different voltage and amperage output. Luckily, because of the USB-C's capability to carry enough power to power many laptops, we are starting to see an adoption of that universal standard.

> **NOTE**   The European Union has made great strides in making USB-C a universal charging port to reduce e-waste. The EU has mandated that by the end of 2024 all phones, tablets, and cameras will have to be USB-C if they are sold in EU countries. In addition, the EU is pushing for all laptops to be the same. As a result, many manufacturers have quickly adopted the USB-C standard so that they do not lose sales in EU countries. Notably, this mandate caused Apple to ditch its proprietary Lightning phone cable and move to USB-C with the release of the iPhone 15.

Like laptops, mobile phones have had a litany of various power cables. There are dozens of proprietary phone cables. Most notably was Apple's Lightning cable, which was the follow-up to the company's proprietary 30-pin connector in use previously. Luckily, with the introduction of the iPhone 15, Apple has moved to the universal standard of USB-C. Most phones out now use USB-C. There are still some proprietary cables out there, but they are fewer than before. Before USB-C, phones started out with almost entirely proprietary adapters, then moved to mini-USB, then micro-USB (refer to Figure 2-11).

Converters vs. Adapters

One important distinction when needing to convert from one type of cable to another is whether you need a converter or an adapter. An **adapter** changes the plug type but must be the same signal. For example, you can go from an HDMI plug on one side to a DisplayPort plug on the other side with an adapter. They are both digital signals, so you are just adapting one plug to the other.

However, you will need a **converter** if going from a digital signal to an analog signal or vice versa. For instance, if you want to go from VGA (analog) to HDMI (digital), you will need a converter. Converters require power and are often more expensive than adapters. There are unscrupulous people on the Internet who will sell you an HDMI-to-VGA adapter where they just rewire the pins to each other. However, it will not work because you can't just send an analog signal to a digital signal without first converting it.

> **NOTE**   This distinction between adapters and converters also applies to electrical plugs. When traveling, people often buy adapters to plug in their equipment to the wall socket that matches the country's specifications. For most electronics, this is fine because most of the power bricks for modern electronics are rated with an input of 100–240 volts. Therefore, the adapter merely changes the plug style for the wall receptacle. However, you need to check the power brick, which is the box that is in the middle between the wall plug and the plug for the device that converts AC to DC, to see what the input range is. Most of North America and parts of South America use 110–120 volts, whereas most of the rest of the world uses 220–240 volts. Again, most modern electronics can accept the full range of voltage input, but you should always double-check first. There are many horror stories of fires because someone plugged a hair dryer into the wall outlet when traveling with an adapter and not a converter. The reason is that most hair dryers are not dual voltage and only accept the voltage of the country where it was bought. In this case, you would need to purchase a converter to convert from one voltage to another, not just an adapter!

Identifying, Installing, and Upgrading Computer Components

Whether you are building a computer, upgrading, or fixing one, it is vital to be able to identify computer components to be successful.

Identifying Computer Components

An IT support technician needs to be able to identify many essential computer components to be able to install or upgrade them. While the following sections do not provide an exhaustive list of every computer component, they include the major components you need to be able to identify.

Processor

The **processor** is the brain of the computer. It processes instructions of the programs sent to it. It is also called a central processing unit, or CPU. Most modern CPUs have multiple cores. These cores act as *almost* independent processors and allow the CPU to process many workloads or tasks at one time. Early CPUs had one core. As a result, it could perform only one task at a time. Today, some high-end CPUs have as many as 96 cores! In many server setups, the motherboards can support multiple processors with each CPU having multiple cores.

In addition, many CPUs are capable of multithreading or hyperthreading. Think of a CPU core as an independent brain. If I have a dual-core CPU, it would be like having two brains with each brain being able to do very different tasks. Multithreading is like having a right brain and left brain in one core. You can perform different tasks in each brain half, but they can't be radically different from each other. For example, with a multithreaded-capable core in this analogy, you could perform simple arithmetic while listening to classical music. However, you would not be able to do calculus while painting a complex scene in oil. Basically, the program being sent to a multithreaded core must be written to take advantage of this multithreading. Otherwise, it would just use another core. So, a dual-core CPU with multithreading has two cores but can split tasks in each core to have a pseudo four-core performance. In fact, Windows 11 shows these multithreaded cores as logical processors, so that a dual-core example would state two cores with four logical processors.

The way that a CPU processes instructions is separated into two camps: CISC and RISC. *CISC* stands for complex instruction set computer, and *RISC* stands for reduced instruction set computer. To simplify this distinction, let's use the analogy of a complex calculus problem. A CISC processor would take the entire problem and work on solving it. In contrast, a RISC processor would break up the problem into smaller chunks and solve it. On one hand, the benefit of a CISC processor is the raw horsepower to deal with complex instructions. On the other hand, a RISC processor has the benefit of energy efficiency and speed in small instruction sets. Traditionally, desktop/laptop computers have used CISC processors, whereas mobile devices have used RISC processors.

> **NOTE** The lines between CISC being for desktops/laptops and RISC being for mobile devices have blurred recently. Apple has released M series processors for its laptops that use a RISC architecture. Meanwhile, Intel has CPUs that advertise performance cores and efficiency cores. The performance cores are CISC, and the efficiency cores are RISC.

The CPU architecture types **x86/x64** versus **ARM** showcase the CISC/RISC division. *ARM*, which stands for Advanced RISC Machine, is RISC, as the name implies, and is used on most mobile devices for energy efficiency. The x86 is an older CISC architecture type that was limited to 32-bit processing. Today, most desktop computers run on x64, also CISC, which allows 64-bit processing and is backward-compatible with 32-bit processing.

NOTE Modern ARM processors are 64 bit and backward-compatible to 32 bit. The x64 is the same but in CISC form. To understand the difference between a 32-bit processor and a 64-bit processor, it is important to understand what each means. Computers work in binary, so a 32-bit processor is capable of understanding 2^{32}, or 4,294,967,295 bits. This is an important number because a 32-bit processor can only understand up to this number in calculations. Therefore, with 32-bit CPUs, you can't have more than 4 gigabytes of RAM installed because the CPU can't understand a larger number. Technically, you can install more than 4 GB, but the processor will only see 4 GB as useable. In contrast, a 64-bit processor can have over 17 billion gigabytes of installed RAM. Remember that 2^{64} is a lot more than double 2^{32}—it's exponentially bigger.

The two CPU socket types for x64 processors are **PGA** and **LGA**. *PGA* stands for pin grid array. A PGA CPU has the pins on the CPU with the motherboard having the holes for the pins to be inserted into (see Figure 2-16). *LGA* stands for land grid array. In this style, the pins are on the motherboard with the CPU having flat contact points for the pins to touch (see Figure 2-17). Traditionally, Intel has supported LGA, and AMD has supported PGA. However, this has recently changed with AMD's new AM5 CPU socket being LGA. Both PGA and LGA have many generations of sockets, so you can't merely put any LGA CPU in an Intel-compatible motherboard. You would need to know whether it is an LGA 1700 or an LGA 1200, among many others.

NOTE You might also encounter a *BGA*, or ball grid array. This style is commonly found on laptops, phones, tablets, and gaming consoles. The CPU is soldered directly to the motherboard with this style.

Figure 2-16   *PGA CPU (the Pins Are on the CPU)*

Figure 2-17   *LGA CPU and LGA Motherboard Socket (the Pins Are on the Motherboard)*

Motherboard

If a processor is the brain of the computer, then the motherboard is the central nervous system. The CPU is installed on a motherboard. The **motherboard** is a large circuit board that is foundational for other components to connect and communicate through. It serves three main functions:

1. **Connectivity:** It allows vital communication between the CPU, RAM, graphics cards (also called video cards), storage devices, and more with the chipset working as the intermediary.

2. **Power Delivery:** The PSU supplies power directly to the motherboard through the 24-pin PSU cable; subsequently, the motherboard delivers power to various connected components such as the RAM, M.2 storage, and some lower-powered graphic cards.

3. **Expansion:** The motherboard often provides slots for expanding functionality like graphic cards, sound cards, video capture cards, Wi-Fi, and more.

Regarding connectivity and how the motherboard communicates between components, this is often done through the **chipset** on the motherboard. Originally, the chipset consisted of the Northbridge and Southbridge chipsets. The Northbridge handles communication between the CPU and extreme time-sensitive components such as RAM and the graphics card. The Southbridge chipset handles communication between the CPU and hard drives, optical drives, I/O ports, and less time-sensitive devices. On modern motherboards, most of the Northbridge's chipset functions have been moved directly to the CPU for speed while remaining functions have been merged with the Southbridge chipset. Today, we rarely refer to Northbridge and Southbridge chipsets and merely call it *the chipset*.

If you are not sure of the processor and/or motherboard in a current machine, the easiest way to identify it in Windows is to press Windows+R to open the Run dialog box. Then type **msinfo32** and press Enter. Here, you will see the CPU/Processor name, the motherboard manufacturer and specific model (labeled as BaseBoard Manufacturer/Product), and more detailed system information. You can also run **systeminfo** from the command prompt to see relevant information. For macOS, you will need to look in the "About This Mac" section. See the "macOS System Tools" section in Chapter 5, "macOS."

RAM

To continue with the analogy of the human body and computer components, **RAM** would be short-term memory. RAM, or random-access memory, is where the operating system stores everything that is currently opened and being used. This includes operating system programs, files that are opened, and web pages currently being displayed in your browser. It is volatile in nature, which means that what is stored in RAM disappears when you restart your computer or shut it down. This is contrasted to storage devices such as hard drives or solid-state drives. Those are long-term storage devices and are nonvolatile. If you have a saved document, it will be saved on a storage device. However, when you open that saved document, the operating system will place a copy of its contents in RAM for speed of accessing it.

When referring to RAM, people often use the term *RAM stick*. A RAM stick is merely a piece of silicone with many memory modules on it that collectively form what is called RAM. While there are various forms of RAM, including the very fast static random-access memory (SRAM) that is used in CPU caches, most RAM being referred to is DDR SDRAM or GDDR SDRAM. *DDR SDRAM*, which stands for Double Data Rate Synchronous Dynamic Random Access Memory, is often shortened to just *DDR RAM* and is used on modern computers. GDDR SDRAM is DDR RAM tuned for graphic cards and often called *GDDR RAM* (short for Graphics DDR RAM). DDR has gone through many iterations. With each iteration, speed and bandwidth have increased. As of this writing, the most modern motherboards utilize DDR5, and the most modern graphic cards utilize GDDR6. It is common that graphics cards utilize newer DDR standards because speed over cost is a priority for modern graphics cards. Also, you usually have lower amounts of RAM on a graphics card than you do on the main system. However, many gaming graphics cards have 16 gigabytes of GDDR, which often rivals what people have installed on their motherboard.

> **NOTE** How much RAM do you need? The short answer is you need enough RAM to comfortably run the programs that you have open at one time. A large chunk of your RAM will be used by your operating system, and the rest will be used by active programs you have open. If you edit videos or play games, you will want more RAM than someone who does minimal web browsing and opens a word processing document sometimes. If you have ever opened just one more tab on your web browser to discover your computer starts running incredibly slow, you probably ran out of RAM. When you run out of RAM, the operating system must write those temporary files to your storage device, which is incredibly slow compared to RAM. On Windows, this would be a file on your operating system drive called *pagefile.sys*. As the programs you use become more complex, the need for more RAM increases. A decade ago, 8 GB of RAM was considered a lot. Today, it is a recommended minimum on most builds.

Peripherals

In addition to a CPU, motherboard, and RAM, computers also have peripherals. **Peripherals** can be both input and output devices. They can also be external or internal. A keyboard is an external, input peripheral device. The devices connected directly to the motherboard are internal peripheral devices. Video/graphics cards, wireless network cards, Bluetooth cards, and even storage devices such as hard drives and solid-state drives are all peripheral devices. These internal peripherals can be integrated on the motherboard from the factory, such as wireless and Ethernet NICs, or installed afterward, such as graphics cards and storage devices. These can be installed in expansion slots such as **PCIe** slots or dedicated ports such as SATA or M.2.

Storage Devices

Traditionally, **hard drives** were the long-term, nonvolatile, storage device in computers. Hard drives are magnetically written storage devices that have a spinning metal platter, almost looking like a miniature metal record player, that reads and writes data. The issues with hard drives are those two defining characteristics. First, hard drives store their information magnetically. This makes them susceptible to magnetic interference, and that interference can even cause data corruption. In fact, the official way to erase a hard drive for recycling purposes is to use a degausser. A degausser creates a strong magnetic field that erases the hard drive. Additionally, magnetic storage will degrade over time, much like an old VHS tape that loses its information over time (it is magnetically stored as well). A hard drive could last 5 years, or it could last 20 years. The problem is that over time data degradation is inevitable.

The second issue with hard drives is the spinning of that metal platter with the moving actuator arm (think of a tone arm on a record player). Because these parts are mechanical in nature, they can break. Are hard drives dead technology? No. In a cost to performance to storage size comparison, hard drives still win when looking at large storage needs. Yes, SSDs perform much faster than hard drives, but as the storage size increases, so do their prices. As of this writing, an 8 TB SSD is three times more expensive than an 8 TB hard drive. For smaller sizes, the price is less of a difference, but the larger sizes see a large difference. Hard drives come in two main form factors: 3.5 inch, which is typical for desktop computers, and 2.5 inch, which is typical for laptops.

Solid-state drive, or **SSD**, is a newer long-term, nonvolatile, storage device in computers. SSDs are neither mechanical nor magnetic. Instead, they use a type of flash memory to store the data. This means there are no moving parts to break and no issue with magnetic fields. While there can still be quality control issues with the actual flash memory modules that are installed that can cause premature failure, they usually have a finite number of read and write cycles. This means that it is normally possible to calculate exactly how long the SSD will last by looking at how many times the SSD has been read/written. There are two main form factors for SSDs: 2.5 inch, the same size as a laptop hard drive, and M.2.

NOTE Hard drives and 2.5-inch SSDs normally plug into the SATA port on a motherboard for data transfer. However, **M.2** is a new form factor for SSDs and can be confusing for those new to the IT field. M.2 is a port that is on the motherboard. It allows an M.2 drive to be directly inserted onto the motherboard. This direct insertion means the drive can get power and transfer data directly from the one M.2 port on the motherboard. Normally, a hard drive and SSD need a data cable plugged into the motherboard and a power cable from the PSU plugged into it. With M.2, you don't need either cable. The often-confusing part for consumers is understanding that M.2 is a form factor. There are two technologies behind M.2. You can have an SSD M.2 or an NVMe M.2 drive. They look identical, but how they transfer data is different. An SSD M.2 transfers data over the SATA interface. This means that it is exactly as fast as what a regular 2.5-inch SSD is because both use the SATA interface. However, an NVMe M.2 drive uses the PCIe interface. This is the same interface your graphics card uses and is substantially faster than SATA. Most M.2 ports on motherboards will accept either technology, so it is important to distinguish between the two. As you can imagine, SSD M.2 is usually cheaper than NVMe M.2.

Installing and Upgrading Computer Components

With the exception of the PSU, you should always wear an antistatic wrist strap and use ESD safety when working with computer components. Whether building a new computer or upgrading components on a computer, it is important to know the relationships between the components. The two sets of relationships you need to understand are form factor and compatibility factor. The following information mainly applies to desktop computers and not laptop/all-in-one computers.

NOTE While technically, you can replace motherboards and processors on laptops and all-in-one computers (where the computer and the screen are one unit), most of them are proprietary. This means that you can replace a motherboard on a laptop, but you will have to buy the motherboard from the laptop manufacturer because even their form factor is proprietary. The only items that are replaceable (usually, because there are exceptions) that aren't proprietary are items such as RAM, optical drive, and maybe the ability to swap out a hard drive with an SSD if both are 2.5-inch form factor.

Form Factor

The form factor relationship is usually defined as the physical dimension relationship between the motherboard, case (sometimes called tower), and PSU. Motherboards come in various physical sizes, such as ATX-E, ATX, Micro ATX, and ITX boards (listed from largest to smallest). As a rule of thumb, the larger the motherboard, the more physical connections and features it has. If you are building a simple home theater computer to play movies and music, you probably don't need an ATX-E but could get away with a smaller board like a Mini-ITX or Mini PC board like the Intel NUC. The motherboard's size will determine the computer case you use as well. A small case designed for a Mini-ITX board will not fit ATX-sized boards. However, a large computer case could fit an ATX-E board all the way down to a Mini-ITX board, but you might have a lot of wasted space inside. You will read terms such as *full-sized tower*, *mid-sized tower*, and *small form factor cases* when researching cases. Unfortunately, there is no agreed-upon consensus on what physical dimensions make up these terms. Some mid-sized towers can hold an ATX board or a Micro ATX, whereas some only support Micro ATX and smaller. Basically, you need to read the case's dimensions to see what size motherboard it can hold. The two most common sized desktop motherboards are ATX and Micro ATX.

In addition to the relationship between the size of the motherboard and the size of the case to hold it, you also need to look at the size of the PSU. Traditional desktop power supply units are ATX PS/2 form factor. These fit in most mid-sized towers and above. There is also the smaller SFX PSU form factor for smaller cases like those that might fit a Mini-ITX board, and the even smaller TFX for some Mini-PC cases. These terms refer only to the physical dimensions of the PSUs. You need to choose the wattage of the PSU based on what you're running inside the computer.

Compatibility Factor

In addition to the form factor compatibility, you also need to look at the compatibility factor. This is especially important when looking at the CPU, motherboard, and RAM relationship. With desktop computers, you basically have two manufacturers of CPUs: Intel and AMD. An Intel CPU will not install on an AMD-compatible motherboard or vice versa. Furthermore, the specific CPU will run only on certain chipsets and socket types on the motherboard. Consequently, if you have a computer with an Intel Core i5-9300 CPU, it must be installed on an Intel-compatible motherboard with an LGA 1151 socket type and a compatible chipset like the H310 chipset. This makes it much harder to upgrade computer components. If you wanted to upgrade that same Intel Core i5-9300 CPU to a newer Intel Core i5-14600, you would also have to replace the motherboard because the socket type changed from an LGA 1151 to an LGA 1700 in that time, and you would need a newer 600 or 700 series chipset.

Using the same example, in addition to changing the motherboard for the new CPU, you will also probably need to change the RAM. The Intel Core i5-9300 compatible motherboards utilized DDR4. Most of the newer Intel boards utilize DDR5. Luckily, the iteration of RAM is not dependent on whether it's an Intel or AMD CPU, but rather on the motherboard and chipset. The new AMD motherboards, utilizing the AM5 CPU socket, have transitioned to using DDR5 while the newer Intel motherboards are starting that transition over to DDR5 as well. The number after the DDR on the RAM denotes a different generation or iteration of the RAM. You cannot stick a DDR4 RAM stick in a motherboard designed for DDR5 RAM because it won't fit. There is a notch in the bottom of the RAM stick that is in a different place on the different generations of RAM. This notch helps to make sure you place the RAM in the correct orientation and to help with putting the wrong generation of RAM in (see Figure 2-18). In DDR5 the notch is closer to the center of the RAM stick, so DDR4 RAM will not insert correctly.

Figure 2-18   *RAM Stick (the Notch in the Bottom Helps Installation Orientation)*

To simplify, before you start assembling a computer or upgrading parts, make sure that you understand the physical form factor relationship of the case, motherboard, and power supply. Additionally, the motherboard, CPU, and RAM must be compatible with each other whether you're building new or upgrading.

Installing/Upgrading: Processor/Motherboard

Always read the motherboard manual to see the exact steps to install a motherboard and the CPU. The model of the motherboard is generally written on the motherboard itself.

To install the motherboard, follow these steps:

1. **For new builds, prepare the case:** Take the side panel of the case and locate the standoffs (threaded metal posts). If they're not preinstalled, screw them into the holes designated for the motherboard size (ATX, Micro ATX, and so on) according to your motherboard manual (some cases have labels next to the holes that state ATX, Micro ATX, and so on, to help with the process).

    For existing builds, double-check the standoffs to make sure they are in the correct position for the replacement motherboard. It is critical that a standoff does not exist where there is not a hole on the motherboard for a screw; otherwise, the standoff could be touching the back of the motherboard and possibly short-circuit it!

2. **Install the rear input/output (I/O) shield:** Some motherboards have this shield or backplate preinstalled on the motherboard itself, but most don't. This metal shield should come with the motherboard and is placed on the rear of the case matching the cutouts for your motherboard's ports.

3. **Place the motherboard:** Lower the motherboard onto the standoffs while making sure the motherboard holes align with the standoff screw holes.

4. **Secure the motherboard:** Screw the motherboard down to the standoffs using the included screws that come with the case. Don't overtighten because you risk unscrewing the standoffs when trying to loosen the screws on top of the motherboard if you need to remove it.

For PGA CPUs, hold the CPU up to the light and carefully look down the rows of pins to make sure none are bent. Don't touch the pins or top of the CPU while doing this because you don't want your finger oils to create hot spots anywhere on the CPU. There are special gloves you can wear when handling the CPU, but wearing an antistatic wrist strap and carefully holding the CPU only on its sides are usually okay as well. If you see a bent pin, you can either return the CPU or try to carefully use a razor blade to bend the pin straight again. Understand that if you do the latter, you run the risk of bending the pin too much and it breaking off because it's thin metal!

For LGA CPUs, make sure the pins are not bent on the CPU socket on the motherboard. This is harder to see than bent pins on a PGA CPU, so you might take a flashlight to shine on the socket to see if you see any bent pins. Unfortunately, if you see a bent pin on the motherboard socket, it is nearly impossible to fix. You will probably be returning the motherboard.

To install the CPU, follow these steps:

1. **Locate the CPU socket:** It's usually a square socket in the center of the motherboard.

2. **Open the socket lever:** Carefully release the lever that secures the CPU in place (refer to your motherboard manual for specifics).

3. **Place the CPU:** Hold the CPU by the edges, aligning the notches or triangles on the CPU with the corresponding markers on the socket. Gently lower it into the socket.

   a. Use zero-force insertion! This means that you merely lower the CPU onto the socket and do not press down. Imagine setting a delicate plate down on a hard counter. You don't drop it down, you don't press it down, you just gently place it down.

   b. Once you've set it down, you can very gently wiggle the CPU from side to side and front to back to make sure it's in place. Sometimes, you will feel it fall into place; this is okay if you didn't put pressure downward when wiggling it. Make sure that you still do not touch the top of the CPU.

4. **Close the socket lever:** Secure the CPU by gently closing the lever.

5. **Apply thermal paste (optional):** If your CPU cooler doesn't come with pre-applied thermal paste, you'll need to put a small, pea-sized amount in the center of the CPU. More is not better!

6. **Place the active cooling:** Install the heat sink/CPU cooler, being sure to follow the directions that came with it. Aftermarket heat sinks are often for various CPU sockets, so be sure to read the directions on those extra carefully.

Installing/Upgrading: RAM/Storage Devices/Internal Peripherals

With DDR RAM, you get the most speed by installing them in pairs. The reason is that motherboards have memory channels. If you are installing a pair of DDR RAM sticks, you will want to install them in the same channel, which is often color coded on the dual-inline memory module (DIMM) slots themselves on the motherboard. The DIMM slots are where you install RAM (see Figure 2-19).

Figure 2-19 *DIMM Slots with Color-Coded Channels*

To install the RAM, follow these steps (make sure computer is off):

1. **Open the locking mechanisms:** On the motherboard, the DIMM slots will have two locking mechanisms that you need to open by flipping outward. Some motherboard DIMM slots have only one side that will open; this is normal.

2. **Find the notch:** RAM sticks have two notches on each side with a single notch on the bottom. This bottom notch needs to line up with a matching notch or ridge on the RAM slot. This helps to correctly orient the RAM and make sure you don't put a different generation of RAM in.

3. **Align and insert:** Hold the RAM by the edges, aligning the notch with the slot's notch and gently slide in evenly before applying pressure.

4. **Apply pressure:** Once it is in position and slid down evenly with very little pressure to just put in position, gently but firmly press the RAM stick further down into the slot until you hear a click from both locking mechanisms on the sides.

On modern computers, you will connect your hard drives, SSDs, and optical drives to a SATA port on the motherboard with a SATA data cable. Figure 2-20 shows a SATA port on a motherboard. In addition to connecting to a SATA data port, you will also need to connect to a SATA power cable coming from the PSU.

Figure 2-20 *SATA Data Port on a Motherboard*

For an M.2 form factor drive, you will install it directly on the motherboard with no additional data or power cable needed. There are different sizes of M.2 with 2280 being the most common. The M.2 port is often located between the PCIe expansion slots on the motherboard.

To install an M.2 storage drive, follow these steps (make sure the computer is powered off and you are using an antistatic wrist strap):

1. **Unscrew the M.2 slot cover:** The M.2 slot might have two small screws holding a cover in place. Remove the screws and the cover if present. Some motherboards

have the cover, and some do not. The cover acts as a heatsink to help keep the drive cool. There is often a thin plastic film on the downward-facing side that needs to be removed to expose the sticky adhesive before placing it back.

2. **Find the correct standoff position:** M.2 comes in many sizes with 2280 being the most common. There should be a standoff located next to a number. This indicates the size of the M.2 drive and what the drive will rest on and be secured to. Remove the standoff and place it into the correct position if not in it already. Some motherboards do not have the standoff preinstalled. If it's not, it will come in a bag with the motherboard. Find it and put it in the correct position. The end with the notch will fit into the actual M.2 port, and the other end will lie down and be secured with one screw in the standoff.

3. **Identify the notch:** Both the M.2 drive and the port/slot will have a notch. These notches must be lined up for proper installation.

4. **Insert the drive:** Carefully insert the M.2 drive into the port/slot at an angle (between 30 and 45 degrees) while aligning the notch on the drive with the notch on the port/slot (see Figure 2-21). Apply gentle pressure at the angle to have it fully inserted. When done correctly, the drive will remain in the angled position when let go.

Figure 2-21 *M.2 NVMe Drive Being Installed*

5. **Tilt and secure:** Once it is inserted, gently tilt the drive down until it lies flat on the standoff on the opposite side of the port. Secure it with the screw in the standoff or from the motherboard bag that contains the standoff and screw. Don't overtighten because it is easy to snap off the standoff.

While some CPUs come with a built-in graphics processing unit (**GPU**) to output video to the monitor, many do not. In this case, you would need to install a graphics or video card. This would be considered an internal peripheral expansion card. Other expansion cards you might want to install would be wireless NICs to connect wirelessly to the Internet if your motherboard doesn't have one built in, video capture cards for editing video, Bluetooth cards for Bluetooth connectivity, audio cards for higher-quality audio output, and more. While external peripherals are usually connected to USB, internal peripherals are usually connected to PCI or PCIe slots/ports located directly on the motherboard. Peripheral Component Interconnect (PCI) is an older technology to connect expansion cards to. It is being replaced by PCI Express (PCIe). PCIe is capable of much faster data transfer as well as more bandwidth of data transfer. There are four PCIe expansion slots you might find on a motherboard: PCIe x1, PCIe x4, PCIe x8, and PCIe x16. The x and the number refer to the number of lanes of data communication the port can use. Typical motherboards often have one or two PCIe x16 slots and one or two PCIe x1 slots. Graphics cards will use PCIe x16 slots because they need more bandwidth than a wireless NIC, which might need only a PCIe x1 slot. If you have a PCIe x8 expansion card and no PCIe x8 slot/port on the motherboard, it will not fit in a PCIex1 slot, but you can use a PCIe x16 slot. It won't fill all the pins, but it will work. See Figure 2-22 for a motherboard with both PCIe x16 and PCIe x1 slots.

Figure 2-22   *PCIe Expansion Slots (Bottom Three Are Older PCI Slots; Above Bottom Three Is PCIe x1, Followed by PCIe x16, and Top Is PCIe x1)*

NOTE   To know if a CPU includes onboard graphics, you need to look at the processor suffix. For example, you might buy an Intel Core i5-14400F. The i5-14400 is the specific model number. The *F* is the suffix. In this case, with Intel, *F* means it does not include onboard graphics and you must buy a dedicated graphics card. If you see a *K*, it means unlocked and can be overclocked for faster performance, which is not covered in this certification and generally advised against because it can cause stability issues. There are many other Intel-specific suffixes, but *F* and *K* are common ones. As a rule of thumb, if the Intel CPU does not have an *F*, it includes at least basic graphic capabilities.

Conversely, no AMD includes graphics unless it has the *G* suffix. The *X* suffix means overclockable and roughly equivalent to Intel's *K* suffix. As with all technology, this is true as of the time of this writing, but both companies are changing and adding suffixes for marketing purposes with each new generational launch of CPUs.

To install an expansion card, follow these steps (make sure the computer is powered off):

1. **Remove the cover screw:** Some cases may have a small screw holding a metal cover plate over the empty expansion slot on the back of the computer case. Remove this screw and the cover plate if present.

2. **Align the card:** Carefully hold the expansion card by its edges or mounting bracket. Align the gold connector edge of the card with the corresponding slot on the motherboard.

3. **Insert and secure:** Gently but firmly press the card straight down into the slot until it's fully seated. You should hear a click from the latch on the slot. Secure the card in place with the screw you removed earlier (if applicable). Don't force the card.

Post Installation Checklist

After you are finished installing or upgrading your PC, there are a couple of steps you should follow:

1. Power on the computer after double-checking all cables and parts are correctly positioned or installed.

2. If a new build, you will need to install an operating system at this point.

3. If you installed Windows, you will need to go to **Device Manager** to make sure you have no missing drivers or issues with your hardware (see Figure 2-23).

    a. In Windows, click the **Start** menu icon and type **device manager** in the search bar to find it. You can also press Windows+R on your keyboard to open the Run dialog box. Then type **devmgmt.msc** in the open box and press Enter/OK. Other ways to reach Device Manager include right-clicking the Windows logo and selecting **Device Manager** from the context menu. They will all get you to the same place.

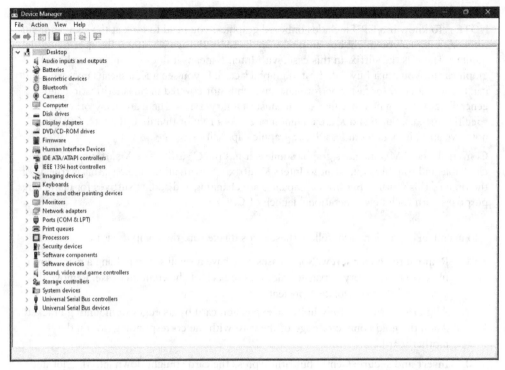

Figure 2-23 *Windows Device Manager*

    b. You will see device categories listed here. If you see a yellow exclamation mark next to an item, you are missing a driver or Windows is using a generic driver. You might also see the yellow exclamation point with the words "Unknown Device" by it. Either way, you will need to fix this. There are two ways to approach this issue.

        i. Right-click the item with the yellow exclamation point and choose **Update Driver Software** from the context menu (the context menu is the right-click menu in Windows). Then choose **Search Automatically for Updated Driver Software** from the next menu. This sometimes will allow Windows to find the correct driver, but you must be connected to the Internet.

        ii. If the previous method didn't work and the device is listed, but it has a yellow exclamation mark by it, you can go to the motherboard manufacturer's website, or the company website if a prebuilt computer, and search for the specific driver. If it states something like Biometric reader, look on the motherboard support website for your specific model and see if there is a fingerprint driver or the like. Download and install the driver and look to see if it is resolved in Device Manager.

        iii. For stubborn drivers or unknown devices, you can right-click the item and choose **Properties**. From there, choose the **Details** tab and select **Hardware Ids**. You can then copy the value and paste it into a search engine.

You will often find what the device is from various sites that cross-reference the hardware ID with the actual device. Do not download a driver from a random site! Always use the motherboard's official support site or the manufacturer's site.

4. After making sure your drivers are installed correctly, update your operating system for optimum performance.

5. Do not throw old parts in the trash! Many computer components contain dangerous chemicals and elements that are harmful to the environment. Always follow e-waste best practices to dispose of old parts. Often, your city's website or local fire department can help direct you to e-waste centers for proper disposal.

Hardware and Peripheral Issues

When you're troubleshooting hardware issues, it is always important to follow the problem-solving process as outlined in the "Problem-Solving Process" section in Chapter 1, "Help Desk." The following sections cover some common issues IT technicians might encounter with hardware and peripheral devices.

Basic Hardware/Software Troubleshooting

One of the most demanding skills of the IT technician is to learn how to troubleshoot hardware and software. These are some basic issues you might encounter. It is by no means a complete list, but more of an example of some issues you might encounter.

Power and Connectivity:

- Verify the device is plugged in securely to a functioning power outlet.

- Ensure all cables (power, data) are properly connected to both the device and the computer.

- Check for any physical damage to the cables or ports.

- Ensure the computer is powered on if it has a power switch.

  - Check to make sure the PSU switch is also in the 1 (or on) position.

  - If the power button on the computer case doesn't seem to work, double-check that the front panel header cables that connect from the case to the motherboard are connected correctly.

  - If you're working on a laptop, ensure it's plugged in or has sufficient battery life. Sometimes, if a laptop battery is malfunctioning or completely dead, the laptop will not turn on even if plugged in. Disconnect the battery from the laptop and plug the laptop into a wall outlet with no battery attached. If the laptop turns on, you need to replace your battery.

Device Status Indicators:

- Many devices have LED lights that indicate their status (e.g., blinking for errors, solid for power on). Consult the device's manual to understand the meaning of the lights particular to the device.

Firmware Updates:

- The most common firmware update for computer hardware is the **BIOS** of the motherboard. The basic input/output system, or BIOS, is a minimalistic operating system that allows a computer to turn on and understand basic devices. It allows various configuration settings including system clock/date, RAM overclocking settings called XMP/DOCP/EXPO depending on the manufacturer, boot order selection, and more. The settings are stored in another chip called the CMOS chip, and the BIOS reads setting changes from the CMOS upon boot. It is important to note that the changes or settings you adjust in BIOS are actually stored in the CMOS chip. The BIOS itself is a special type of read-only memory (ROM) chip called an EEPROM, which is short for electrically erasable programmable read-only memory. You can easily cause your computer to not boot if incorrect settings are applied in the BIOS. Therefore, if you do cause an issue, you can unplug your computer, pull the CMOS battery, and clear those configurations. Without a BIOS chip on the motherboard, your computer would do nothing when you turn it on. When you turn on your computer, the BIOS recognizes basic devices like a monitor, keyboard, mouse, RAM, and storage devices, and then does a power-on self test (POST) to make sure the devices are working. POST then passes on the startup process to the boot loader on your storage device that begins actual loading of the operating system.

  Having a basic understanding of BIOS is important because it is vital to your computer's performance. It used to be that you would not update your BIOS firmware unless you were having a problem. This is called **flashing**. Unfortunately, in the past decade, motherboard manufacturers are racing to put out new motherboard models for the seemingly endless choices of CPUs and chipsets that Intel and AMD have been releasing. As such, many new motherboards have critical errors upon release. Therefore, you might have to flash, or update the firmware, of your BIOS.

- Benefits of firmware updates involve improved performance, bug fixes, and new features added to the hardware.

- Possible dangers of firmware updates include faulty updates that can brick your device. *Bricking* is a term meaning to cause it to become permanently nonoperational. Also, not obtaining the firmware from a trusted source like the motherboard manufacturer's website directly could open the possibility of malware being installed at the hardware level, which is extremely dangerous.

> **NOTE** If you are going to flash your motherboard to update the BIOS, make sure to get the update only from the manufacturer's website. Also, it is advisable to have it plugged into an uninterruptable power supply (UPS) while performing the update. If power cuts out during the process, you could end up with a device that is completely dead. Luckily, many motherboard manufacturers have backup BIOS files and ways to restore the BIOS if the updating process goes bad. However, you should never rely on those mechanisms because they can fail too.

Software Compatibility:

- If devices are working properly on Windows, check the Device Manager to see if the drivers are loaded and working (refer to Figure 2-23).

- Check whether the software you're trying to use meets your system's specifications. Look for information on processor type (32 bit versus 64 bit), minimum RAM, graphics card compatibility, and required disk space.

 ## Peripheral Troubleshooting

A multitude of issues can arise with peripherals. While the following list is not exhaustive, here are some common issues:

- **Printers:**

  - **Drivers:** Always install your printer driver before plugging in or setting up your printer.

  - **Connectivity:** Ensure the printer is connected properly (USB, Wi-Fi) and turned on.

  - **Multifunction Devices:** Consult the printer's manual for specific instructions on using its scanning, copying, and faxing functions. Drivers have notoriously been problematic for all-in-one or multifunction printers.

  - **Loading Paper:** Refer to the manual for instructions on loading paper based on the paper size and type (tray selection).

  - **Paper Jams:** Carefully follow the manufacturer's instructions on clearing paper jams to avoid damaging the printer. As a rule, never pull jammed paper out the opposite way as it was going through the rollers. Paper jams are often caused by rollers that are losing their special coating that grips the paper; you might have to replace the worn printer roller.

  - **Print Queue:** Access the print queue from your computer (**Settings > Printers & Scanners**) to view and manage printing jobs. You can cancel or restart stuck jobs there.

  - **Ink Replacement:** For inkjet printers, consult the manual for instructions on replacing ink cartridges specific to your printer model. Before replacing inkjet cartridges, try to run Clean Printhead from your printer's menu. This will often help alleviate streaking or faded text/graphics.

  - **Toner Replacement:** For laser printers, consult the manual for instructions on replacing toner cartridges specific to your printer model.

- **Fax:**

  - Most modern computers lack built-in fax functionality. If you need to fax from your computer, you can rely on websites that will allow you to upload a document to be faxed from their service, or you will need to buy a dedicated fax machine or a multifunction printer that includes fax capabilities.

- If you have a multifunction printer with fax capabilities, but you cannot send a fax out, check that your printer is plugged into a telephone port with an RJ-11 cable. Also note that many Internet-based telephones (IP telephones) can be problematic when faxing because they can have jitter, or unevenness in transmission speed, that faxes can't account for.

- **Headphones/Microphones:**

  - Check the connection (wired or wireless) and ensure the volume is turned up on both the device and your computer.

  - Test the microphone using the Sound Settings in Windows.

  - Make sure the right Sound Output is selected in Sound Settings in Windows. For example, if you have speakers built into your monitor, you will want to make sure the Sound Output is HDMI or DisplayPort and not speaker output.

- **External Drives:**

  - Verify the drive is properly connected and recognized in File Explorer.

  - Some external drives require additional power (a separate power adapter).

- **Scanners:**

  - Like printers, scanners often need specific software to function. Install the scanner driver and software from the manufacturer's website.

- **Webcams:**

  - Ensure the webcam is enabled in your computer's settings and privacy settings.

  - Check whether applications have permission to access the webcam.

- **Keyboard/Mouse (wired/wireless):**

  - Try using a different USB port for wired connections.

  - Replace batteries for wireless keyboards/mice.

  - If using a Bluetooth wireless keyboard/mouse, ensure you have a Bluetooth receiver on your computer because not all desktop computers come with a Bluetooth expansion card built in. Begin by pairing the device to get it to work.

  - For wireless keyboards/mice, move your wireless router away from your computer because many wireless peripherals operate in the 2.4 GHz range, which is one Wi-Fi frequency your router uses for network connectivity.

- **Teleconferencing Devices:**

  - One main issue you might encounter with teleconferencing devices such as Cisco's Webex Desk Pro screens is insufficient bandwidth. If the video call is lagging or dropping out, try to switch from a wireless connection to a wired connection. If this doesn't help, you might need to check your Internet speed and possibly upgrade your Internet plan for a faster connection.

- If the device is not recognized by your operating system, try updating drivers and/ or using a different port for connection.

- **Tactile/Interactive Input Devices:**

  - Touch screens can lose calibration, which can cause inaccurate touches. Use the device's built-in settings to recalibrate the screen.

  - Clean dirty or wet input devices with a microfiber cloth.

  - Check for physical damage to the device itself.

  - Check for loose cables.

  - Check for outdated drivers.

  - Check for firmware updates to the device itself.

Exam Preparation Tasks

As mentioned in the Introduction, you can customize your strategy for exam preparation. Suggested tasks include the exercises here, Chapter 9, "Final Preparation," and the exam simulation questions on the companion website.

Review All Key Topics

Review the most important topics in this chapter, noted with the Key Topic icon in the outer margin of the page. Table 2-2 lists a reference of these key topics and the page numbers on which each is found.

Table 2-2   Key Topics for Chapter 2

Key Topic Element	Description	Page Number
Paragraph	Electrical shock	34
Paragraph	ESD	36
List	How to use a fire extinguisher; P.A.S.S.	38
Paragraph	Repetitive Strain Injuries	38
Paragraph	Ergonomics	38
Paragraph	Interfaces	39
Paragraph	Ports	40
Paragraph	HDMI	42
Paragraph	DisplayPort	42
Paragraph	DVI	43
Paragraph	VGA	44
Paragraph	USB Form Factors	45
Paragraph	USB-C	46
Paragraph	Ethernet cables	47
Paragraph	Power cords	49
Paragraph	Adapters	50

Key Topic Element	Description	Page Number
Paragraph	Converters	50
Paragraph	Processor	51
Paragraph	Motherboard	53
Paragraph	Checking processor and motherboard	53
Paragraph	RAM	54
Paragraph	Peripherals	55
Paragraph	Storage devices	55
Paragraph	SSD	55
Paragraph	Form factor of computer components	56
Paragraph	Physical form factors and compatibility factors	58
List	Installing a motherboard	58
List	Installing the CPU	58
List	Installing RAM	60
Paragraph	Built-in GPU or dedicated graphics card	62
List	Post-installation checklist	63
List	Basic hardware/software troubleshooting	65
Paragraph	Firmware updates	66
Paragraph	Software compatibility	67
Section	Peripheral Troubleshooting	67

Define Key Terms

Define the following key terms from this chapter and check your answers in the glossary:

adapter, amps, ARM, BIOS, chipset, converter, Device Manager, DisplayPort, driver, DVI, ergonomics, ESD, flashing, GPU, hard drive, HDMI, input/output device, interface, LGA, M.2, motherboard, Ohm's law, P.A.S.S., PCIe, peripheral, PGA, pixel, port, processor, proprietary, PSU, RAM, RJ-45, RSI, serial port, SSD, STP, threat actors, Thunderbolt, USB, USB form factors, USB-C, UTP, VGA, volts, x86/x64

References

Anker Innovations, "How to Identify Different Types of USB Cables: A Brief Guide," https://www.anker.com/blogs/cables/how-to-identify-different-types-of-usb-cables-a-brief-guide

Cisco, "What Is Power over Ethernet (PoE)?," https://www.cisco.com/c/en/us/solutions/enterprise-networks/what-is-power-over-ethernet.html

Geeks for Geeks, "Types of Computer Ports," https://www.geeksforgeeks.org/types-of-computer-ports/

CHAPTER 3

Networking and Network Connectivity

This chapter covers the following topics:

- **Locate Basic Network Information:** This section describes how to understand and locate basic network information about the hosts you are maintaining.

- **Basic End-to-End Network Connectivity:** This section covers the basics of local area and wide area networks, ensuring a basic working knowledge of network systems.

- **Connectivity Testing:** This section explains how to test to ensure that a device is correctly working on a network.

- **Multifactor Authentication:** This section describes how to use multifactor authentication to secure a network connection.

This chapter is all about the network. You will learn how to locate basic information about the network that your devices are connected to and learn how to identify information about your hosts on the network; this information will assist you when troubleshooting those devices. You will learn how to verify the network information and perform connectivity testing across the local area network (LAN) and wide area network (WAN), both with IPv4 and IPv6 networks, and be able to identify the differences between each type. Finally, you will learn how to establish access to network resources using multifactor authentication to further secure the connections.

The chapter covers information related to the following Cisco Certified Support Technician (CCST) IT Support exam objectives:

- 2.2 Assist end users in using tools to locate information about their device

- 3.1 Assist users with establishing access to network-based resources

- 3.3 Examine basic end-device connectivity to the network

"Do I Know This Already?" Quiz

The "Do I Know This Already?" quiz allows you to assess whether you should read this entire chapter thoroughly or jump to the "Exam Preparation Tasks" section. If you are in doubt about your answers to these questions or your own assessment of your knowledge of the topics, read the entire chapter. Table 3-1 lists the major headings in this chapter and their corresponding "Do I Know This Already?" quiz questions. You can find the answers in Appendix A, "Answers to the 'Do I Know This Already?' Quizzes."

Table 3-1 "Do I Know This Already?" Section-to-Question Mapping

Foundation Topics Section	Questions
Locating Basic Network Information	1–4
Basic End-to-End Network Connectivity	5–9
Connectivity Testing	10, 11
Multifactor Authentication	12

CAUTION The goal of self-assessment is to gauge your mastery of the topics in this chapter. If you do not know the answer to a question or are only partially sure of the answer, you should mark that question as wrong for purposes of the self-assessment. Giving yourself credit for an answer you correctly guess skews your self-assessment results and might provide you with a false sense of security.

1. Which of these reflects the purpose of a hostname?

   a. It determines which IP address to use for a device.

   b. It is a unique label identifying a device on a network.

   c. It allows **nslookup** to find your device.

   d. It is not needed in IPv6 networks.

2. Why would an IT support technician need to know information about the processor of a user's machine?

   a. Different processors may require different versions of the software.

   b. Different processors have different speeds.

   c. Manufacturers use different processors that are incompatible with one another.

   d. Some processors can't run operating systems.

3. RFC 1918 defines IP addresses that can be used by anyone. Which of these is true for these address blocks?

   a. Network Address Translation (NAT) is used when going from the private network to the public Internet.

   b. You will never have the same network address as your neighbor.

   c. Linux, Mac, and Windows machines cannot use the same network address blocks.

   d. Internet of Things (IoT) devices such as light switches should always be given RFC 1918–compliant addresses because they cannot run IPv6.

4. IPv6 is written in hexadecimal notation. Which of the following is true of hexadecimal?

   a. Hexadecimal is newer than decimal, so it is better.

   b. Decimal numbers are shorter than hexadecimal numbers.

   c. Binary numbers are shorter than hexadecimal numbers.

   d. Hexadecimal numbers are base 16, and each represents a value from 0 to 15.

5. Which is true of a LAN versus a WLAN?

   a. A LAN uses wired connections, and a WLAN uses wireless connections.

   b. A LAN is on one site, and a WLAN is on multiple sites.

   c. A LAN and a WLAN are the same thing with different names.

   d. LAN uses copper cables, and a WLAN uses fiber-optic cables.

6. SSID is the network name for what type of network?

   a. A WLAN

   b. A WAN

   c. A LAN

   d. A fiber-optic cable

7. DNS provides what capability to the users?

   a. Names can be provided to users who have an IP address.

   b. IP addresses can be provided to users who have a URL.

   c. Top-level servers are accessible only through DNS.

   d. Physical phone books have been replaced with DNS.

8. DHCP provides what services to an IPv4 network?

   a. APIPA network addresses

   b. IPv6 addresses

   c. IPv4 addresses, subnet masks, default gateways

   d. Time server information only

9. IPv6 uses SLAAC to assign IPv6 addresses. How does the device know what range to create the IPv6 address within?

   a. APIPA provides the range of addresses.

   b. Neighbor solicitation messages give the range.

   c. Router solicitation (RS) messages give the range.

   d. Neighbor advertisement messages give range information.

10. The **ping** command is used to do which of these?

   a. Verify connectivity with a remote device

   b. Test whether a router can reach the DHCP server

   c. Determine your IP address

   d. Show a device's subnet mask

11. The **traceroute/tracert** command is used to extend ping functionality in what way?

   a. Shows the same information as ping with no changes

   b. Shows the time to the first router hop only

   c. Shows the FQDN of your own device

   d. Shows the time, distance, and FQDN of each device along the way to the destination

12. What does multifactor authentication allow a site to require?

   a. Only a password to access a site before allowing access

   b. Use of multiple methods to verify identity before allowing access

   c. A physical key instead of a password

   d. An app to log in the user instead of a password

Foundation Topics

Locating Basic Network Information

It is important for IT support technicians to know how to locate information about the devices they are maintaining to troubleshoot more efficiently and effectively. By keeping track of the device hardware, software, and configuration information, IT support technicians will be better able to serve the customers and get them back up and running when problems occur. As you follow the troubleshooting steps, remember that gathering information is one of the important steps, and the following sections will help you gather that information.

The OSI Model

The **Open Systems Interconnect (OSI) model** describes the basic conceptual framework by dividing network communications into seven layers. By breaking down the communications into the seven layers, the model simplifies that complexity and helps explain what is happening logically, providing a universal language for computer networking.

Diverse technologies can communicate using standard protocols. Each layer has its own responsibilities and functions. When the functions of the layers are broken down, the users don't have to worry about functions at higher or lower layers of the model.

Troubleshooting is simplified because an IT support technician can concentrate on a layer-by-layer approach, ensuring that each layer is functioning properly, without having to worry about the interrelationship between the layers themselves.

Figure 3-1 shows the OSI model. Data is interpreted "up" the layers as it is received and "down" the layers as it is transmitted.

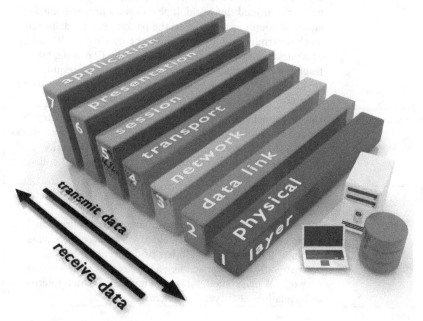

Figure 3-1 *OSI Model*

Each layer of the OSI model operates independently of the other layers and has its own tasks to perform. Once done with its own tasks, the individual layer passes the information to the next layer up or down, depending on whether the packet is inbound or outbound. As an IT support technician, you will use the layers of the OSI model to help you troubleshoot network-related issues. Table 3-2 details what each layer defines.

Table 3-2 OSI Model Layer Definitions

Application Layer (Layer 7)	Defines the communications services to applications. The only layer to interact with the user.
Presentation Layer (Layer 6)	Defines the syntax or language (.txt, html, .jpg, mp4), encryption or decryption, and compression or decompression of data.
Session Layer (Layer 5)	Defines how to establish, manage, and terminate conversations. It provides dialogue control between nodes. It also supports simplex, half-duplex, and full-duplex communications.
Transport Layer (Layer 4)	Defines the reliability of a network by choosing either the connection-oriented Transmission Control Protocol (TCP) or the connectionless User Datagram Protocol (UDP). It provides mechanisms for the reordering of the incoming data stream when packets arrive out of order, reassembly of the data if the packets fragmented during transmission, error recovery, and flow control.
Network Layer (Layer 3)	Defines end-to-end delivery of packets. It uses logical addressing (IP addressing, using either IPv4 or IPv6) to identify endpoints and to provide connectivity to millions of networks around the world. It also defines how routing works and how routes are learned so the packets can be delivered (path determination) by examining the destination IP address of a packet, comparing that address to the IP routing table, fragmenting the packet if the outgoing interface requires smaller packets, and queuing the packet to be sent out to the interface. It breaks collision and broadcast domains.
Data Link Layer (Layer 2)	Defines specifications and protocols for getting data across a link or medium. It provides physical addressing, media access control (MAC), logic link control (LLC), error detection, and frame assembly. It also helps relieve congestion and collisions on a network segment.
Physical Layer (Layer 1)	Defines the physical characteristics of the medium (electrical, light, or wireless). It defines connector and interface specifications, as well as the medium (cable) requirements. Connectors, pins, use of pins, electrical voltage, encoding, and light modulation are all part of different physical layer specifications for sending a bit stream on a computer network. When something is unplugged, it is often referred to colloquially as a "Layer 1 problem."

The TCP/IP Model

Like the OSI model, the **Transmission Control Protocol/Internet Protocol (TCP/IP) model** is designed to simplify understanding of how networks are designed and configured. Note that, while it shares a name with the TCP/IP protocol stack used for all Internet-based communication, the model itself can be generalized to refer to any network-based communication. Like the OSI model, each of the layers of the TCP/IP model works independently to manage different aspects of communication, allowing the IT support technician to troubleshoot the layers separately and more efficiently.

Remember, the purpose of the TCP/IP model is to describe what is happening in your network communication. You will use this to troubleshoot more efficiently and effectively.

Figure 3-2 shows the layers of the TCP/IP model.

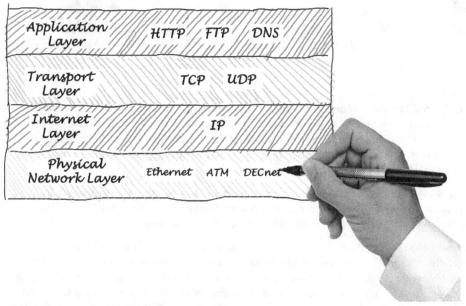

Figure 3-2 *Layers of the TCP/IP Model*

Shown side by side in Figure 3-3, the two models are similar. This is no accident; although they were originally intended as an engineering exercise, reality has grown to favor the models. In other words, the engineers who designed and built the devices really liked the layer concept behind the models and made the real world match the models. It is a case of real life reflecting a proposed theoretical best-case scenario.

Locating Information About the Device

To help troubleshoot issues with the user device, it is important that the IT support technician be able to find key information about that device. This information includes configuration information but also includes information about the physical device itself. All of this is important toward troubleshooting and resolving the problems that the IT support technician is working on resolving.

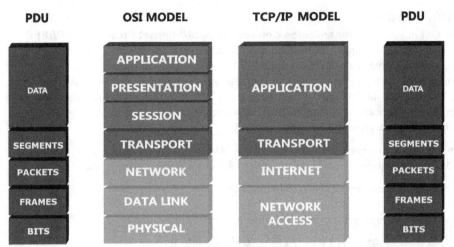

Figure 3-3 *The OSI and TCP/IP Models Side by Side; Note That They Describe the
Same Thing in Different Ways*

Host Name

A **hostname** (note that some operating systems list this as two words, *host name*, but they
mean the same thing) is a label assigned to a device that is connected to a computer network. It must be unique on the network, allowing the device to be easily differentiated by
other network devices. It is most often related to the DNS name that the computer or other
network-enabled devices receive but does not have to be.

It is important to realize that hostnames are not related to IP addresses. Hostnames are
designed to be human-readable though it is not uncommon for them to have numbers and
abbreviations within them as well. IP addresses are purely numbers.

Generally, the network administrator (which could be you, the IT support technician,
especially in a small organization) will provide the hostname, following a set of conventions.
Please review these with your organization so you are clear not only on the naming schema
but also on which names have already been used. Part of the documentation for your workplace will include the hostname for each device, and a separate list should be maintained to
help ensure that you don't inadvertently duplicate a name. Note that except in a very, very
few situations, hostnames cannot include spaces, but you can use hyphens and underscores
instead as needed.

If set up properly, hostnames can be pushed through to your Domain Name System (DNS) to
provide a **fully qualified domain name (FQDN)**. This is not required for operation on the
network but can provide additional security, especially for servers, because it is a much more
precise way of addressing a specific device within a network.

If a host has a FQDN, you can find its hostname by querying the DNS server. To do this,
access a command prompt and type **nslookup** [{ *IP address* | *URL* }], where *IP address* rep-
resents the IP address of a remote device with a FQDN and *URL* represents a URL for which
you wish to get the DNS information. While the example in Figure 3-4 shows **nslookup** with
an IPv4 address, the process is the same with IPv6.

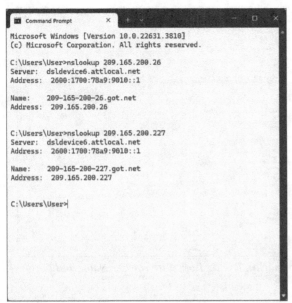

```
Command Prompt          ×    +  ∨                  –   □   ×

Microsoft Windows [Version 10.0.22631.3810]
(c) Microsoft Corporation. All rights reserved.

C:\Users\User>nslookup 209.165.200.26
Server:   dsldevice6.attlocal.net
Address:  2600:1700:78a9:9010::1

Name:     209-165-200-26.got.net
Address:  209.165.200.26


C:\Users\User>nslookup 209.165.200.227
Server:   dsldevice6.attlocal.net
Address:  2600:1700:78a9:9010::1

Name:     209-165-200-227.got.net
Address:  209.165.200.227


C:\Users\User>
```

Figure 3-4 *Results of Using* **nslookup,** *Showing the FQDN for the Devices Found*

Figure 3-4 shows the results of **nslookup example.com** and **nslookup 209.165.200.225.** Note that the FQDN returns a hostname that includes the IP address separated by dashes. This is not unusual for public-facing IP devices.

Processor Type, Memory, Disk Space, and OS Version

When you're an IT support technician, knowing the version of the hardware and **operating system** software running on a client's machine is useful so that you can help troubleshoot errors they are receiving. Sometimes errors occur because of misconfigurations. Sometimes patches, updates, and software versions are available only for specific machine types. You will need to find out the pieces of information for your users.

If your organization has a standard for hardware, you will likely already know or easily be able to find this information. In other cases, however, you will need to be able to find this out. Luckily, it's easy to find.

Windows 10 and 11 keep most of this information in the System Information dialog box, under System Summary. Figure 3-5 shows an example of one such dialog, with the OS Name and Version at the top and **processor** highlighted. In the left-hand column, you can select the entries where you can find the Memory and Storage installed on the device.

To find this same information on a Mac, go to the About This Mac screen, then look in the Overview tab, or go to the **System > About** dialog. Device Name shows the hostname. The line for Processor will be called either Chip or Processor depending on OS version. Memory or Installed RAM (depending on the OS version) shows the amount of memory. Figure 3-6 shows an example of the About This Mac screen with the Overview tab showing. To check hard drive space, go to **General Settings**, then select **Storage**. Note that, by default, this will give storage across all drives as a summary (not an issue if you have only one drive installed).

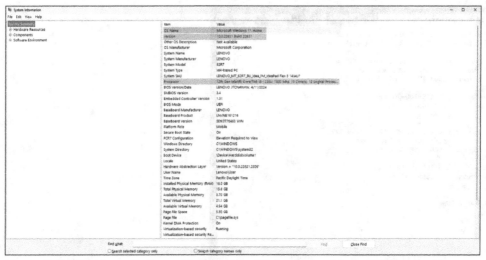

Figure 3-5   *Windows 11 System Information Dialog Box, with the OS Name and Processor Lines Highlighted*

Figure 3-6   *About This Mac Dialog Box with the Processor Line Highlighted*

For Linux, you can find the CPU information by typing **lscpu** on a terminal line. The specific information will be on a line in the Vendor ID section, under Model Name. There is a lot of additional information available about the CPU speed, and so on, that you don't get using other operating systems. Figure 3-7 shows an Ubuntu terminal having run the **lscpu** command. The **df** command can be used to get disk space. The **top** command can be used to see the status of memory. There are also GUI-based tools such as hardinfo and System Monitor that will give you this information as well, but they are not installed by default in every Linux instance.

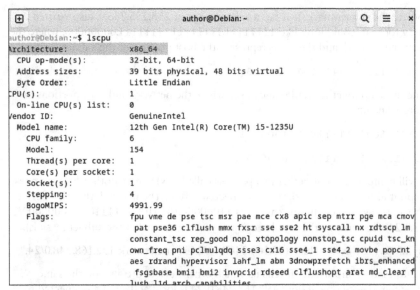

```
author@Debian:~
author@Debian:~$ lscpu
Architecture:                 x86_64
  CPU op-mode(s):             32-bit, 64-bit
  Address sizes:             39 bits physical, 48 bits virtual
  Byte Order:                Little Endian
CPU(s):                       1
  On-line CPU(s) list:       0
Vendor ID:                   GenuineIntel
  Model name:               12th Gen Intel(R) Core(TM) i5-1235U
    CPU family:             6
    Model:                  154
    Thread(s) per core:     1
    Core(s) per socket:     1
    Socket(s):              1
    Stepping:               4
    BogoMIPS:               4991.99
    Flags:                  fpu vme de pse tsc msr pae mce cx8 apic sep mtrr pge mca cmov
                            pat pse36 clflush mmx fxsr sse sse2 ht syscall nx rdtscp lm
                            constant_tsc rep_good nopl xtopology nonstop_tsc cpuid tsc_kn
                            own_freq pni pclmulqdq ssse3 cx16 sse4_1 sse4_2 movbe popcnt
                            aes rdrand hypervisor lahf_lm abm 3dnowprefetch ibrs_enhanced
                            fsgsbase bmi1 bmi2 invpcid rdseed clflushopt arat md_clear f
                            lush_l1d_arch_capabilities
```

Figure 3-7 *A Linux Terminal Showing the Results of the* **lscpu** *Command*

IP Addresses

IP addresses enable devices to communicate on networks. Part of OSI Layer 3, the TCP/IP Network layer, these are logical addresses that provide a way for devices to find one another on the network. There are two parts: network and host. The network portion allows the network devices such as routers to know which network segment contains the device, and the host portion identifies the specific device. Your network manager (which could be you!) will have divided the network into subnetworks for actual use. Most devices receive their IP addresses automatically via DHCP or similar methods, as discussed later in this chapter. No two devices can have the same public IP address.

There are two major variants of IP addresses in use: IPv4 and IPv6. A device can use one or both, a process called dual stacking. They each have network and host portions.

IPv4

IPv4 consists of 32 binary bits, written in **dotted decimal notation** as **decimal** numbers representing four **binary** octets (like bytes) separated by periods. While older, it is still extremely common, and you will see it in your everyday work as an IT support technician. Eventually, it will be replaced by IPv6, but that is expected to take decades.

Using a Subnet Mask

The network portion of an IPv4 address is defined by the **subnet mask**. This determines whether the destination host is on the local subnetwork or is on a remote network. It is easiest to see this in binary, where the subnet mask is compared against the IPv4 address. For instance, let's consider IP address 192.168.248.143. It translates to 11000000.10101000.111 11000.10001111 in binary. The decimals are here to make the binary easier to read, but the computer doesn't use them:

```
11000000.10101000.11111000.10001111  (192.168.248.143)
```

Now let's look at the subnet mask. If it has a subnet mask of 255.255.255.0, also written as /24, the binary for that would look like 11111111.11111111.11111111.00000000, where the ones represent the network and the zeros represent the host portion of the subnet mask:

```
11111111.11111111.11111111.00000000  (255.255.255.0)
```

Now, let's line these up together, and you can see where the network and host portions of the IPv4 address line up:

```
11000000.10101000.11111000.10001111

11111111.11111111.11111111.00000000
```

The system will combine them together in a process called ANDing; if both values are ones, the one is kept; if either value is zero, the value becomes zero. The network that this device belongs to, then, is easy to see. In this case, it is 11000000.10101000.11111000.00000000/24 (192.168.248.0/24) (because you always have to tell your readers what the subnet mask is).

Another way of saying this is: "Host 192.168.248.148/24 is on network 192.168.248.0/24."

Why is this information important? It tells us which other devices are also on the same network. Any other device on network 192.168.248.0/24 is local and can be connected to directly. Connecting to any device outside of the local network requires you to go through a gateway router (most often called a **default gateway**) because those hosts are not on the same network as this device. You need to ensure that your router's default gateway address is in the same subnet with your device. This default gateway is your network's egress point to the rest of the world; if it isn't configured correctly, your device can't get its packets out.

Public vs. Private IPv4

By using **private IPv4 addresses**, an organization can use as many IPv4 addresses as they need internally and needs only one public IPv4 address that everyone shares. This approach substantially reduces the need for public IPv4 addresses, which have largely been exhausted. Many organizations use this approach for security reasons as well, since devices using private IPv4 addresses are "invisible" to devices outside the organizational network without translation.

For this reason, it is not uncommon to have the same 192.168.x.x range at your home or small business and at your friend's house; each network uses the same IPv4 RFC 1918 private address range. You could get the same exact IPv4 address in these locations without it being an actual problem.

The IPv4 RFC 1918 private address ranges include

    Class A: 10.0.0.0 to 10.255.255.255

    Class B: 172.16.0.0 to 172.31.255.255

    Class C: 192.168.0.0 to 192.168.255.255

Network Address Translation

A process called **Network Address Translation (NAT)** "translates" the private range into a public range before it goes onto the public Internet. This is generally done by a router at the network edge. The NAT router keeps track of which device has asked for which public service and automatically retranslates and reroutes packets appropriately.

There are a lot of addresses available. IT support technicians need to know them in order to tell whether a device is using a private or public IP address, so you know to look at NAT translation as a possible cause of trouble.

IPv6

IPv6 is newer than IPv4. It consists of 128-bit addresses, written as eight groups of four **hexadecimal** (base 16) digits each, separated by colons and shortened where possible, because even in hexadecimal these numbers get long. For example, *2001:0db8:0000:0000:0 000:8a2e:0370:7334* can be shortened to become *2001:db8::8a2e:370:7334*.

The rules for shortening IPv6 addresses are straightforward: (1) Remove leading zeros. If an octet has zeros at the beginning, just remove them. For instance, 00f0 becomes f0 without changing the value. But that's not the same as 00f, which *would* change the value. That also lets you shorten 0000 to just a single 0. (2) When you have long sequences of all zeros, replace all of them with a colon. In the example, three sequences are all zeros. All three sets are replaced with a double colon. Remember, though, you can only do this once (otherwise, you wouldn't know how many zeros were removed). That does mean that an address of :: or ::1 is valid (and is actually the loopback address). Compare the IPv6 address in the preceding example, and you'll see how it works in real life.

Finding your IPv4 or IPv6 address is simple and straightforward for most operating systems. For Windows, you will open a command prompt and type **ipconfig /all** to get full information for all your network interfaces. For Mac, you can find it in the System Settings under **Network**, then select **Wi-Fi** or **Ethernet**, then **Details** and scroll down. For Linux systems, open a terminal window and enter the command **ifconfig** or **ip addr** and press Enter. Note that **ifconfig** is deprecated on many Linux systems, so it is not always available.

Figure 3-8 shows a portion of the results of a Windows command prompt running the command **ipconfig /all**. Notice that the hostname is also available here.

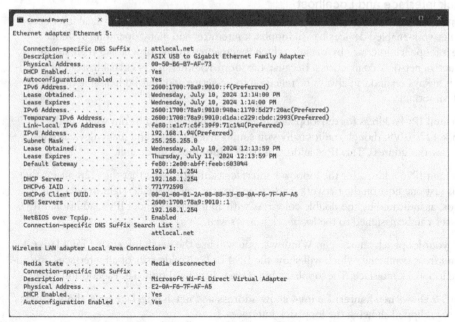

Figure 3-8 *Running* ipconfig /all *on a Windows Command Line*

MAC Address

The media access control address, called a **MAC address**, is a physical address, represented by Layer 2 of the OSI model and the Network Access layer of the TCP/IP model. Each network interface has its own MAC address, which is used as an address within a network segment. Unlike an IP address, which can be used to identify a device outside of a network segment, a MAC address is used only within a particular network segment and is not routable. To reach a particular device, a packet is addressed with the MAC address as well as the IP address. If the device is in the local network, the MAC address is that of the device and is in the local network, and the packet is sent directly to that device. If the device is in a remote network, the MAC address is that of the default gateway with the remote device's IP address, and the default gateway will forward the packet to the destination.

In general, a MAC address is assigned by a manufacturer and is 48 bits, represented by six groups of two hexadecimal (base 16) digits, separated by hyphens, colons, or spaces. Because they are typically assigned by manufacturers, they are often referred to as *burned-in* or *physical* addresses. On a particular network segment, you cannot have two devices with the same MAC address, just like you cannot have two devices with the same IP address on an organizational network.

Figure 3-8 shows the MAC address for each interface, referring to it as a physical address. Note that Windows uses the hyphen to separate the octets. Other operating systems may use colons or spaces, but the meaning is the same. You can change MAC addresses if needed, but that is rare and unusual.

Because the MAC address is assigned by the manufacturer, you can generally tell the manufacturer of a device by its MAC address. This tip can help with troubleshooting of devices because it will help you determine if you have the correct network driver for a network device.

Loopback Interface and Localhost

A **loopback** interface is a special software-only interface that mimics a physical interface. Most network-enabled devices have a loopback interface, and many operating systems enable a loopback interface by default, which is active regardless of whether there are any other active network connections. Because the loopback interface is virtual instead of physical, it is always on and can always be relied on to be active and thus addressable during troubleshooting.

The default IPv4 address for the loopback interface technically can be anywhere in the network 127.0.0.0/8, though traditionally you simply use 127.0.0.1, and many devices will only allow this address. This IPv4 address is named **localhost** by default.

The default IPv6 address for the loopback interface is ::1/128. Note that the /128 means that there is just one host on the network, and except for the one at the far right in binary, it is all zeros, as indicated by the double colon. As with all interfaces under IPv6, additional IPv6 addresses can be assigned to the loopback port as well.

To see your loopback interface in Windows, you will use the **netsh interface [ipv4 | ipv6] show address** command, which will show the IPv4 or IPv6 addresses of all interfaces, including the loopback interface. The loopback interface is listed as Loopback Pseudo-Interface.

Figure 3-9 shows **netsh interface ipv4 show address** and **netsh interface ipv6 show address** being run, clipped showing the loopback interfaces.

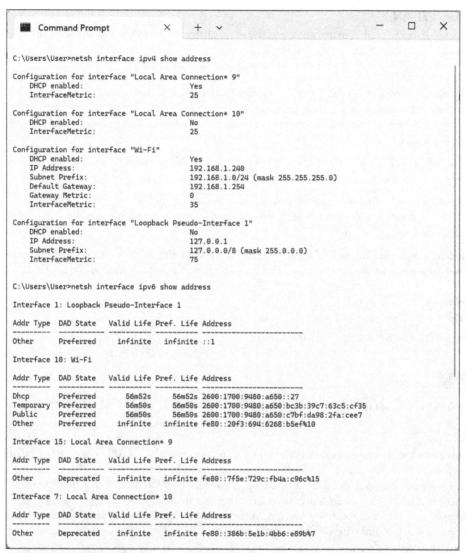

```
Command Prompt            ×    +  ∨                            —   □   ×

C:\Users\User>netsh interface ipv4 show address

Configuration for interface "Local Area Connection* 9"
    DHCP enabled:                    Yes
    InterfaceMetric:                 25

Configuration for interface "Local Area Connection* 10"
    DHCP enabled:                    No
    InterfaceMetric:                 25

Configuration for interface "Wi-Fi"
    DHCP enabled:                    Yes
    IP Address:                      192.168.1.240
    Subnet Prefix:                   192.168.1.0/24 (mask 255.255.255.0)
    Default Gateway:                 192.168.1.254
    Gateway Metric:                  0
    InterfaceMetric:                 35

Configuration for interface "Loopback Pseudo-Interface 1"
    DHCP enabled:                    No
    IP Address:                      127.0.0.1
    Subnet Prefix:                   127.0.0.0/8 (mask 255.0.0.0)
    InterfaceMetric:                 75


C:\Users\User>netsh interface ipv6 show address

Interface 1: Loopback Pseudo-Interface 1

Addr Type  DAD State    Valid Life Pref. Life Address
---------  -----------  ---------- ---------- ------------------------
Other      Preferred     infinite   infinite ::1

Interface 10: Wi-Fi

Addr Type  DAD State    Valid Life Pref. Life Address
---------  -----------  ---------- ---------- ------------------------
Dhcp       Preferred     56m52s      56m52s 2600:1700:9480:a650::27
Temporary  Preferred     56m50s      56m50s 2600:1700:9480:a650:bc3b:39c7:63c5:cf35
Public     Preferred     56m50s      56m50s 2600:1700:9480:a650:c7bf:da98:2fa:cee7
Other      Preferred     infinite   infinite fe80::20f3:694:6268:b5ef%10

Interface 15: Local Area Connection* 9

Addr Type  DAD State    Valid Life Pref. Life Address
---------  -----------  ---------- ---------- ------------------------
Other      Deprecated    infinite   infinite fe80::7f5e:729c:fb4a:c96c%15

Interface 7: Local Area Connection* 10

Addr Type  DAD State    Valid Life Pref. Life Address
---------  -----------  ---------- ---------- ------------------------
Other      Deprecated    infinite   infinite fe80::386b:5e1b:4bb6:e89b%7
```

Figure 3-9   *A Command Prompt Running the* **netsh interface ipv4 show** *Address and* **netsh interface ipv6 show** *Address Commands*

Basic End-Device Network Connectivity

Modern devices are connected to one another to facilitate communication. While there are many methods to do this, building and campus networks can be divided into a handful of large groups: local area networks (LANs) and wireless local area networks (WLANs). Regardless of size, the key point is that they are in a single, limited area—defined by a campus or building. If connection is made beyond that, the term wide area network (WAN) or metropolitan area network (MAN) is used. A WAN or MAN will connect multiple LAN networks together.

LAN vs. WLAN

Devices are connected in many ways, but the main difference is important: wired versus wireless. That is the focus of the following sections.

LAN

A **local area network (LAN)** refers to a collection of devices connected in one physical location, such as a building, office, or home, and overseen by one central administrative organization—like you, the IT support technician. LANs can be small or large and may have several segments.

These segments can be connected via copper cabling, usually Category 5, 6, or 7, or via fiber-optic cabling, and are interconnected using network switches.

LANs are connected to WANs using routers. In home and small business networks, they often use network devices containing both routers and switches, and many of these also contain wireless access points.

Standard icons describe each of these devices, as shown in the following figures. Figure 3-10 shows a standard network router icon. Figure 3-11 shows a standard network switch icon.

Figure 3-10   *The Standard Icon for a Router*

Figure 3-11   *The Standard Icon for a Workgroup Switch*

WLAN

A **wireless local area network (WLAN)** refers to a segment of a LAN connected by Wi-Fi or other wireless connection. Wi-Fi connections are radio based, but some other types of WLAN are optical, usually infrared. The most important characteristic is that they connect devices to a LAN via a wireless access point, either as a dedicated device called a wireless bridge or via a combined gateway device. Many home and small business networks use combined wireless and wired network devices.

The **service set identifier (SSID)** is the name by which your WLAN is known. Often this is the same as the overall network name, but that isn't required. Most home and small business networks use the default SSID configured by their ISP.

Many individuals and most large organizations will customize their SSID. You may use up to 32 alphanumeric characters to customize the SSID, and these names are case sensitive. Spaces and special characters are permitted but discouraged in an SSID name due to potential incompatibilities with some devices. Hiding your SSID is possible but does not provide any security advantages.

You should secure your SSID with the strongest encryption available. As of this writing, that is WPA2 and WPA3. Avoid the oldest, WEP and WPA, unless you absolutely must. In that case, you should put devices that require the older WEP and WPA encryption into their own

SSID and provide a firewall between them and the rest of the network, because these older devices prompt additional security concerns on the wireless network.

Be sure to change the WLAN password and keep it secure. Change your router admin login credentials to ensure that only those authorized can access the system. If you have visitors who need network access, consider setting up a Guest network just for them. This way, you ensure that guest and professional traffic remains segregated on your network.

Standard icons represent wireless network devices on your network. Figure 3-12 shows a standard wireless bridge icon. Figure 3-13 shows a standard wireless router icon, representing what a person might see in a home or small business network. Figure 3-14 shows a wireless access point, which an organization might install in a room separately from a router. Often mounted on walls and ceilings, these wireless access points provide wireless access far away from the routers and switches of the network. Figure 3-15 shows a wireless gateway router. It contains an Internet router, network switch, and wireless access point all in one box. Many Internet service providers (ISPs) will provide these to their clients. These are very common in homes and small businesses.

Figure 3-12   *The Standard Icon for a Wireless Bridge Device*

Figure 3-13   *The Standard Icon Representing a Wireless Router, Which Could Include a Gateway Router*

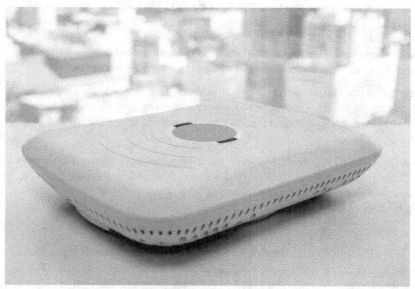

Figure 3-14   *A Standalone Wireless Access Point*

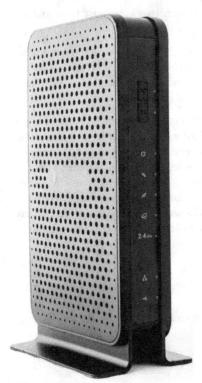

Figure 3-15   *A Wireless Gateway*

DNS

You can think of a **Domain Name Service (DNS)** as being kind of a phone book for the Internet. People think of and remember names better than numbers. Computers think only in numbers. DNS translates names to numbers and numbers to names. Specifically, DNS translates domain names into IP addresses so your web browsers and other Internet-bound traffic (email and so on) can know where to send a request for Internet resources.

As discussed earlier, devices must have their own IP addresses for them to be found online. DNS servers eliminate the need to memorize all those IP addresses. Instead, people just need to remember the website names, and the DNS will translate that into the needed IP addresses.

Not every device needs to be registered with DNS (remember, devices registered in this way have what is called a FQDN). After all, not every device needs to be found on the Internet. However, devices such as servers need to be registered with DNS whenever you want them to be reachable by domain name.

When a user wants to connect to a site on the Internet, the following steps occur:

1. The user types the web address they are seeking into the web browser. If this website is not in the local machine's DNS cache, this becomes a query that goes to the DNS Recursive Resolver server (often just called DNS Server on an individual machine).

2. If the resolver does not have the web address in its cache already, the resolver server queries a DNS root nameserver.

3. The root server responds to the resolver with the address of a top-level domain (TLD) DNS server. These are responsible for all domains at the top level, such as .com, .net, and store information for these domains.

4. The resolver makes a request to the TLD for the domain.

5. The TLD server responds with the IP address of the domain's nameserver.

6. The recursive resolver sends a query to the domain's nameserver.

7. The nameserver returns the IP address for the domain, along with additional information as appropriate.

8. The DNS resolver then responds to the web browser with the IP address and puts the new IP address and domain name in its cache, just in case they are asked for again.

9. The browser then makes a request to the IP address of the website it is seeking.

10. The destination web server returns the web page to the originating web server.

Note that each server will cache the domain information so that the nameservers are not overtaxed with queries. If cached, that cached data is provided at each step instead of just sending the resolver on to the nameserver.

DHCP

Dynamic Host Configuration Protocol (DHCP) is a way of automatically issuing IP addresses and other information to devices instead of having to configure them manually. It is used mostly in IPv4 networks; it is based on the much older BOOTP protocol, which you may still see reference to occasionally but is rarely used. The concept is that you can automatically allocate network addresses and configurations to host devices, allowing them Internet access without the need for manual intervention and configuration.

DHCP can be configured to assign IP addresses, default routers (also referred to as gateways), subnet masks (for IPv4 configurations), DNS servers, time servers, and certain other elements. Most DHCP services are set to dynamic allocation, where devices are assigned an IP address for a specified amount of time, called a **DHCP lease**, which must be renewed if the device needs to have continued Internet access (such renewal is automatic and is part of the DHCP process). The length of the lease is set by the network administrator—which could be you as the IT support technician. Because these DHCP leases expire, large numbers of devices can share relatively small blocks of IP addresses at locations such as conference centers, airports, coffee shops, and hotels, which would otherwise not be able to accommodate the large numbers of visitors over time.

The DHCP lease is simple in practice: when a new host comes onto the network, it will request an IP address from a DHCP server by sending a DHCP DISCOVER (Broadcast) message. If there is no DHCP server on the local network, the router will forward this via a DHCP relay agent to the DHCP server, which will send back a DHCP OFFER (unicast), which the router will relay to the host. This has a proposed IP address and other information. If acceptable to the host (which may have multiple DHCP OFFER messages from multiple DHCP servers to choose from), the client sends a DHCP REQUEST (broadcast) back to the DHCP server it is accepting the offer from. The DHCP server then responds with a DHCP ACK (acknowledgment) (unicast), which has all the information the host needs to configure its IP address stack.

Figure 3-16 shows the process of a host getting an IP address from a DHCP server.

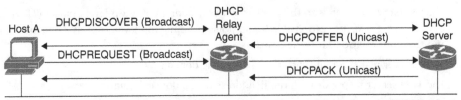

Figure 3-16   *The Process of an IPv4 Device Getting an Address from a DHCP Server*

DHCPv6

DHCPv6 operates a little differently. DHCPv6 offers two different methods of operation: stateful and stateless configuration. Stateless is also known by the acronym SLAAC, which stands for Stateless Address Autoconfiguration, discussed in the following paragraphs.

Unlike IPv4, where the client needs to learn everything about its IP configuration from the DHCP server, under IPv6 it learns its prefix and routing from the router itself via the router advertisements, leaving the DHCPv6 servers to do other things.

Otherwise, the stateful DHCPv6 is pretty much the same as with IPv4: the DHCPv6 server assigns IPv6 addresses to clients and keeps track of them, and issues DNS, time server, and other information as needed.

Stateless (SLAAC) DHCPv6 servers don't do addressing. Instead, the devices allocate their IPv6 addresses automatically via autoconfiguration (detailed further in the next section). Domain name, DNS servers, time servers, and other information are issued via DHCP.

Self-Assigned IP Addresses

Sometimes devices can issue their own IP addresses, whether running IPv4 or IPv6.

IPv4 APIPA

If you have an IPv4 device that is in the 169.254.x.x range, that means that the device has not been able to get a valid IP address from the DHCP server and does not have an IP address manually assigned to it. In this case, you know that something is wrong—often a loose or missing cable or otherwise missing network connection. Something is not working. This information narrows down the problem to the connection.

In this case, the IPv4 device has assigned itself an address using a process called **Automatic Private IP Addressing (APIPA)**, where it generates a random IP address in the 169.254.x.x range and then looks for another device using it. If there is a conflict, it tries again until it finds one no other device is using. This solution is intended as a temporary fix until it can get access to a DHCP server. It is almost always not what you want.

When your IPv4 devices get the 169.254.x.x addresses, you know that something is wrong with their network, so you can narrow down your troubleshooting to Layer 1 of the OSI model or Network Access layer of the TCP/IP model: you already know that the device doesn't have access to the DHCP server.

IPv6 Autoconfiguration

Under IPv6, automatic addressing is not a problem. Instead, a process called **Stateless Address Autoconfiguration (SLAAC)** automatically configures the interfaces. IPv6 uses

Neighbor Discovery Protocol (NDP), which uses router messages to help configure IPv6 devices automatically. The router will send out **router solicitation (RS)** and **router advertisement (RA)** messages, which help the IPv6 devices know what configuration information to use.

As with APIPA in IPv4, IPv6 SLAAC uses a process to ensure that there are no duplicate IPv6 addresses. For IPv6, this process is called Duplicate Address Detection (DAD), and uses **neighbor solicitation** and **neighbor advertisement** messages. Like router solicitation and router advertisement, these messages help devices learn about one another.

IPv6 Link-Local Addresses

Unlike with IPv4, IPv6 interfaces often have multiple IPv6 addresses. These include a link-local and a global address. They often have temporary IPv6 addresses as well, which will expire after a period elapses. Link-local addresses are used only within the local network and are not routed (they share this trait with the 169.254.0.0/16 network in IPv4). However, whereas in IPv4 you will only see the 169.254.x.x network appear when the interface cannot get an IPv4 address, you will always see an IPv6 link-local address alongside the other IPv6 addresses. If you refer to Figure 3-8, you will see that there is a link-local IPv6 address configured.

All link-local addresses are in the range FE80::/10, which means that they start with the binary 1111 1110 10. This makes them easy to identify (and this is important for your certification exam).

A device may use the same link-local address on multiple interfaces, so long as the same link-local address is not reused by multiple devices on the same network. In that respect, it is the same as any other address: don't duplicate addresses on the same network segment. That is different from any other addresses you may have used in the past, however, and it can be confusing to see multiple interfaces with the same link-local address.

Private IPv6 Networks

IPv6 segment FD00::/8, designated for /48 routing blocks, can be used to create multiple subnets. This capability allows an organization to subnet any number of private IPv6 networks as needed. These are not globally routable. FC00::/7 (which includes the FE80::/10, mentioned earlier as link-local addresses) are reserved for unique local addresses. Any other IPv6 addresses are globally routable addresses.

Where IPv4 uses 127.0.0.0/8 as its loopback interface, IPv6 reserves the ::1 for its loopback. Loopback interfaces are useful for troubleshooting purposes.

Connectivity Testing

To determine whether a device is actively on the network, you have several options. We previously discussed the idea of using **ipconfig** or **ip address** commands (depending on the device) to determine if the device has an IP address on the correct network. Another set of tools can be used to determine if a device has connectivity with the entire network and, if not, where the break in connectivity is occurring.

ping/ping6

The command **ping/ping6** tests the connectivity between any two points on the Internet. This tool measures the round-trip time for messages sent from an originating host to the destination and echoed back again. It does this by sending an **Internet Control Message Protocol (ICMP)** ping packet to the destination device and waiting for an **ICMP echo reply**.

Usage is simple, though it has extensibility that can make it a powerful tool. At its basic level, you simply type the command **ping** { [URL] | [IPv4 address] | [IPv6 address] }. Some very old systems require **ping6** { [URL] | [IPv6 address] } or **ping -6** { [URL] | [IPv6 address] } when working with IPv6 addresses, but that is largely deprecated and merged into the **ping** command, so it is unlikely you will see that except in very old devices.

If the remote device is reachable, the response (the echo) will start appearing, with information about the remote device and the time it took. An IT support technician can use the time field to help determine network issues.

Ping packets have been implicated in denial-of-service (DoS) and distributed-denial-of-service (DDoS) attacks, overwhelming victim systems with ICMP echo requests in what is called a *ping flood*. Because of this, some administrators restrict ICMP ping partially or completely. Some go so far as to block all ICMP entirely, but that limits other network troubleshooting that runs over ICMP.

You can ping via URL, IPv4, or IPv6 address. Figure 3-17 shows an IPv6 ping to example. com via its URL; because IPv6 is the default address for example.com, that is what is used for the ping. Figure 3-18 shows an IPv4 ping to example.com via its IPv4 address. Both ping queries go to the same device.

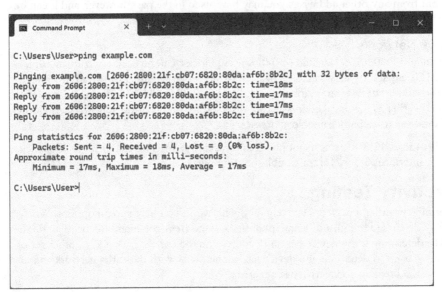

Figure 3-17 *IPv6 Ping to example.com via the URL*

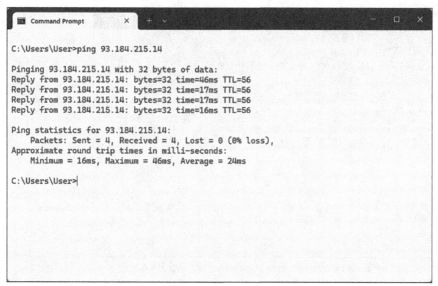

Figure 3-18 *IPv4 Ping to example.com*

traceroute/tracert

The command-line interface commands **traceroute** and **tracert** are used for displaying routes and paths of packets across an IP network. The command will respond with the round-trip time of the packet received from each host along the path to the destination, providing information about each of the remote routers that are encountered along the way.

It operates by sending ICMP echo request packets to the remote system with differing lengths of time before they expire, a concept called *time to live*; once a packet expires, the expiring router responds that the packet expired and returns its information. These are related to the ping packets discussed previously. That information is then displayed in the **traceroute** screen.

Some remote devices will not respond with their data; that is to be expected. Most will respond, and traceroute/tracert will attempt to get their FQDN for you to display that information along with their IP address.

Note that traceroute/tracert operate the same regardless of whether you are using IPv4 or IPv6. You can use the **tracert** { [*URL*] | [*IPv4 address*] | [*IPv6 address*] } command (note the similarity to the **ping** command). Some very old devices may want to see the **traceroute6** or **tracert6** command, where the syntax there would be **tracert6** { [*URL*] | [*IPv6 address*] }, but these are only for very old systems, and it is unlikely you would see those very often.

Figure 3-19 shows an IPv6 traceroute to example.com using its URL. Figure 3-20 shows an IPv4 tracert to example.com (via its IPv4 address). The route is almost the same, as you can see in the DNS addresses provided; they are reaching the same destination server.

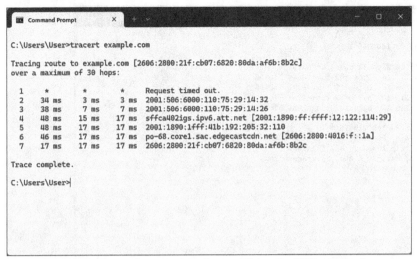

Figure 3-19 *A Traceroute to example.com Using Its URL via IPv6*

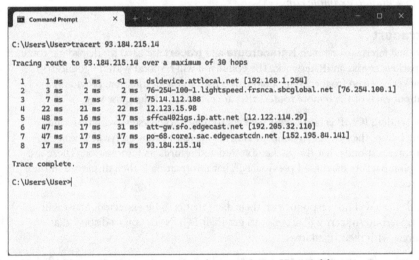

Figure 3-20 *A Traceroute to example.com via Its IPv4 Address*

nslookup

The **nslookup** command enables an IT support technician to query the DNS server directly from the command line. It allows you to see the mapping between domain name, IP address, and other DNS records.

By querying DNS records with nslookup, you can determine whether errors exist within the DNS records on a particular system or within DNS and can use this information to help diagnose and troubleshoot connectivity errors. Where records do not exist within DNS, this shows you that the problem is within the DNS queries themselves and gives you a direction in which to troubleshoot.

Note that the nslookup query is to the local DNS server, not to anything cached on the local machine. You also can see if connectivity to the local DNS server is broken. The syntax is **nslookup** { *URL* | *IPv4 address* | *IPv6 address* }.

Figure 3-21 shows an nslookup of example.com using the command **nslookup example.com**. Note that the results show both an IPv4 and IPv6 binding to the name; these are the same IPv4 and IPv6 addresses from the ping and tracert in the earlier figures.

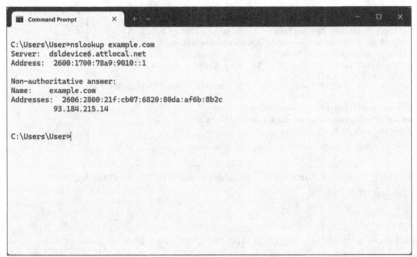

Figure 3-21 *The Results on* **nslookup example.com,** *Where You Can See the IPv4 and IPv6 to the Site*

netstat

The **netstat (network statistics)** command tells you about network statistics for your TCP/IP network, including routing tables, connections, and protocols in use. It is useful for finding problems in the network and the amount of traffic on segments and ports. By default, it will show each IPv4 and IPv6 connection in use. The command may be used by itself, **netstat,** or with additional parameters. It is largely deprecated because other existing tools provide more useful data.

iproute2

If you are managing Linux devices, you need to know about **iproute2**. This collection of tools allows you to control and monitor networking within Linux. In fact, many Linux distros no longer have the older **ifconfig** in favor of the tools that come with **iproute**.

ip

The most useful tool within iproute2 is **ip address**. At first glance it looks as if this is equivalent to using **ipconfig**, but it is much more powerful. Figure 3-22 shows the result of a Linux terminal running the **ip address** command, which shows the interfaces and associated information, including IPv4 and IPv6 addresses. Note that this is equivalent to the **ip address show** command.

```
author@Debian:~$ ip address
1: lo: <LOOPBACK,UP,LOWER_UP> mtu 65536 qdisc noqueue state UNKNOWN group default qlen
1000
    link/loopback 00:00:00:00:00:00 brd 00:00:00:00:00:00
    inet 127.0.0.1/8 scope host lo
       valid_lft forever preferred_lft forever
    inet6 ::1/128 scope host noprefixroute
       valid_lft forever preferred_lft forever
2: enp0s3: <BROADCAST,MULTICAST,UP,LOWER_UP> mtu 1500 qdisc fq_codel state UP group def
ault qlen 1000
    link/ether 08:00:27:e2:ec:80 brd ff:ff:ff:ff:ff:ff
    inet 192.168.1.93/24 brd 192.168.1.255 scope global dynamic noprefixroute enp0s3
       valid_lft 86332sec preferred_lft 86332sec
    inet6 2600:1700:78a9:9010::f/128 scope global dynamic noprefixroute
       valid_lft 3533sec preferred_lft 3533sec
    inet6 2600:1700:78a9:9010:2ac7:77d0:6fac:35fc/64 scope global temporary dynamic
       valid_lft 3534sec preferred_lft 3534sec
    inet6 2600:1700:78a9:9010:a00:27ff:fee2:ec80/64 scope global dynamic mngtmpaddr nop
refixroute
       valid_lft 3534sec preferred_lft 3534sec
    inet6 fe80::a00:27ff:fee2:ec80/64 scope link noprefixroute
       valid_lft forever preferred_lft forever
author@Debian:~$
```

Figure 3-22 *A Linux Terminal Running the* **ip address** *Command, Displaying All Interfaces and Their Configuration*

ip address

You can do a lot more with the **ip** command. You can manually add an IP address to an interface, for instance. Remember that you need to be running at elevated permissions (sudo) in order for this to work. The general syntax is **[sudo] ip address add** { *ipv4 address/mask* | *ipv6 address/prefix* } **dev** { *IFNAME* } (where *IFNAME* is the Interface name), which gives you the following examples to place an address on the Ethernet 0 Interface:

IPv4:

[sudo] ip address add 209.165.201.5 dev e0 will add the IPv4 address to the interface.

The same is true for IPv6 addresses:

[sudo] ip address add fe80::1 dev e0 will add the IPv6 address to the Ethernet interface. Note that you won't usually need to do this due to APIPA.

Remember, loopback interfaces, by default, have the IPv6 address of ::1/128, and the IPv4 address of 127.0.0.1/8.

ip neighbor show

The other devices that a device knows about are called *IP neighbors*. Using the **Address Resolution Protocol (ARP)**, you can get a list of all the neighbors the device knows about. ARP is used for translating IP addresses into physical (MAC) addresses, so it is very useful to check when troubleshooting; any errors in the ARP table will cause issues getting to local network devices, including the default gateway. The **ip neighbor show** command shows all the local entries in the ARP table. An IT support technician using **ip neighbor show** can see whether the device sees the other devices on its immediate network, including the router, and thus is able to communicate with other local devices.

ss

iproute2 has a utility called **ss**, which shows socket statistics. Like netstat, running **ss** will show a list of all network processes and their port numbers, along with other details about the connections.

Figure 3-23 shows **ss -u -a** running under Debian Linux. In this case, the figure shows just UDP packets, but with both IPv4 and IPv6 network protocols in use. There are a lot of additional options, expressions, and filters that can extend the use of the **ss** command.

```
┌─────────────────────────────────────────────────────────────────────────┐
│  ⊞                        author@Debian: ~              Q  ≡   ✕         │
├─────────────────────────────────────────────────────────────────────────┤
│ author@Debian:~$ ss -u -a                                                 │
│ State  Recv-Q Send-Q               Local Address:Port        Peer Address:│
│ Port                               Process                                │
│ UNCONN 0      0                        0.0.0.0:631               0.0.0.0:  │
│ *                                                                         │
│ UNCONN 0      0                        0.0.0.0:56333             0.0.0.0:  │
│ *                                                                         │
│ ESTAB  0      0                192.168.1.93%enp0s3:bootpc     192.168.1.254:│
│ bootps                                                                    │
│ UNCONN 0      0                        0.0.0.0:mdns              0.0.0.0:  │
│ *                                                                         │
│ UNCONN 0      0        [fe80::a00:27ff:fee2:ec80]%enp0s3:dhcpv6-client [::]:│
│ *                                                                         │
│ UNCONN 0      0                           [::]:40806                [::]:  │
│ *                                                                         │
│ UNCONN 0      0                           [::]:mdns                 [::]:  │
│ *                                                                         │
│ author@Debian:~$                                                          │
│                                                                           │
│                                                                           │
│                                                                           │
│                                                                           │
└─────────────────────────────────────────────────────────────────────────┘
```

Figure 3-23 *Results of Running the **ss -u -a** Command in a Linux Terminal; Note That This Command Shows All IPv4 and IPv6 Connections Using UDP*

Firewall

Firewalls protect network-attached devices by monitoring incoming and outgoing network traffic and determining if the traffic is legitimate. If legitimate, the traffic is allowed; if the traffic is not legitimate, it is blocked. Think of them as the first line of defense on a network. They can be hardware, software, Software as a Service (SaaS), or cloud-based (either public or private cloud); this last type is often referred to as a *virtual firewall*. Generally, network devices with firewalls are shown with icons having a brick wall. Figure 3-24 shows an example of an icon of a router with a firewall. Note the brick pattern; when you see this on an icon, you know the device should have a firewall installed.

Figure 3-24 *The Standard Icon of a Router with Firewall*

When users have trouble connecting to services, the issue could be the firewall inadvertently blocking traffic where it should not. In this case, the IT support technician will need to investigate what type(s) of firewall(s) exist between the client system and the remote system and what type of traffic is being blocked.

For instance, it is not uncommon for ICMP ping traffic to be blocked by a firewall. This reduces unnecessary network traffic and limits DoS attacks. However, a misconfiguration that removes all ICMP traffic could interfere with legitimate operation of network administration and error code transmission across the network. Similar restrictions could happen for any other type of protocol blocks that might inadvertently creep into configurations by accident, causing a user to lose connectivity to remote systems. By understanding how firewalls work and where they might be placed, the IT support technician can troubleshoot more efficiently and effectively.

The main types of firewalls are described in Table 3-3.

Table 3-3   Firewall Types

Firewall Type	Description
Proxy firewall	A proxy firewall takes each packet, caches it, and passes it along, using its own interface IP information in place of the originating system. It thus protects the originating system(s) completely from the outside networks. In busy networks, proxy firewalls can get bogged down, affecting throughput.
Stateful inspection firewall	Added to a gateway router, the stateful inspection firewall inspects each packet as it comes through the router and compares the state, port, and protocol against allowed and blocked packet types. Decisions are made based on defined rules and context, using information from previous connections and packets. These are relatively simple to configure and operate.
Unified Threat Management (UTM) firewall	The UTM firewall combines a network firewall with email, stateful inspection, intrusion prevention, antivirus, and other firewall options, providing a unified solution to protection of the network. While more expensive up front, the unified management appeals to a lot of businesses that otherwise would not have access to dedicated firewall appliances.
Next-generation firewall (NGFW)	NGFWs use network intelligence to control access using stateful inspection, integrating intrusion prevention system (IPS), application awareness and control, URL filtering, and other techniques that address evolving threats. The NGFW is ready to tackle the next generation of challenges.
Threat-focused NGFW	These firewalls are like traditional NGFWs (see the preceding description) but have more advanced threat detection. The user and IT support technician will know which assets are most at risk, be able to quickly react to attacks, detect evasive or suspicious activity with network and endpoint event correlation, decrease time from detection to cleanup, and ease administration with unified policies.

Firewall Type	Description
Virtual firewall	Virtual firewalls are deployed as virtual appliances in the cloud. They protect cloud environments and virtualized infrastructure inside a data center that would be difficult to protect physically. By being virtual, they can adapt quickly to the changing network environment and help cloud-based virtual servers and software-defined networking (SDN) be more efficient and effective.

Multifactor Authentication

When you're authenticating across a network, it is not enough anymore to just have a username and password. Security makes an additional layer of authentication more critical than ever to help prevent unauthorized access.

The components of **multifactor authentication (MFA)** are based on something you know, something you have, and something you are.

Usernames and Passwords

Username and password are the something you know; this is why it is so important to not share your username and password with others, and to change your password if it is hacked or stolen. This includes secret questions or a PIN code.

Physical Keys

It is important to verify something you have. This could include entering a code from an app on your mobile phone (because you have the phone; see next section); security token (often called **FIDO**, or **Fast IDentity Online**, tokens); display cards; hardware fobs (similar to security tokens); or security keys.

FIDO tokens are available from many vendors; your workplace will settle on one that is right for your organization. Many of these plug in to your device via a USB port or via a Bluetooth connection, making it unnecessary for you to do more than press a button, enter a code, or scan your fingerprint to authenticate. For these, you do not even need to type the passcode into your device to verify.

Figure 3-25 shows a FIDO token; when you press the button, the code appears, and you can enter it into your computer.

Figure 3-25 *A FIDO Token*

Authentication Apps

Multifactor authentication apps are available from multiple sources, and many different vendors support them. Apple embeds one into its iOS for the iPhone and iPad devices. Microsoft embeds one into the Outlook app for iOS and Android. Google and Microsoft each have their own authenticator apps. There are several standalone security and authentication companies such as Duo, Yubico (which also makes FIDO keys), Aegis, Authy, and OTP that have their own authenticator apps. Many password managers such as LastPass, Bitwarden, and others have their own authenticator apps; most of them can be used with other sites as well.

When verifying identity with apps or tokens, you are verifying who you *are*, the third piece of multifactor authentication. This can be done with a password on your device or app, but is more often done via face recognition, fingerprint scans, retinal scans, and the like. Some devices and sites are instituting voice recognition into their verification schemes. Still others look for behavioral patterns. The Android pattern lock, for instance, looks not just at the specific pattern of dots but also at the method by which the user touches the dots to unlock the device. A different user will move their fingers slightly differently, and the device may not unlock for them, even if they have touched the same sequence of dots.

Other Methods

Sometimes you will be prompted to enter a code that was emailed or sent to you via **Short Message Service (SMS)**. This code is then entered as an additional layer of security for the login. While this is a good additional method of authentication, it is important to remember that both email and SMS are considered insecure. They are better than nothing at all, but FIDO tokens or apps are better methods.

One additional caution: phishing campaigns often ask that you forward the information from these authentication emails and SMS messages to the phishers to allow them to hack your account. This scenario is much less likely with the physical keys or the authentication apps for two reasons: (1) either the token code is never given to you (in the case of physical FIDO keys, which are plugged directly in to your device) or (2) the code changes periodically (every 30 seconds or 1 minute), thus rendering any emailed code useless very quickly. Emailed and SMS-based codes often do not expire quickly, sometimes being valid for 24 hours or more.

Exam Preparation Tasks

As mentioned in the Introduction, you can customize your strategy for exam preparation. Suggested tasks include the exercises here, Chapter 9, "Final Preparation," and the exam simulation questions on the companion website.

Review All Key Topics

Review the most important topics in this chapter, noted with the Key Topic icon in the outer margin of the page. Table 3-4 lists a reference of these key topics and the page numbers on which each is found.

Table 3-4   Key Topics for Chapter 3

Key Topic Element	Description	Page Number
Paragraph	Hostnames	78
Paragraph	Identifying the operating system, processor, disk space, and quantity and type of memory of a device	79
Section	IPv4	81
Section	Using a Subnet Mask	81
Section	Public vs. Private IPv4	82
Paragraph	IPv6	83
Paragraph	MAC address	84
Paragraph	LAN	86
Paragraph	Wireless LAN	86
Paragraph	DNS	88
Paragraph	DHCP	89
Paragraph	DHCPv6	90
Paragraph	ICMP ping	92
Paragraph	The **tracert/traceroute** command	93
Paragraph	The **nslookup** command	94
Paragraph	The **netstat** command	95
Paragraph	The **iproute2** suite	95
Paragraph	The **ip address** command	96
Paragraph	The **ss** utility	97
Paragraph	Firewalls	97
Paragraph	Multifactor authentication	99
Paragraph	Physical keys	99
Paragraph	Authentication apps	100
Paragraph	Other authentication methods	100

Define Key Terms

Define the following key terms from this chapter and check your answers in the glossary:

Address Resolution Protocol (ARP), Automatic Private IP Addressing (APIPA), binary, decimal, default gateway, DHCP lease, DHCPv6, Domain Name Services (DNS), dotted decimal notation, Dynamic Host Configuration Protocol (DHCP), FIDO (Fast IDentity Online), firewall, fully qualified domain name (FQDN), hexadecimal, hostname (host name), ICMP echo request/reply, Internet Control Message Protocol (ICMP), IP address, iproute2, IPv4, IPv6, local area network (LAN), localhost, loopback, MAC address, multi-factor authentication (MFA), neighbor advertisement, Neighbor Discovery Protocol (NDP), neighbor solicitation, netstat (network statistics), Network Address Translation (NAT), next-generation firewall (NGFW), nslookup, operating system, Open Systems Interconnect (OSI) model, ping/ping6, private IP address, processor (CPU), proxy firewall, router

advertisement (RA), router solicitation (RS), Service Set Identifier (SSID), Short Message
Service (SMS), ss, stateful inspection firewall, Stateless Address Autoconfiguration
(SLAAC), subnet mask, Transmission Control Protocol/Internet Protocol (TCP/IP) model,
threat-focused NGFW, traceroute/tracert, Unified Threat Management (UTM) firewall,
virtual firewall, wireless local area network (WLAN)

Command Reference to Check Your Memory

This section includes the most important configuration and EXEC commands covered in this
chapter. It might not be necessary to memorize the complete syntax of every command, but
you should be able to remember the basic keywords that are needed.

To test your memory of the commands, cover the right side of Table 3-5 with a piece of
paper, read the description on the left side, and then see how much of the command you can
remember.

The 100-140 CCST IT Support exam focuses on practical, hands-on skills that are used by
networking professionals. Therefore, you should be able to identify the commands needed to
configure and test.

Table 3-5   Configuration Commands

Task	Command Syntax
Find a hostname from the DNS server	**nslookup [{** *IP Address* **|** *URL* **}]**
Find the CPU info in Linux	**lscpu**
Get disk space in Linux	**df**
Get memory allocation in Linux	**top**
Find IP information for all interfaces: Windows	**ipconfig /all** or **ipconfig**
Find IP information for all interfaces: Mac	**ifconfig** or **ip address**
Find IP information for all interfaces; Linux	**ip address**
Show the loopback interface in Windows	**netsh interface [ipv4	ipv6]**
Ping a remote device to verify connectivity	**ping {** [*URL*] **|** [*IPv4 address*] **|** [*IPv6 address*] **}**
Ping a remote IPv6 device to verify connectivity (old method)	**ping6 {** [*URL*] **|** [*IPv6 address*] **}** or **ping -6** **{** [*URL*] **|** [*IPv6 address*] **}**
Trace the path of a packet through the network to a remote device	**tracert {** [*URL*] **|** [*IPv4 address*] **|** [*IPv6 address*] **}**
Trace the path of an IPv6 packet through the network to a remote device (old method)	**tracert6 {** [*URL*] **|** [*IPv6 address*] **}**
Look up a host in the DNS server to see mapping between the URL and IP address	**nslookup {** *URL* **|** *IPv4 address* **|** *IPv6 address* **}**
Find network statistics for your device	**netstat**
Define a new IPv4 or IPv6 address on an interface in Linux	**[sudo] ip address add {** *ipv4 address/mask* **|** *ipv6* *address/prefix* **} dev {** *interface ID* **}**
Show all entries in the ARP table	**ip neighbor show**
Show socket statistics in Linux	**ss** (part of the **iproute2** suite)

References

AWS, "What Is MFA?" https://aws.amazon.com/what-is/mfa/

AWS, "What Is OSI Model?" https://aws.amazon.com/what-is/osi-model/

Baturn, D., "Task-Centered iproute2 User Guide," https://baturin.org/docs/iproute2/

Cisco, "DHCP Overview," https://www.cisco.com/en/US/docs/ios/12_4t/ip_addr/configuration/guide/htovdhcp.html

Cisco, "What Is a Firewall?" https://www.cisco.com/c/en/us/products/security/firewalls/what-is-a-firewall.html

Cisco, "What Is a LAN?" https://www.cisco.com/c/en/us/products/switches/what-is-a-lan-local-area-network.html

Cisco, Loopback Interfaces, https://www.cisco.com/c/en/us/td/docs/security/asa/asa919/configuration/general/asa-919-general-config/interface-loopback.pdf

Cloudfare, "What Is DNS? How DNS Works," https://www.cloudflare.com/learning/dns/what-is-dns/

Geeks for Geeks, "TCP/IP Model," https://www.geeksforgeeks.org/tcp-ip-model/#

Kuznetsov, A. "Ss(8)," *Manpages.com*, https://manpages.debian.org/testing/iproute2/ss.8.en.html

Lenovo, "What Is a Hostname?" https://www.lenovo.com/us/en/glossary/hostname/

Microsoft Ignite, "Understand TCP/IP Addressing and Subnetting Basics," https://learn.microsoft.com/en-us/troubleshoot/windows-client/networking/tcpip-addressing-and-subnetting CHUCK

NetworkLessons, "Cisco DHCPv6 Server Configuration," https://networklessons.com/ipv6/cisco-dhcpv6-server-configuration

Vigderman, A., and G. Turner, "What Is SSID?" *Security.org*, https://www.security.org/vpn/ssid/

WhatIsMyIP.com, "Why Do I Have the 169.254 IP Address?" https://www.whatismyip.com/169-254-ip-address/

Wikipedia, "Iproute2," https://en.wikipedia.org/wiki/Iproute2

Wikipedia, "IPv6 Address," https://en.wikipedia.org/wiki/IPv6_address#Stateless_address_autoconfiguration_(SLAAC)

Wikipedia, "Nslookup," https://en.wikipedia.org/wiki/Nslookup

Wikipedia, "Ping (network utility)," https://en.wikipedia.org/wiki/Ping_(networking_utility)

Wikipedia, "Traceroute," https://en.wikipedia.org/wiki/Traceroute

CHAPTER 4

Windows OS

This chapter covers the following topics:

- **Resolving Common Windows OS Systems Issues:** Users will have issues with the operation of the Windows operating system itself. This section looks at common issues and solutions.

- **Resolving Common Application Issues:** The section covers installing and uninstalling software from different sources, including collaboration and productivity software.

- **Windows System Tools:** This section looks under the hood to discover what is going on with the operating system to help diagnose problems.

- **Windows Security Tools:** The section describes how to secure a Windows installation with Active Directory to allow multiple users to use the same Windows computer and continue the security after deployment in the field.

- **Mapping Cloud Drives:** The section explains how to map drives to simplify management.

Solving problems with Windows devices is part of what you will do as an IT support technician most workdays. This chapter assists you with what you need to troubleshoot common Windows OS systems issues, including connectivity and configuration; installation of software; passwords and other security concerns; and directory and shared drives. Throughout, you will see how your current skills will apply in the workplace and allow you to be the best IT support technician and serve your users better.

The chapter covers information related to the following Cisco Certified Support Technician (CCST) IT Support exam objectives:

- 2.2 Assist end users in using tools to locate information about their device

- 3.1 Assist users with establishing access to network-based resources

- 4.1 Assist users in resolving Windows operating system issues

- 4.5 Assist users in resolving common application issues

"Do I Know This Already?" Quiz

The "Do I Know This Already?" quiz allows you to assess whether you should read this entire chapter thoroughly or jump to the "Exam Preparation Tasks" section. If you are in doubt about your answers to these questions or your own assessment of your knowledge of the topics, read the entire chapter. Table 4-1 lists the major headings in this chapter and their corresponding "Do I Know This Already?" quiz questions. You can find the answers in Appendix A, "Answers to the 'Do I Know This Already?' Quizzes."

Table 4-1 "Do I Know This Already?" Section-to-Question Mapping

Foundation Topics Section	Questions
Resolving Common Windows OS Systems Issues	1–11
Resolving Common Application Issues	12–14
Windows System Tools	19
Windows Security Tools	15–16
Mapping Cloud Drives	17–18

CAUTION The goal of self-assessment is to gauge your mastery of the topics in this chapter. If you do not know the answer to a question or are only partially sure of the answer, you should mark that question as wrong for purposes of the self-assessment. Giving yourself credit for an answer you correctly guess skews your self-assessment results and might provide you with a false sense of security.

1. Why is understanding Windows OS configuration critical for IT support technicians?
    a. It helps them install new software.
    b. It ensures they can set up new hardware.
    c. It allows them to assist users with common system issues.
    d. It makes them proficient with network security.

2. What can be adjusted in the Display Settings dialog of the control panel?
    a. Sound settings
    b. Display resolution, brightness, scaling, and orientation
    c. Network display settings
    d. User accounts

3. What is the purpose of moving display icons to represent their position on the desk?
    a. To update the display drivers
    b. To adjust the brightness settings
    c. To accurately reflect their physical position
    d. To improve network connectivity

4. Why does Windows encrypt system drives with BitLocker?
    a. To improve system performance
    b. To allow faster boot times
    c. To prevent unauthorized use
    d. To enable remote access

5. Where is the BitLocker recovery key saved when BitLocker is automatically enabled on a modern Windows device?
    a. In the user's Microsoft account
    b. On a USB drive
    c. In the system BIOS
    d. On a printed piece of paper

6. What is one of the best methods to improve the stability and security of a Windows system?

   a. Increasing system RAM

   b. Upgrading hardware components

   c. Changing the desktop wallpaper

   d. Keeping the system up-to-date with the latest Windows updates

7. Why do web browsers cache pages?

   a. To speed up loading times and minimize bandwidth consumption

   b. To increase the security of the browser

   c. To store user passwords

   d. To improve the appearance of web pages

8. What problem might occur if the cache data becomes outdated or corrupt?

   a. Loading or formatting issues on some websites

   b. Slower Internet speed

   c. Increased system memory usage

   d. Frequent browser crashes

9. What is the purpose of the End Task feature in Task Manager?

   a. To restart the computer

   b. To update a program

   c. To close an unresponsive program and all associated tasks

   d. To change system settings

10. How can you make permanent changes to the boot order of a device?

   a. Through the Windows System Configuration utility

   b. By entering BIOS or UEFI and adjusting the Boot Order settings

   c. By selecting the boot device from a menu during startup

   d. By adjusting settings in the Device Manager

11. What is the purpose of the Windows accessibility features?

   a. To enhance the visual design and aesthetics of the operating system

   b. To support productivity, creativity, and ease of use for all users, regardless of their vision, hearing, dexterity, mobility, focus issues, or other needs

   c. To provide advanced graphics and gaming performance

   d. To limit user access to specific applications and settings

12. What is the first step to take when troubleshooting issues with collaboration applications?

   a. Check connectivity to the Internet and the collaboration app

   b. Restart the computer immediately

   c. Contact the collaboration app's support team

   d. Reinstall the collaboration app

13. What should you do if a locally installed software application is not working properly?

    a. Uninstall and reinstall the application

    b. Perform a repair installation using the original installer

    c. Contact the software's support team

    d. Reinstall the operating system

14. What is the primary function of Active Directory?

    a. Connect users with network resources and manage permissions and access within a Windows domain environment

    b. Monitor network traffic and performance

    c. Install and update software applications

    d. Configure hardware settings and drivers

15. What is the primary purpose of the **GPUpdate** command in Active Directory environments?

    a. To manually update Group Policy settings for computers and users in an Active Directory domain

    b. To install updates for Windows operating system

    c. To synchronize user data across devices

    d. To back up Group Policy settings to a file

16. How do security groups simplify user management in Active Directory?

    a. By allowing users to access resources across multiple domains

    b. By categorizing users into educational and administrative roles

    c. By transferring permissions to groups so that users inherit permissions from the group

    d. By managing users and groups on a local device

17. What is the purpose of the Add Network Location wizard in Windows?

    a. To map local drives to network drives

    b. To connect to an SMB share via the web

    c. To find and connect to an Internet-based network location or web-based drive

    d. To configure system updates and network settings

18. What is the primary purpose of AWS Simple Storage Service (S3)?

    a. Storing and managing large amounts of data in data lakes and buckets

    b. Running virtual machines

    c. Hosting web applications

    d. Managing databases

19. What information can be found in the System Information window in Windows?

    a. Log entries of system events

    b. Network configuration details

    c. Processor details and installed hardware/software

    d. Active network connections and their statuses

Foundation Topics

Resolving Common Windows OS Systems Issues

The main issues that IT support technicians must deal with on an ongoing basis have to do with the Windows operating system configuration. One could even refer to this as the "bread and butter" of the IT support technician. Understanding how to assist users in the common Windows OS configuration and systems issues is critical to your success as an IT support technician, and knowing how to make your users feel comfortable coming to you with the relatively simple configuration issues will make them comfortable coming to you with more complex questions as well.

Display Settings

Displays are also called monitors. For this section, we use the term *display*. If you are accustomed to using the term *monitor*, realize that in the Windows PC world, these two terms refer to the same thing.

Adjusting settings of Windows displays is a deceptively simple task. At first, this task might seem so simple that anyone should be able to do it without assistance; however, your users may contact you when they come across issues with screen resolution or other problems, so knowing how to check and adjust the Windows displays is important. In addition, if a **display** should be showing but is not, knowing how to troubleshoot the missing display is important for the IT support technician.

There are several methods to see what displays are available to a system. Press the Windows key, type **Display**, and select **Display Settings** to call up the system control for the display, as seen in Figure 4-1. This dialog allows you to adjust settings for each attached display, including placement (if there are multiple displays), brightness, scaling, display resolution, orientation, and advanced display information. As you can see in Figure 4-2, users and IT support technicians can see advanced information about their display and adapter. To select a different display, select the display icon at the top of the screen. To see which display is which, select the Identify button. If using multiple displays, you can position them relative to their physical position by dragging the display icons to the correct relative positions and then clicking Apply.

Troubleshooting Missing Display Issues

If a display should be showing but is not, one option is to select the Detect Other Display button. If this approach doesn't work (the message is "We didn't find another display"), the user or IT support technician should look to other options to resolve the issue.

Ensure that the display is not disabled (see Figure 4-3). If a display or its adapter is disabled, enable it first, since nothing else you try will work.

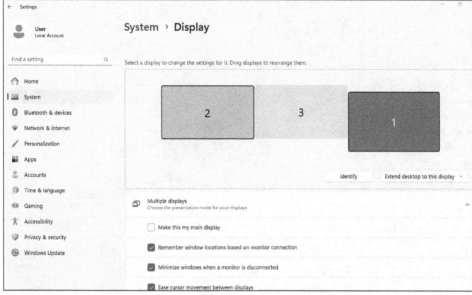

Figure 4-1   *The Display Control with Three Displays Available*

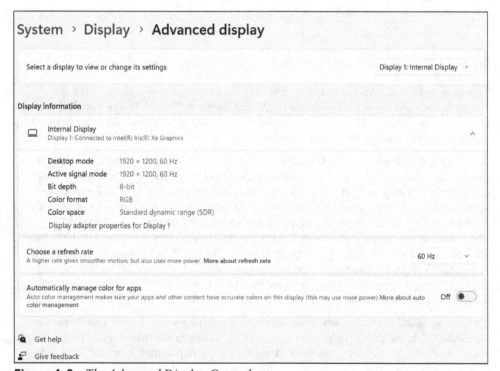

Figure 4-2   *The Advanced Display Control*

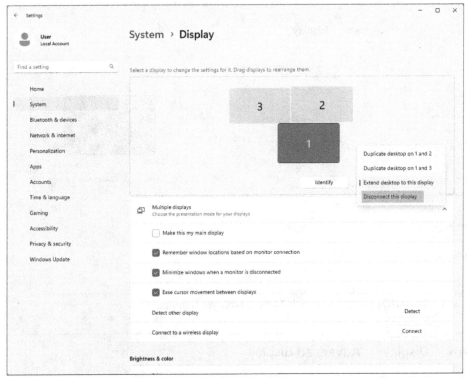

Figure 4-3 *Multiple Displays Can Be Disabled by "Disconnecting" the Display*

Assuming that the display has not been disabled, the first place to start is to check the cabling (please review the OSI reference model in Chapter 8, "The IT Professional"; this is Layer 1 of the OSI model—the physical layer). Look to see if the device is plugged in both to power and the video port of your computer.

This piece is the simplest and most complex to review because desktop display power cords sometimes appear to be plugged in when they are partially disconnected. Luckily, trouble-shooting them is easy, since desktop displays also light up when power is available. If no light comes on when the power button is triggered, power is not available to the device. Even if it looks as though the device is plugged in securely, the plug itself may have worked its way loose and may need to be reseated in the socket. If the power light still does not come on, replacing the power cable is an easy thing to try. These cables do wear out over decades of use, although that is uncommon, but it is not uncommon for power cables to be reused when swapping displays themselves because they tend to be universal and difficult to fish out from behind workstations.

If power is available to the external display, check the display cable. Ensure that it is securely fastened at both ends. If the cable goes to a docking station rather than directly to the com-puter, ensure that it has power too. As with power cables, unplugging from each end and then replugging the cables can ensure a secure connection, and can help ensure that the correct cable is being used, especially on a crowded desktop with several cables available.

If adjusting power cabling does not solve the problem, look for a set of controls on the display itself that will allow the user to adjust the brightness settings. It is possible that the display is working fine but has its brightness turned down. If this is the case, nothing else would fix the problem because, from the perspective of the computer, the display is working fine; the display simply is turned down too much for the user to see.

If it is still not showing an image after you confirm that the external display has power, the correct display cable is attached, and the brightness is turned up, then a restart of the computer is in order. A restart often fixes the problem because it allows the computer to take stock of all peripherals installed, including displays, and install updated drivers.

If a restart still does not solve the issue, try swapping cables, beginning with the video cable (remember: by this time, you have confirmed that you have power because you have a power light). Swapping out the display cable is a tried-and-true method that may solve the issue.

If the problem continues to persist, it is time to try swapping out the display itself. Use a known good display with the existing cables. If you now have an image on your display, you know that the problem is with the old display, and you have resolved the issue; all you need to do is to configure the settings within Windows (see the earlier section "Display Settings") and discard the old, broken display according to your organization's policies. Your user then can get back to work. If the problem is still not resolved, start over within Windows; you might have a defective display port, or you might have otherwise disabled the output within Windows, and it will take more troubleshooting to resolve the issue and perhaps an escalation to another IT support technician for assistance.

Multiple Displays

If a user has multiple displays, the steps are similar. The only difference is that you will need to pay attention to the method by which the multiple displays are connected and ensure that each of them is working before attempting to connect the next display. Figure 4-3 shows multiple displays attached with the Disconnect This Display option highlighted. Ensure that each display you wish to use is not disconnected before moving forward. When you wish to use the display again, simply click the display icon and select Extend Desktop to This Display to re-enable it. Move the display icons to represent their position on the desk. Be sure to select the Apply button to save your changes.

Connecting to a Wireless Display

Users can also connect wirelessly to displays and other Windows PCs by using the Connect button in the Connect to a Wireless Display section. This approach does the same thing as pressing Windows+k, allowing the user to connect to an external **wireless display**. The user simply selects the wireless display from the list provided. In some cases, the user will need to input a code (like a password) that appears on the wireless display to confirm the connection. Wireless displays are often used in conference rooms to connect to conference room screens and projectors. Figure 4-4 shows the connection screen with a TV being used as a conference room display.

Figure 4-4   *The Connection Screen*

Brightness

There are several ways to adjust the **brightness** of a display. You can adjust it from the Display controls, as seen in Figure 4-5. This approach works well for internal laptop displays and for some other displays with on-screen controls that can be used to adjust their brightness. If users are unable to see the content on their screen, sometimes the reason is that the screen brightness has been turned down all the way.

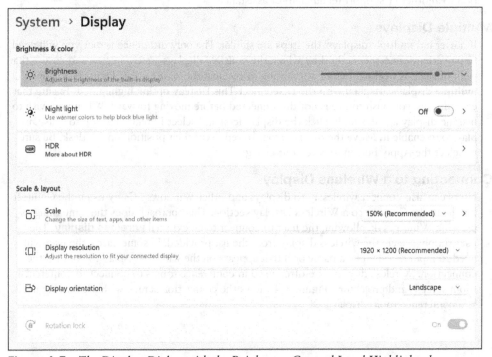

Figure 4-5   *The Display Dialog with the Brightness Control Level Highlighted*

If this is the case, there will be manual controls on the display itself. These buttons will activate an on-screen display like Figure 4-6, allowing the IT support technician or user to adjust contrast and brightness directly on the display.

Figure 4-6   *A Brightness Control Slider That Might Be Seen on a Display*

BitLocker

Windows encrypts system drives to prevent unauthorized use. Usually, this is a very good thing; unauthorized use of your drive is almost always a bad thing. However, sometimes a corrupt boot sector will cause a **BitLocker** error to creep in, and you will need to unlock it with the unlock code. Luckily, Microsoft has made it straightforward to recover a locked system.

Generally, BitLocker will be automatically enabled under one of the following circumstances:

- You have a modern Windows device that automatically enables device encryption. In this case, when BitLocker is activated, the recovery key is automatically saved to the user's Microsoft account. This is the most common method of having BitLocker activated on a device.

- An owner or administrator manually activated BitLocker (also called device encryption) through the Settings app. In this case, the recovery key was saved to a location of the owner's or administrator's choice and might not be automatically available in the owner's or administrator's Microsoft account.

- A work or school organization managing the account activated BitLocker protection; in this case, that organization likely has the BitLocker recovery key. If it is not in the user's personal Microsoft account, the IT support technician or user will need to contact that organization's help desk to get the recovery key.

It is rare to be asked for the BitLocker recovery key unless something has gone wrong. Perhaps the user has attempted to install a different operating system on the device. Perhaps the user has a corrupt hard drive. There are other possibilities. What is most important is that help be delivered quickly to allow the user to get back to work.

The first step is to find the BitLocker recovery key. The user needs to log in to their Microsoft account, go to https://account.microsoft.com/devices/recoverykey, and select Devices from the left-hand pane. This pane should show all the devices your Microsoft ID has been logged in to and for which you may have a BitLocker ID.

If the necessary device is not available on either the user's account or that of the IT support technician, you will need to contact the network administrator to get a BitLocker key because you do not have access.

If the necessary device is available, select the device and then View Bitlocker Keys from the dialog. Figure 4-7 shows a sample of a Devices screen with the View Bitlocker Keys button visible. It assists in recovery after a sector failure of a hard drive or other error occurs.

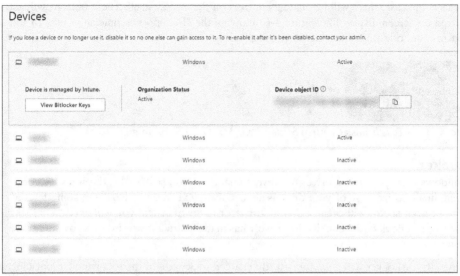

Figure 4-7   *The Microsoft Account with All Devices for Which the BitLocker Codes Are Known and Can Be Shown*

Some organizations and individuals prefer to store their BitLocker recovery codes (remember, these are also called *recovery keys*) on paper or on a USB flash drive. If you have ever logged in to your Microsoft account for work from your personal computer, it is possible that your recovery key is saved to that Microsoft account for work as well.

Because Microsoft Support cannot create, re-create, or supply a BitLocker recovery key, a totally lost key will result in the need for Windows Recovery. Thus, it is imperative that you have access to it just in case. Logging in to Windows from a Microsoft account is the easiest method.

Windows Update/Microsoft Update

One of the best methods to improve stability of a Windows system is to keep it up-to-date with the latest Windows updates. While there are cases where Windows updates have interfered with specialized software, for the average user these cases are rare, so it is generally recommended that most users install all released updates. For some versions of Windows, the broader Microsoft Update utility is used instead when dealing with non-Windows updates.

Enterprises can control the updates that are being installed in the Active Directory Group Policy. This is done by controlling the updates available from within the Windows Server Update Services (WSUS). This allows administrators, including IT support technicians if that is part of your job scope, to test released updates prior to allowing your users to install the updates. By controlling the updates available to users, the organization can have a chance to test the updates prior to pushing them out to users for installation and can ensure that all users have all requisite updates as well.

Most users, including home and small business users, will not have access to an Active Directory domain to control the updates. For these users, the IT support technician should ensure that all updates are installed. To do this, the IT support technician should have the user go to the **Settings > Windows Update.** If any updates are available, they will appear on this screen. This is also where changes can be made to the options, including the option to install updates for other Microsoft software. Figure 4-8 shows a Windows Update screen. The sample system is up-to-date. While the system is not receiving updates as soon as possible, they will be installed within a week or so of release under this configuration.

Figure 4-8 *A Windows Update Screen*

Finally, it should be noted that sometimes updates are available here for software not produced by Microsoft. Many manufacturers will use the **Windows Update/Microsoft Update** Service to provide updates for their products. This helps to streamline installation to their users. Because it is easier for the users to receive the latest updates, and since the update servers and services are hosted by Microsoft and are already configured and running, it helps ensure that each user is running the latest version of the software, thus reducing support costs for the individual companies involved.

Keeping your Windows software up-to-date is a critical piece toward keeping your machine healthy and operating properly.

Application Updates

In addition to the applications that update via Windows Update/Microsoft Update, most other software runs its own update service. Sometimes this updating happens automatically, but it is not uncommon for users to need to initiate the update manually.

The easiest way to update manually is from within the application. When in Google Chrome, for instance, selecting About Chrome will trigger the update process. Figure 4-9 shows the update in progress, where Chrome is automatically downloading and installing the latest update for Chrome. Chrome will finish installing the update when it is restarted, either by the user right away or when the entire system is shut down or restarted.

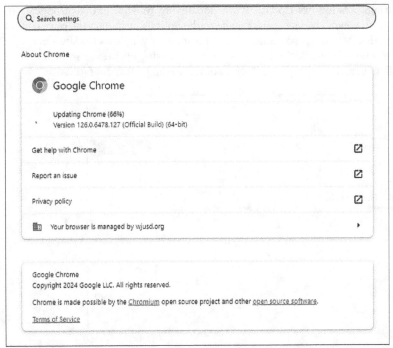

Figure 4-9   *Update to Google Chrome in Progress*

Other software will have a discreet Check for Updates menu item. In Adobe Acrobat, this item resides in **Help > Check for Updates,** as shown in Figure 4-10. This is a fairly typical method that many varieties of software show the Check for Updates option.

Figure 4-10   *The Menu Item to Check for Updates Within Adobe Acrobat*

Other software operates in a similar manner. Some even have automatic update capabilities. For instance, Google Chrome will prompt the user when it is out of date. Other software will update on its own cycle as determined by the manufacturer.

The Browser Cache

Web browsers **cache** pages to speed loading when you access a page again. That way, they do not need to load images and other common elements. This process speeds up browsing and minimizes bandwidth consumption.

Unfortunately, sometimes the cached data becomes outdated or corrupt and causes issues such as loading or formatting issues on some websites. If this situation occurs, you will need to clear the browser cache.

To clear the browser cache in Microsoft Edge, go to the three dots at the right-hand edge (the More menu) and select Settings. From there, select Privacy, Search, and Services. Select the Choose What to Clear button in the Clear Browsing Data Now section. Note that you can clear data from just the past hour or even periods of time longer than that also. Figure 4-11 shows part of the Settings screen with the Choose What to Clear button highlighted.

Figure 4-11   *The Microsoft Edge Settings Window*

In Google Chrome, go to the three dots in the upper-right side of the page and then select Settings. From there, select Privacy and Security. The selection is called Delete Browsing Data. As with Edge, you will have the opportunity to select a period of time as well as what type of data to be deleted. In Figure 4-12 the Google Chrome Delete Browsing Data dialog shows types of data available for deletion as well as time range available.

Other web browsers have similar procedures and options for clearing the browser cache.

Task Manager

At its most basic level, the Windows **Task Manager** lets you see all the processes running on a Windows system and make simple changes, including quitting them. It is a useful tool for troubleshooting and making simple repairs on the fly.

Launching the Task Manager

There are multiple methods to launch the Task Manager, but the easiest is pressing Ctrl+Shift+Esc. You can also press Ctrl+Alt+Delete and select Task Manager from the options that appear. Alternatively, you could select Task Manager from the Windows menu. Right-clicking the toolbar will also give you the option to open the Task Manager in most systems after Windows 10. You can also access the Task Manager by selecting **Control Panel > All Control Panel Items > Windows Tools**. Figure 4-13 shows a Task Manager window. Figure 4-14 shows a Task Manager window with a submenu of one of the tasks open. In this submenu, you can see many of the possible options for working with individual tasks.

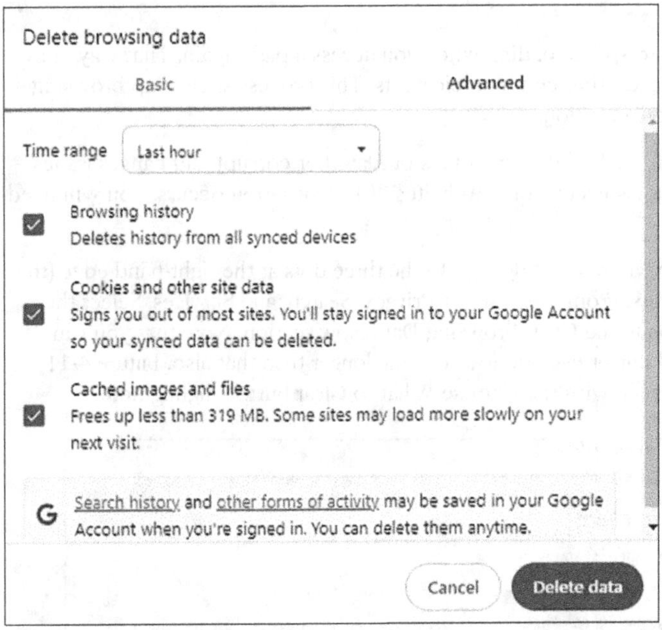

Delete browsing data

| Basic | Advanced |

Time range   [Last hour   ▼]

☑   Browsing history
     Deletes history from all synced devices

☑   Cookies and other site data
     Signs you out of most sites. You'll stay signed in to your Google Account
     so your synced data can be deleted.

☑   Cached images and files
     Frees up less than 319 MB. Some sites may load more slowly on your
     next visit.

G   Search history and other forms of activity may be saved in your Google
     Account when you're signed in. You can delete them anytime.

                                      (Cancel)   (Delete data)

Figure 4-12   *The Google Chrome Delete Browsing Data Dialog*

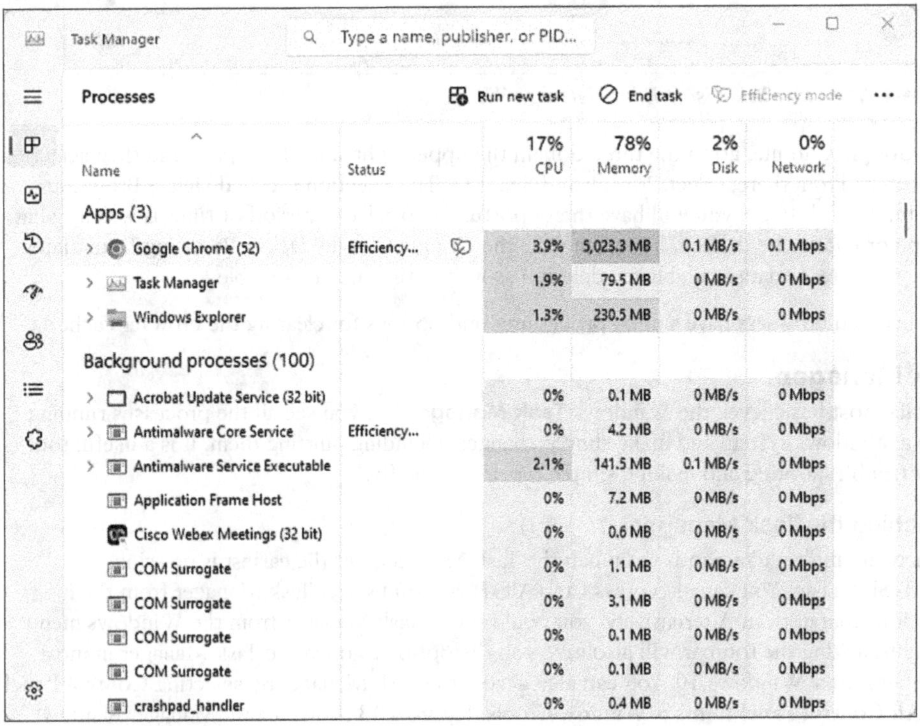

Task Manager	🔍 Type a name, publisher, or PID...		— ☐ ✕		
Processes		🔲 Run new task ⊘ End task Efficiency mode •••			
		17%	**78%**	**2%**	**0%**
Name	Status	CPU	Memory	Disk	Network
Apps (3)					
> ◉ Google Chrome (52)	Efficiency... 🍃	3.9%	5,023.3 MB	0.1 MB/s	0.1 Mbps
> ▨ Task Manager		1.9%	79.5 MB	0 MB/s	0 Mbps
> ▤ Windows Explorer		1.3%	230.5 MB	0 MB/s	0 Mbps
Background processes (100)					
> ▢ Acrobat Update Service (32 bit)		0%	0.1 MB	0 MB/s	0 Mbps
> ▣ Antimalware Core Service	Efficiency...	0%	4.2 MB	0 MB/s	0 Mbps
> ▣ Antimalware Service Executable		2.1%	141.5 MB	0.1 MB/s	0 Mbps
▣ Application Frame Host		0%	7.2 MB	0 MB/s	0 Mbps
▣ Cisco Webex Meetings (32 bit)		0%	0.6 MB	0 MB/s	0 Mbps
▣ COM Surrogate		0%	1.1 MB	0 MB/s	0 Mbps
▣ COM Surrogate		0%	3.1 MB	0 MB/s	0 Mbps
▣ COM Surrogate		0%	0.1 MB	0 MB/s	0 Mbps
▣ COM Surrogate		0%	0.1 MB	0 MB/s	0 Mbps
▣ crashpad_handler		0%	0.4 MB	0 MB/s	0 Mbps

Figure 4-13   *A Task Manager Window*

Figure 4-14 *A Task Manager Window with a Submenu of One of the Tasks Open*

End Task

One of the most important tools within the Task Manager is the idea of ending a task. If a program has become unresponsive, selecting it from within the Task Manager and clicking End Task will end all associated tasks and force the program to close completely. Once closed, the program will often allow you to restart and work normally. At the very least, the offending program will no longer be in the way and the computer can restart normally.

Switch To

You can also switch to a task. Many programs use cryptic names in Task Manager, and it can be difficult to tell which entry belongs to which program. The Switch To option allows you to see quickly which program is related to which process.

Run New Task

You can even start new programs (tasks) from within the Task Manager. Simply select Run New Task and type the program executable name. Note that you will need to know the exact name of the executable file. For instance, to launch Google Chrome, you would type **chrome.exe** in the Run New Task dialog.

Tabs

Several tabs on the left side of the Task Manager contain additional information about the processes:

- The **Processes** tab is the default that appears when the Task Manager is first launched. It shows a list of all running applications, including background applications and the processes they are using. This includes CPU, memory, disk, network, and other resource usage information.

■ The **Performance** tab shows CPU, memory, disk, network, and GPU allocation in real time. Charts will show allocation across time. By default, this tab shows the last 60 seconds. When you are troubleshooting issues with a system, this tab can show which system resources have been in use and help you see if a system is still overwhelmed by a rogue program.

■ The **App History** tab displays information about which apps have been used by the current user over time. It is limited to Microsoft Store apps but can be useful for tracking down frequently used apps and programs that might be causing issues on the machine.

■ The **Startup** tab lists all apps that start upon sign-in of a user. This information is very useful because some are launching processes in the background and taking up resources unnecessarily. From this screen you not only can see all processes but also can disable unnecessary or unwanted startup applications.

■ The **Users** tab shows all logged-in users, how many of the system resources they are currently using, and which applications they are using. If multiple users are currently logged in to a device, that will serve to slow it down and you can diagnose issues this way. From this screen you can also force a logout of the other users.

■ The **Details** tab shows detailed information about all the processes running. Like the Processes tab, it shows all the processes. Unlike the Processes tab, it shows details such as the status, the user who initiated the process, and other information about the process.

■ The **Services** tab is limited to system services. You will find this information in the Services management console also at services.msc, and you will manage these services there. These tasks help the operating system itself to run efficiently. While you can make changes here, it is recommended that you avoid making direct changes to this tab unless you are an expert, since unexpected issues can occur if changes are made directly to the services on this tab.

Using the Task Manager can make the work of an IT support technician easier and more efficient. Quitting troublesome programs when they crash is a godsend, and being able to look at startup programs to see if any rogue programs have inserted themselves in the startup queue can be useful and helpful to your users.

Back Up to the Cloud

According to the adage, there are two types of hard drives: those that will fail and those that have failed. Because of this, it is important to back up any data you want to keep. In the past, this was done by backing up files to external disks, flash drives, optical media, and tape drives. In the modern era, most end users will back up to cloud-based drives. As an IT support technician, you will need to configure this process for your users or walk them through the process of doing so.

Sync Files to OneDrive

Microsoft makes it convenient to **sync** user files directly to **OneDrive**. Note that while this is the same location where your OneDrive files are stored while working within Microsoft Office 365, this process makes a backup of all files, not just Office documents. By default, OneDrive does a full sync of all files in the OneDrive folders you select to back up. This tool enables users to use multiple devices, including mobile, and have access to all files from all devices. The use of the term *backup*, then, is not as precise as it might otherwise seem.

To configure the backup/sync process, launch the OneDrive app on the computer. The Back Up Folders on This PC dialog will appear, as shown in Figure 4-15. Select which of the folders you wish to back up and click Start Backup to begin the backup.

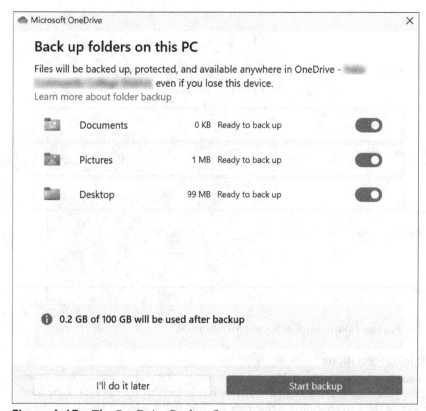

Figure 4-15 *The OneDrive Backup Screen*

This same app can also be used to start sharing your OneDrive, which will now appear as a drive location in your File Explorer.

All local files in the selected folders will sync, and stay in sync, with your OneDrive.

Use Google Drive for Backup

Google Drive is a popular cloud-based tool. For those with Enterprise-level accounts, it can be configured as a backup device as well. Simply go to the Google Admin Console, and from there, select **Menu > Apps > Google Workspace > Drive and Docs > Features and Applications.** Select Drive and then Back Up and Sync to enable backup of a user's files directly to their Google Drive. The user will need to log back in to their Google account and launch the Google Drive app to configure the backup.

Use Dropbox for Backup

For those users who prefer to use Dropbox, it can be used to back up to the cloud as well. Install the Dropbox desktop app on your device. Once it is installed, log in to Dropbox. You will see the Dropbox icon on the taskbar at the bottom-right edge of the screen. Right-click and you will be able to select Backup, which gives you the ability to designate a location on your device that needs to be backed up. Figure 4-16 shows the configuration screen for Dropbox backup.

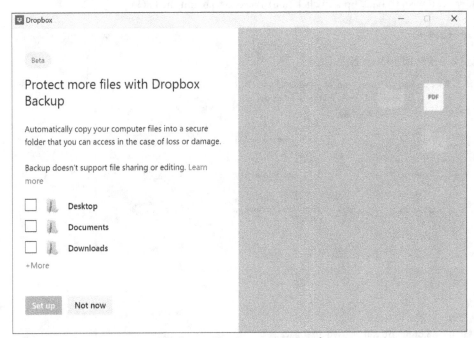

Figure 4-16 *The Backup Configuration Screen for Dropbox*

Other Cloud Backup Solutions

Other cloud backup solutions are available, and most will work the same way as these examples. In addition, your organization may have a custom solution that operates the same way. The most important thing to remember is that only the files in the selected folders will be backed up; users who store files in folders other than these will still lose their data when the drive fails, or they get a new computer. It is critical that they learn to either use their cloud drive exclusively or use these backed-up folders exclusively; otherwise, you cannot guarantee the viability of their data, and some will be lost in the future.

Boot Sequence

Most of the time, you will want to boot a device from the internal hard drive. However, sometimes you will need to boot from other devices, either to run diagnostics or to install specific hardware or software images that require booting from either a flash drive or the network. To do this, you will need to adjust the **boot sequence/boot order**.

If you want to make permanent changes to your boot order, you should go into **BIOS** or **UEFI** itself to make the change. This way, you and your user do not have to worry about which Windows instance will attempt to boot on startup. For most Dell systems, pressing F2 will enter the BIOS or UEFI configuration screens; other manufacturers use a different key combination. This key combination is displayed on system startup, and you may need to press the key(s) multiple times before the combination is read by the system.

Once you are in BIOS or UEFI, go through the menus and look for Boot Order or Boot Settings or similar language, and you will see the options. Select the order you would like to boot your device. Each startup, the device will look in this order for an operating system.

To make a change to the boot order on a temporary, one-time basis, there will be a set of keys to press on startup. On most Dell computers, this has traditionally been the F12 key. Other brands may use other keys, and you may need to press the key more than once to get your device to recognize it. When the computer is partway through the boot process, you will be presented with a list of all possible boot options (even if a boot device is not present); select the desired option, and the device will attempt to boot from that device. Under older BIOS, this is usually not a problem. Under newer UEFI, which replaces BIOS, your boot order may not be as configurable for security reasons.

For devices with UEFI, you have additional choices. You can use the F12 or other key to select a boot device to attempt at startup (which is useful if you are booting from the network), or you can configure the boot device from within Windows itself. Go to the System Configuration control by pressing Windows and typing **msconfig**. Select the Boot tab at the top of the screen, and you will see all Windows installations. If you do not see the Windows installation you want to boot from, you will need to ensure that it is installed correctly.

Boot to Safe Mode

When things are not working properly, you will want to boot your system into **Safe Mode**. This mode disables most startup devices and third-party drivers, leaving only a limited number of known-good and known-stable drivers to run the system, helping ensure stability. In this way you can start repairing the crashed operating system that otherwise might not be booting at all or might be restarting randomly.

Remember: if the problem does not occur in Safe Mode, that means that default drivers and settings are not the problem. If the problem does occur during Safe Mode, you know that the problem is with Windows itself or with one of those default drivers and settings, and is much bigger than just third-party software, drivers, and configurations.

To boot into Safe Mode, you will need to go to the Settings panel (Windows+i or Windows and then type **Settings**), then go to System, then select Advanced Startup. Figure 4-17 shows the Advanced Startup button highlighted. When you restart after selecting this button, you will be given the option to start in Safe Mode.

Often the system is too unstable to get to the controls and reach the button. In that instance, you can get to the Safe Mode prompt from the Login prompt. At the sign-in screen, hold down the Shift key while clicking the on-screen Power button and then selecting Restart.

On restart, you will have the option to select **Troubleshoot > Advanced Options > Startup Settings > Restart.** Pressing 4 or F4 should allow Safe Mode, and pressing 5 or F5 should allow Safe Mode with Networking.

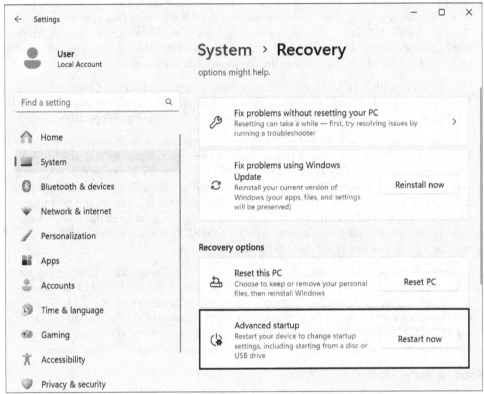

Figure 4-17   *The System Recovery Control with Advanced Startup: Restart Now Button Highlighted*

If your device can't even make it to the Login screen, and instead fails to boot entirely, Windows will automatically boot into the **Windows Recovery Environment (WinRE)** after three failed boot attempts. In the WinRE Advanced Options, you have the option to select Safe Mode and Safe Mode with Networking.

Power Management

Advances in power management have made newer Windows devices much more efficient and allow for fine-tuning of power usage and management, as well as allowing users to access their devices faster upon startup from sleep states rather than having to wait for the device to boot from a fully off state. This can result in substantial power savings and longer battery life in mobile devices. Figure 4-18 shows the Energy Recommendations screen where a user or an IT support technician can adjust power management options.

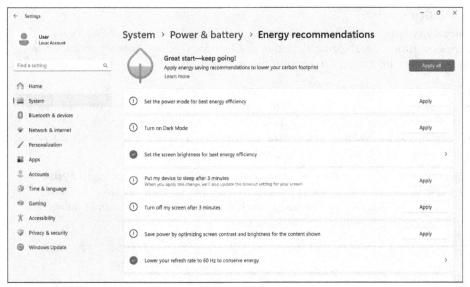

Figure 4-18   *The Energy Recommendations Window*

Windows power management has the following direct benefits:

- Startup and shutdown delays are eliminated due to the computer not needing to perform a full system shutdown and boot when entering and exiting a sleep state.

- In this version, unlike prior versions of sleep, automated tasks can run during the sleep state. Using the Task Scheduler, users can schedule applications to run specific tasks using a process called *waitable timers*.

- Per-device power management is enabled, allowing devices not in use to power down independently of devices that are being used. This capability can substantially improve power savings of individual devices, even when the device is in operation, because individual components can power down independently.

- Power efficiency is substantially improved, especially on mobile devices. This improved power consumption saves money through lower energy costs and improves battery life. It also increases the life expectancy of components.

- **Power schemes**, alarms, and specific battery options are configured through the Power Options applications of the Control Panel. All power management activities are coordinated at this one combined app.

By adjusting the power consumption of a device, a user can save not only energy but also wear and tear on their machine, while at the same time see improvements to productivity by not having to boot their machine each time they need to use it. These improvements combine to substantially improve the usability of the device.

Accessibility

Accessibility features support productivity, creativity, and ease of use for all users, regardless of their vision, hearing, dexterity, mobility, focus issues, or other needs. Various available features are designed to improve the success of all users.

Vision

For individuals who have trouble seeing the default screen size and colors, Windows has a variety of built-in tools available to assist. To adjust the size of just the text on the screen, select **Settings > Accessibility > Text Size** and then use the slider to adjust the text size. Click the Apply button to lock in the change.

If individuals would like to make everything on the screen larger, go to **Settings > System > Display** and select Scale; adjust the percentage to scale the entire screen. Note that each display can be scaled separately as needed, which is good for different size and resolution of external displays. Figure 4-19 shows the scaling available.

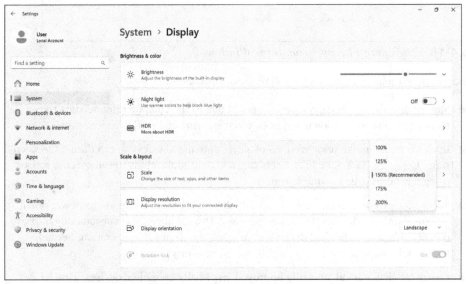

Figure 4-19 *The Scaling Available, Which Will Scale All Visuals on the Displays*

Higher-contrast options also are available. Selecting **Settings > Accessibility > Contrast Themes** will allow you to choose from high-contrast themes. You can also customize the available themes from this control. Figure 4-20 shows the **Contrast Themes** screen where a user or an IT support technician can choose from the high-contrast themes and edit them as needed to improve access for individual users.

The mouse pointer can be edited to make it easier to see. Several options are available in the **Settings > Accessibility > Mouse Pointer and Touch** control. They include changing the look of the mouse pointer, changing the size of the mouse pointer, and adding a touch indicator when using a touch screen. You also can go into the Mouse and Trackpad settings, which will allow you to add a mouse trail and adjust the speed. Figure 4-21 shows the Mouse Pointer and Touch control with options for the mouse pointer.

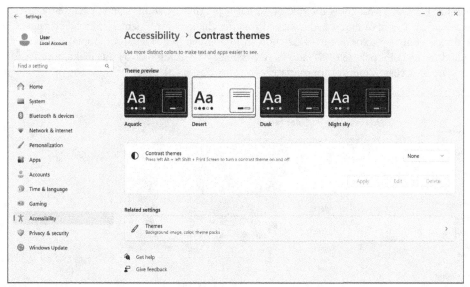

Figure 4-20   *The Contrast Themes Screen*

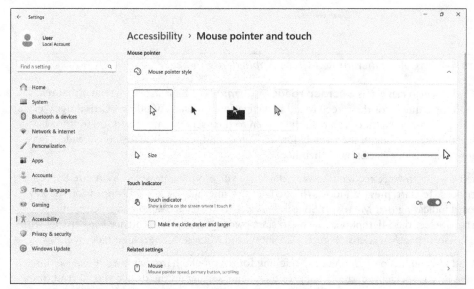

Figure 4-21   *The Mouse Pointer and Touch Control Window*

The **screen magnifier** can be used to enlarge a single portion of the screen. Pressing Windows + + (plus sign) will open the magnifier and magnify a portion of the screen where the mouse pointer is located. Pressing Windows + - (minus sign) will open the magnifier and make the screen smaller at the mouse pointer. Once it is open, you can use the magnifier as needed to magnify text at the mouse pointer location.

Color filters are used to make photos, text, and colors easier to see. Turning on **Settings > Accessibility > Color Filters** will allow you to adjust the color filters. The color filters change the screen color palette to help the user distinguish between things that differ only by color. For users who know their color deficit type, this capability can substantially enhance their use of Windows, since it reduces the chance of misidentifying objects that are divided only by color. Figure 4-22 shows a Red-Green (red weak, protanopia) color filter applied to the color palette of Windows Accessibility. Features such as this make it easier for everyone to access Windows appropriately.

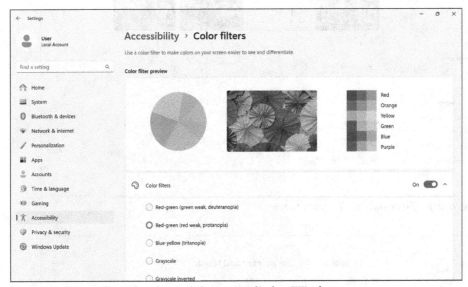

Figure 4-22 *Color Filter for Red-Green Applied to Windows*

Windows also can act as a **screen reader**. *Narrator* is a built-in screen reader that reads aloud the contents of the screen to aid in navigation. Pressing Windows+Ctrl+Enter will start or stop Narrator. Narrator can read the screen to the user. Narrator is a good tool for basic narration needs, though the visually impaired may find that dedicated screen readers have more features that better meet their needs.

Text-to-speech voice recognition is available via voice typing, powered by Azure Speech services. To start, press Windows+h (the h key); a microphone key will appear on the keyboard indicating that Microsoft Speech Services has been activated and voice typing is active. Select the Microphone button to start voice typing. (This sentence was written with Microsoft speech services.) Figure 4-23 shows the Microsoft Speech Services window.

Windows can be controlled via eye tracking for those who have that need. Because this capability is specialized, the IT support technician setting up the device should read through the instructions on the Microsoft website for specific instructions. Knowing that it is built into the operating system is important, since it is a valuable accessibility feature.

Hearing

By default, Windows assumes that the user will be listening in **stereo audio**. However, since many users listen with only one headphone or earbud, this can be a problem. To change to **mono audio**, go to Settings > Accessibility > Audio and switch to the Mono Audio toggle. Figure 4-24 shows the Audio settings control panel. From here, you can set the system to mono audio, to flash parts or all of the screen when audio notifications come in, and go to other audio controls.

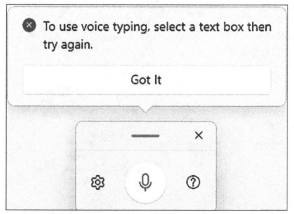

Figure 4-23 *Microsoft Speech Services Window*

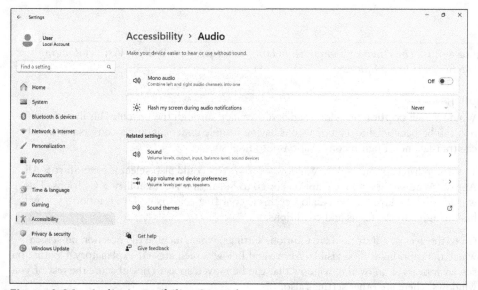

Figure 4-24 *Audio Accessibility Control*

From the same Audio control, users can set the screen to flash when audio alerts come in. The settings include having the title bar flash, the active window flash, or the entire screen flash. This capability substantially improves the chances that a notification will be noticed.

By default, Notifications dismiss themselves after 5 seconds. To keep them around longer, go to the Visual Effects control in Accessibility (**Settings > Accessibility > Visual Effects**) and then select a different time in the Dismiss Notifications After This Amount of Time setting. Your options range from the default 5 seconds up to 5 minutes. Figure 4-25 shows these options.

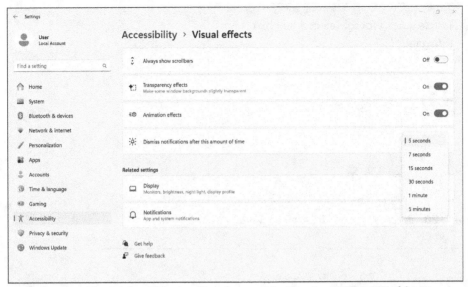

Figure 4-25 *The Dialog Showing How Long a Notification Will Be Visible, Ranging from 5 Seconds to 5 Minutes*

Captions

Windows can **caption** live video and audio coming through the system. This live transcription can be beneficial to anyone who is having trouble understanding a conversation. It also can translate non-English conversations into English.

To turn on live captions, select Windows+Ctrl+l. You could also select it from **Start > All Apps > Accessibility > Live Captions** or go to **Settings > Accessibility > Captions**. This will activate the Live Caption dialog. If this is your first time using Live Captions, you will have to agree to the terms and conditions.

Go to the gear to adjust the Live Captions settings, which include the position on-screen where the captions will be visible. Above and Below screen are self-explanatory. Floating on-screen appears as an overlay window that can be moved so as to not obscure the rest of your windows. There are other settings also.

The Microphone can be used to capture speech in captions. When turned on, any audio heard locally will be captioned. Note that if any other sound is being produced by your device, either from an app on the device or from a web conference, for instance, audio being received by the microphone will be ignored in favor of the remote audio.

To caption languages other than English, you will need to ensure that the correct **language pack** is installed. In the Captions Settings gear, select any desired language to be captioned. If it is not downloaded already, allow it to be downloaded. This will download the language pack for the target language and allow the language to be displayed on the screen. Because it downloads the full language pack, you will also have access to the language throughout other Windows applications, including dictionaries.

If you have a Copilot+ PC, Live Captions can be used to translate audio. The process is much the same: install the correct language pack for the target language you wish to translate from. Once installed, the Copilot+ PC will allow you to translate from those languages into English.

For Live Captions, the captioning is done locally on your device and not sent to the cloud.

Dexterity and Mobility

If you have a touch screen, you can set Windows to use gestures to manipulate the device. Some of these **gestures**, such as pinch in/pinch out to zoom in/zoom out, are common across a multitude of devices. Others, such as swiping with three fingers up the screen to show all open windows, are less common. Many of the gestures work on the touchpad as well as the screen.

Table 4-2 lists the actions and gestures for screen control, and Table 4-3 lists them for the touchpad.

Table 4-2   Screen Control Gestures

Action	Gesture
Select an item	Tap the screen.
Scroll	Place two fingers on-screen and slide up or down or vertically side to side.
Zoom in or out	Place two fingers on the screen and pinch in (zoom in) or out (zoom out).
Show more commands (like right-clicking)	Press and hold the item.
Show all open windows	Swipe with three fingers up the screen.
Show the desktop	Swipe with three fingers down the screen.
Switch to the last open app	Swipe with three fingers left or right on the screen.
Open the notification center	Swipe with one finger from the right edge of the screen.

Table 4-3   Touchpad Gestures

Action	Gestures
Select an item	Tap the touchpad.
Scroll	Place two fingers on the touchpad. Slide horizontally or vertically.
Zoom in or out	Place two fingers on the screen and pinch in (zoom in) or out (zoom out).
Show more commands (like right-clicking)	Tap the touchpad with two fingers OR press down in the lower-right corner (which is where the right button would be).
Show all open windows	Swipe up with three fingers on the touchpad.
Show the desktop	Swipe down with three fingers on the touchpad.
Switch between open apps or windows	Swipe with three fingers left or right on the touchpad.

You can adjust these gestures from the control panel by selecting **Settings > Bluetooth & Devices > Touchpad**. Select three-finger gestures to adjust the three-finger gestures, four-finger gestures to adjust those. Figure 4-26 shows the **Bluetooth & Devices >Touchpad** control with the three-finger and four-finger control settings active. From here, you can set what each swipe command will do.

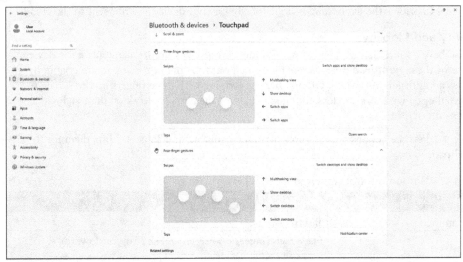

Figure 4-26   *The Touchpad Control with the Three-Finger and Four-Finger Controls Visible*

On-Screen Keyboard

The **on-screen keyboard** is available whenever you need access to a keyboard but don't have access or cannot use a physical keyboard. This tool is also useful to the IT support technician when the physical keyboard is broken or the drivers are inactive. Note that tablet computers have a version of the on-screen keyboard called a *touch keyboard*.

To open the on-screen keyboard, go to **Windows > Settings > Accessibility > Keyboard** and turn on the On-Screen Keyboard toggle. Figure 4-27 shows the Keyboard control where you can enable the on-screen keyboard. Figure 4-28 shows the on-screen keyboard.

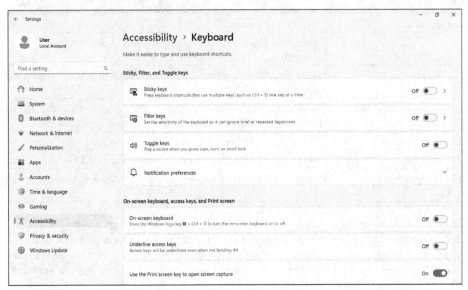

Figure 4-27   *Accessibility Keyboard Control Area*

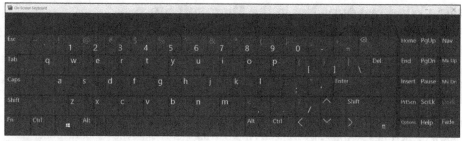

Figure 4-28 *On-Screen Keyboard*

Resolving Common Application Issues

One of the major roles of an IT support technician is to resolve problems with user applications. Remember again: Users will not need to contact the help desk unless something is not working. Applications are one of the major places where users experience their machine not working.

Installing Windows Apps from the Microsoft Store

The **Microsoft Store** (formerly the **App Store** or **Marketplace**) is where many of the main apps will be available to Windows users. To access the Microsoft Store, simply go to **Windows > Store** and select Microsoft Store from the options presented. Figure 4-29 shows the Home screen of the Microsoft Store. From the options on the left-hand side, you can choose from categories of apps, and from the search bar at the top, you can search for specific apps or categories to install.

Figure 4-29 *Home Screen for the Microsoft Store*

Most of the expected applications are available, including Microsoft Office 365, Microsoft Defender, MovieMaker, and Acrobat Reader. Games such as Among Us and Flight Simulator are also available. Users can access movies and other entertainment from within the Microsoft Store as well. If updates are available, they can be retrieved from within the Library section of the Microsoft Store.

Installing Windows Apps Not in the Microsoft Store

You might need an application that is not in the Microsoft Store. In this case there are several options.

The easiest is to go to the publisher's website and download it. The installer should prompt for permission to install, which usually requires an administrator password, and the software should install.

If the software is not installing as expected, there are two things to check. First, go to **Windows > Settings > Apps > Advanced App Settings** and adjust the selection under Choose Where to Get Apps. Figure 4-30 shows the Choose Where to Get Apps drop-down. If you are having trouble finding and/or installing an application, check the settings in this drop-down.

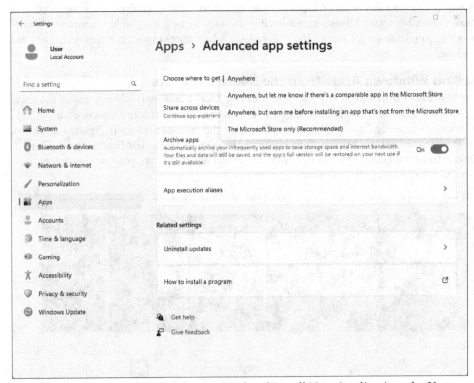

Figure 4-30 *How to Adjust Where to Find and Install New Applications for Your Windows PC*

Some users have a version of Windows called Windows S, which further locks the system. To unlock these systems, refer to the latest online instructions on the Microsoft website; as of this writing, there is an app that will make the change for you. Search for "Switching out of S mode in Windows," and you will find the appropriate instructions. Note that this change is irreversible; once you have left S mode, you cannot go back into it.

When installing software applications other than from the Microsoft Store, be cautious. Unknown software locations can carry viruses and other malware to your computer. In a networked enterprise environment, they can cause havoc on users and impact productivity. For this reason, use only approved software sources. A best practice is to restrict access to only IT support technicians and other IT personnel for installation of software and ensure that end users do not have administrative access to install software on their devices.

Email

Email is a critical tool in the modern workforce. Users who are unable to access their email accounts will often call the help desk, frustrated that they cannot get their work done because of lack of access to their email.

Follow the troubleshooting steps when troubleshooting email problems. Here are some things to look for:

- Check the Internet connection. Because email requires an Internet connection to operate, lack of Internet access to other sites means that the email will not work either. This should be the first thing you check as an IT support technician.

- Verify the email settings. Usernames and passwords are often case sensitive. If the user is using a locally installed email client such as Outlook, Thunderbird, or Microsoft Mail, ensure that the server settings are correct. Be sure to double-check the port numbers in addition to the IP addresses. These are usually available on the email provider's website. Double-check the firewall settings to ensure that **SMTP** and other email protocols are not being blocked at the network level.

- Test the email client or app itself. Perhaps the app itself is not functioning properly. An easy way to do this is to send an email to yourself at a known good email address. If this test doesn't work, switch to a different email program and then a different email account on the same program on the same computer; if that test works, the problem is somewhere within the account settings. Remember, you will need the account credentials and email settings to set this up on the client computer.

- Clear your cache and cookies, as discussed previously. Whether using a separate email client or accessing email in your web browser, the cache and cookies can cause issues. Clearing them can help solve problems.

- Malware could have caused a problem. Scan your device for malware to ensure that isn't interfering. If you end up having malware, sanitize your system and then change the password to your email and other accounts. Assume that your email password was compromised. If your ISP was blocking your email due to the malware, a password reset may unlock the block.

- If none of that works, you will need to contact your email service provider directly. If everything works except the actual email, and you are certain that it is not anything on the device itself, contacting your email provider for assistance is recommended. Because email providers have many clients, review the entire list again before contacting them, just in case you have missed something. This is especially true of the email settings (especially IP addresses of the servers) and passwords (which are case sensitive).

Collaboration Applications

The modern world revolves around **collaboration**; we rely on collaboration environments to do our jobs effectively. When those don't work, business doesn't get done, or at the very least does not get done as effectively and efficiently.

As you troubleshoot issues with **collaboration applications**, you can take several steps to help you narrow down what is wrong:

- First, look to the connectivity. Is your device connecting to the Internet and to the collaboration app itself? If not, that is the first item to repair, and will likely fix the issue. Deleting the cache may be necessary as well.

- Sometimes the app will not load, but you have confirmed connectivity with the collaboration site. In this case, clear the cache and refresh the page. A restart of the collaboration app is recommended if you are not using the browser-based version.

- Some collaboration apps will have their own logging tools, which will help you diagnose the problem and which can be sent to the help desk of the collaboration app company to assist with their troubleshooting of your issue.

- Sometimes the server at the collaboration app provider is the issue. After clearing the cache, quit the app and start it again, or refresh the app window in the web browser.

- Sometimes the network firewall gets in the way of the collaboration app communicating with the back-end servers. Check to see if an update to the firewall is causing a new issue. If that is the case, you may need to reconfigure something at the firewall to allow the collaboration app to function.

- Be sure you are using the latest version of the collaboration app or web browser. If you get too far out-of-date, the app may refuse to run, insisting instead that you run a later (newer) version. These updates should be quick and easy and not take much time and will get you bug and security fixes as well as access to new features.

Productivity Applications

Sometimes your office and other **productivity applications** stop working properly. To troubleshoot these, you need to be able to follow your troubleshooting steps (refer to Chapter 1, "Help Desk") and look at certain other elements to narrow down what is wrong.

If the software is installed locally on the device, a first step is to do a repair installation. The original installer, usually located in the folder where the program itself is installed, can be used to redo the installation. Unlike an original installation, this type of installation simply overwrites corrupt files but does not change locations or settings. For Microsoft Office, you can find this by selecting **Control Panel > Programs > Programs and Features**, right-clicking Microsoft 365 (for Office 365), and then selecting Change. This sequence brings up a dialog that prompts you to select which type of repair to initiate. Figure 4-31 shows the dialog for starting a repair of Microsoft 365 and Office programs. Select Quick Repair first to fix most things; Online Repair will take longer but can fix most other problems.

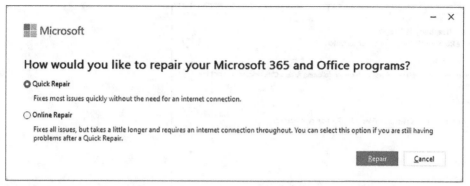

Figure 4-31 *Dialog Asking How to Repair Microsoft 365 and Office Programs*

This solution works for many programs as well. Figure 4-32 shows the results of selecting Change when right-clicking from the Uninstall or Change a Program Control dialog, where users can begin a repair of Adobe Acrobat. They can modify, repair, or remove the application from this dialog.

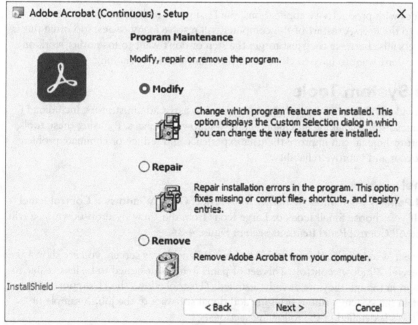

Figure 4-32 *Adobe Acrobat Program Maintenance Window*

Some applications will only have the option to uninstall from this dialog. In that case, uninstalling and then reinstalling the app will often fix the problem. Note that sometimes this fix will erase the user's data, so be sure to back up all user files before beginning. Figure 4-33 shows the Raspberry Pi Imager Uninstall window with Uninstall as the available option. Rather than allowing a reinstall, it only allows an uninstall. Uninstall and then reinstall the software if the imager is not working correctly.

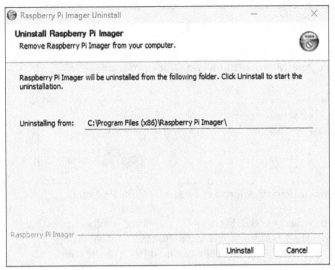

Figure 4-33 *Raspberry Pi Imager Program*

For other issues with productivity applications, the IT support technician should be sure to listen closely to the user. A restart of the computer will resolve many issues; too often this is a step that users miss because they just forget the step or don't want to lose other work on their device or don't want to have to close other programs currently running.

Windows System Tools

Windows provides a variety of tools that are designed to assist administrators, including IT support technicians, in managing and maintaining Windows instances. By using these tools, the IT support technician can improve the user experience and reduce or eliminate problems before they occur and improve reliability.

Control Panel

The **Control Panel** is where most Windows tools reside. Go to **Windows > Control Panel** to access it. If you choose Small Icons or Large Icons from the View By drop-down, you will be able to see All Control Panel Items, as seen in Figure 4-34.

When you select Windows Tools from the All Control Panel Items screen, you are shown the display for several Windows controls. This set of panel items is designed to be less visible to the end users even though they are already installed. This tool allows the IT support technician to maintain the system without bringing additional software to the job. A sample of some of the tools is detailed in the following sections.

System Information

We discussed the System Information dialog box briefly in Chapter 3, "Networking and Network Connectivity." In the System Information dialog, the system shows significant information about the installed operating system, the processor, and other hardware and software installed and attached to the system. You can see what drivers are installed for which components and what types of hardware and software are installed and available.

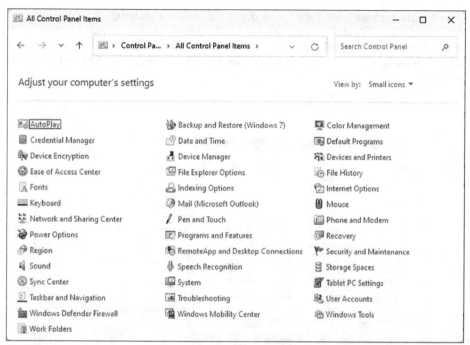

Figure 4-34 *All Control Panel Items Window, with All Control Panel Items Displayed as Small Icons*

Event Viewer

The **Event Viewer** shows logs of events that have occurred within the Windows environment. These logs are designed to help trace problems that have occurred. Log entries are usually entered when errors occur, and the software has been designed to assign a log entry to the Event Viewer.

There are multiple categories of error messages. *Warnings* tell the IT support technician about a problem that is occurring to ensure that problems are addressed but do not have to be addressed immediately. *Errors* tell the IT support technician that something more serious has gone wrong; if the error persists, one or more peripherals will cease to function or will function with errors that will impede the user experience. *Information* items provide information about an event that is taking or has taken place. This is just information but can be useful when troubleshooting the point at which an issue first began. *Cryptographic* logs are identified with a gold key symbol and reference any entry related to encryption. Figure 4-35 shows the Event Viewer screen with **Custom Views > Administrative Events** highlighted, showing a series of warnings available.

ipconfig

The **ipconfig** command is used to display information about currently connected network devices. It is discussed more fully in Chapter 3, but in the context of Windows system tools, **ipconfig** is used to verify connectivity at Layers 1, 2, and 3 of the OSI model. By going to a command prompt (**Windows > Command Prompt**) and typing **ipconfig**, the IT support technician can verify the type of network(s) the device is attached to and the IPv4 and IPv6 addresses in use. Comparing these against the expected values can give insight into problems at the network level. Figure 4-36 shows the results of **ipconfig** on a device. Note that both network cards attach to the same network. **ipconfig** shows summary address and port information. **ipconfig /all** shows more detailed information. Figure 4-37 shows the results of **ipconfig /all** on a device, showing complete information about the interface and its addressing.

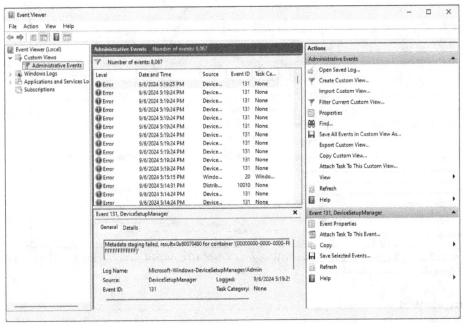

Figure 4-35   *The Event Viewer Window*

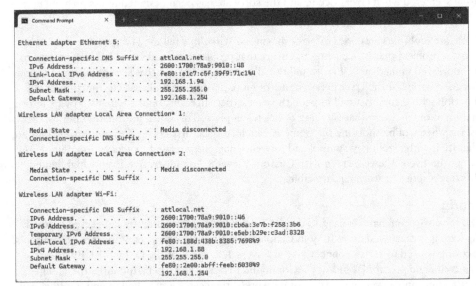

Figure 4-36   *The Results of ipconfig on a Device*

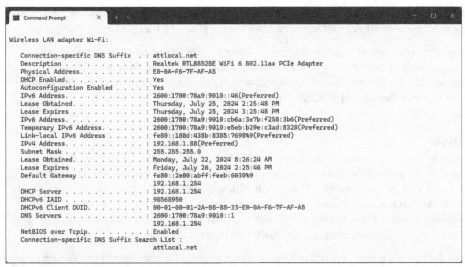

Figure 4-37 *The Results of* **ipconfig /all** *on a Device, Showing Detailed Address and Interface Information*

Windows Security Tools

Windows comes with a variety of tools to help system administrators update and maintain systems, including pushing software as well as system and security updates to devices and to user accounts.

Active Directory

Active Directory (and its cloud-based cousin, **Azure AD**) connects users with the network resources they need to get their work done. It is a directory, or database, that contains information about the entire Windows domain environment, including which users and computers exist on the system and who and which are allowed to do and access what services and other network components. This database is stored on a server called a **domain controller**, and a network will have at least two for redundancy. All data is mirrored on each domain controller. Details about user accounts might include a person's job title, phone number, and password alongside their permissions, for instance.

Each person who attempts to log in to the Windows domain is authenticated against Active Directory and is then allowed access only to their specific data as allowed. In the AAA security framework (discussed in depth in Chapter 7, "Security"), this represents the authentication and authorization portions. The third A of the security framework, accounting, is outside the scope of the IT support technician certification but can also be configured within Active Directory. Users can authenticate anywhere within the domain on any authorized system and have access to their files and other resources, and the authentication can be part of a single sign-on process across the entire domain. When these files are stored in a central server, backups are simplified as well.

Active Directory Group Policy

While it is unlikely that a new IT support technician will be responsible for setting up the Active Directory itself, the technician will be responsible for maintenance of user accounts and permissions of workstations. Your organization will give you specific details regarding how these are to be set up. The important part for an incoming IT support technician is that all the configuration of Active Directory is within the scope of the AD Group Policy.

This centralized user and rights management control simplifies security as well through a process called Active Directory, or AD, Group Policy. **AD Group Policy** defines how computers and users can interact with Windows Update to obtain updates from **Windows Server Update Services (WSUS)**. These computers and users are collectively called WSUS clients.

GPUpdate

Changes made to AD Group Policies are made in Group Policy Objects (GPOs). When changes are made to these GPOs, they should automatically push out to user machines when the device or user account checks for updates. However, sometimes the updates to AD Group Policy do not update a user device or login, or the IT support technician needs to force an update to the device or user account or set of devices or accounts sooner than the expected update timetable. In that case, **GPUpdate** is the tool to use.

GPUpdate forces a manual update to Group Policy settings for computers in an Active Directory domain. The IT support technician or user must be in either the command prompt or PowerShell to run the commands. Go to **Windows > PowerShell** or **Windows > Command Prompt** and select any of the following. There are two main styles of the command, with variants of each:

- **gpupdate** updates all GPOs that are new or have changes since Group Policy was last checked.

- **gpupdate /force** updates to the client for every applicable GPO from the closest domain controller. It will process *all* the GPOs, regardless of whether they have had any changes. This makes it a useful tool when troubleshooting; if a GPO setting has become corrupted on an end device or user account, the **gpupdate /force** command will overwrite and thus fix this corruption.

- One caveat: This update can take a long time, especially for large domains. There could be literally thousands of GPOs that apply to a single computer. If you have a specific user you want to update, you can use the **gpupdate /target:user** command. If you have a specific device, you can use the **gpupdate /target:computer /force** command; in this last example, the GPOs for the computer will be processed, but only those that apply to this specific device.

- Some GPOs require that a user log off or the device reboot. This can be done at the GPO screen as well. Using the **gpupdate /target:user /logoff** command will perform the GPUpdate and then log off. Using the **gpupdate /target:computer /boot** command will install the updates and then reboot the device.

Because many IT support technicians work remotely from the users they support, the GPUpdate can also be run remotely. This also allows the IT support technician to push an update to many users and devices at the same time.

For this, the IT support technician must be in PowerShell by going to **Windows > PowerShell**. The syntax is **Invoke-GPUpdate -Computer "[computer name]" -Target "[username]"**.

If you are trying to update a single computer called TestComputer01, with a user named User, your command line would read **Invoke-GPUpdate -Computer "TestComputer01" -Target "User"**.

ADGPUpdate

Macs and Linux devices can also join Active Directory domains. If this is the case in your environment, you would use **ADGPUpdate** to force the Group Policy update in the same way that GPUpdate would do it. Some sample options include

- **adgpupdate**, which will refresh the GPOs in the system.

- **adgpupdate -target Computer**, which will update only computer GPOs.

- **adgpupdate -target User**, which will refresh only user GPOs.

Local Security Policy

The local security policy of a system is a set of security information about the local device. It includes domains trusted to authenticate login attempts, user accounts authorized to access the system, rights and privileges assigned to those accounts, and the security auditing policy.

Within an Active Directory domain, a local security policy is configured with tools including the Local Group Policy Editor as part of the Group Policy Objects and the Local Group Policy Editor, which helps configure security at the individual system level. This allows security to be applied at the group and individual system levels.

Creating New Users

One of the most important jobs of the IT support technician is creating new users. To do this, you will need to go to the Administrative Tools in Active Directory. Go to **Windows > Control Panel > System and Security** and then select Administrative Tools. From the tools, select Active Directory Users and Computers. This location is referred to as ADUC.

In the left pane of the ADUC, right-click the folder where you want the new user account. Select New and then User. Type in the details of the new user, following username conventions for your organization. When you select Next, you will be prompted to enter a password and select password options. These fields might be prefilled for you via inherited permissions. Figure 4-38 shows a New User screen for the new user IT Support. User accounts can be configured with names (First, Middle, Last, Full Name) and Password, but also Display Name (for those who go by a different name, for instance), Office, Phone Numbers, Job Title, and Department information. Direct reports can be configured to streamlining of teams from within the domain itself. Myriad other fields (including some custom fields) might be included, all of which are designed to streamline how users interact with one another and with the devices within the Active Directory domain.

Enabling and Disabling User Accounts

The left-hand pane of the ADUC can also be used to enable and disable individual user accounts. Right-click an individual user account. If it is disabled, Enable Account will be an option. If it is already enabled, Disable Account will be available.

Figure 4-38   *The Active Directory New User Screen for User IT Support*

Adding Passwords

User **password** resets are among the most common elements that IT support technicians will be asked to perform. Users can perform this task themselves most of the time, but sometimes they will forget (especially after vacation), and it is important that the IT support technician knows how to guide the users through the process.

There are several methods users can use to change their own password. Among the easiest (and oldest) methods: pressing Ctrl+Alt+Delete and then selecting Change Password and following the prompts. The user will need their existing password and a new one. Group Policy can be used to set parameters regarding length and complexity.

Most users will go to **Start > Settings > Accounts > Sign-in Options** and then scroll down to Password. If a user is on an Active Directory domain, the system may prompt additional options. For users who are not on a domain and who have not set a password, the device will prompt the user to click Add to add a password. Figure 4-39 shows the Sign-in Options window where a user can add a password.

Users can enter new passwords or change them, or they can configure **facial recognition, fingerprint recognition, PIN, physical security keys**, and **picture passwords**. These options are always available on personal devices and are available on domain devices if permitted by the network administrator. Physical security keys are discussed in the section on FIDO security keys in Chapter 3.

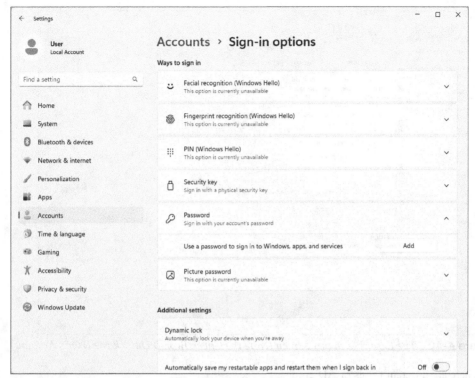

Figure 4-39 *The Sign-in Options Window*

Resetting Passwords

IT support technicians can reset user passwords on Active Directory domain networks. This capability is important if the user forgets their password or otherwise needs it reset. The IT support technician should go to **Active Directory Console > Active Directory Users and Computers Console (ADUC)**. This is the same location where new users are entered. Simply find the user who needs the new password, right-click their name, and select Reset Password from the pulldown.

The user often has locked their account while attempting to enter an incorrect password. Check the **Unlock the User's Account** check box once you have entered a new password (if needed, this location is also where you can select **Lock a User Account**). Best practice is to also check the box for User Must Change Password at Next Login. Click OK to finish resetting the password. Figure 4-40 shows the Reset Password screen. Note the check box to unlock the user's account.

Active Directory Groups

Active Directory administrators uses groups to simplify the administration of users and computers. This capability allows them to assign access rights to entire groups of systems or users at once, rather than one at a time. Changes can be made to the entire group rather than to each individual, streamlining the work.

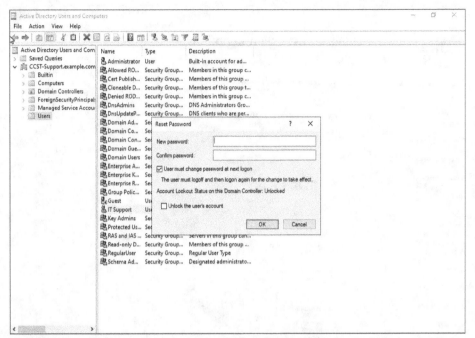

Figure 4-40   *The Reset Password Screen (Note the Check Box to Unlock the User's Account)*

There are different types of AD groups:

- **Distribution groups** are used to organize users into groups to send common messages or emails. These groups are great for groups that need to receive common message types and can receive messages on their devices broadcasted directly from within AD as well.

- **Security groups** are used to simplify user management. Permissions can be transferred directly to groups of users, which then inherit the permission of the whole group, instead of the AD administrators having to individually grant permissions to each individual user.

- **Universal groups** include AD users and groups from different AD domains in the same AD forest (the overarching entity for the enterprise). Users of this universal group can access network resources belonging to any other domain in the same forest.

- **Global groups** allow categorization of users based on their roles in the organization. An educational institution, for instance, might have global groups for students, faculty, staff, and administrators. Because they can nest within one another as well, faculty could be further subdivided by school or department (or both), students might be divided by grade level or graduation year, and staff might be divided by function, with HR and maintenance being separate global groups within the global staff group. The network resources would also be divided and named with similar groupings.

- **Domain local groups** allow admins to include users and groups from multiple domains to share access to network resources. They can also use domain local groups to assign user permissions to resources such as printers.

- **Local groups** can access resources on the local device only. These do not require a domain controller; they're not part of Active Directory at all.

- **Dynamic groups** simplify AD group management by automatically adding and removing users based on specified criteria. These are often scripted in PowerShell due to an absence of native built-in AD tools.

- **Special identity groups** are like security groups, but membership is managed automatically. When a user accesses a resource, they are automatically logged in to the special identity group and the permissions are inherited. If they do not need to access the specific resource, they are never added to the specific group.

When users have trouble accessing specific resources, the IT support technician should check to ensure that they are in the correct AD group to access the resource. If they are not, that is a simple fix: verify that they have permission to access the resource, then add them to the group, then run **gpupdate** or **gpupdate /force** to immediately update the group policy on the user account. Verify that the user now has access to the resource and log the fix.

Verifying AD Permissions

To verify Active Directory permissions, an IT support technician should verify the groups that a particular user, using a particular device, is a member of. One way to do this is to go to **Windows > Command Prompt** and then type **whoami /groups**, which will give the groups that the device belongs to. Figure 4-41 shows the results of a **whoami /groups** command for a device not on an AD domain.

```
Command Prompt                                                                            _  □  ×

C:\Users\User>whoami /groups

GROUP INFORMATION
----------------

Group Name                                                    Type              SID            Attributes
============================================================= ================= ============== ===========================================================
Everyone                                                      Well-known group  S-1-1-0        Mandatory group, Enabled by default, Enabled group
NT AUTHORITY\Local account and member of Administrators group Well-known group  S-1-5-114      Group used for deny only

BUILTIN\Administrators                                        Alias             S-1-5-32-544   Group used for deny only

BUILTIN\Users                                                 Alias             S-1-5-32-545   Mandatory group, Enabled by default, Enabled group
NT AUTHORITY\INTERACTIVE                                      Well-known group  S-1-5-4        Mandatory group, Enabled by default, Enabled group
CONSOLE LOGON                                                 Well-known group  S-1-2-1        Mandatory group, Enabled by default, Enabled group
NT AUTHORITY\Authenticated Users                              Well-known group  S-1-5-11       Mandatory group, Enabled by default, Enabled group
NT AUTHORITY\This Organization                                Well-known group  S-1-5-15       Mandatory group, Enabled by default, Enabled group
NT AUTHORITY\Local account                                    Well-known group  S-1-5-113      Mandatory group, Enabled by default, Enabled group
LOCAL                                                         Well-known group  S-1-2-0        Mandatory group, Enabled by default, Enabled group
NT AUTHORITY\NTLM Authentication                              Well-known group  S-1-5-64-10    Mandatory group, Enabled by default, Enabled group
Mandatory Label\Medium Mandatory Level                       Label             S-1-16-8192
```

Figure 4-41   *The Results of **whoami /groups** Running on a Device That Is Not on an Active Directory Domain (Note the Default Groups That Exist in Windows)*

Within the Active Directory domain, individual objects and users get their permissions via a process called *permission inheritance*, inheriting permissions from parent objects and their own specific permissions.

Viewing Active Directory Permissions

One method to see permissions is to use the Server Manager. To use this method, go to Server Manager, then click the Tools menu, then select Active Directory Users and Computers from the dropdown. Locate the object whose permissions you wish to check, which could be a device or a user. Right-click and select Properties. Click the Security tab to see the permissions. The tab will tell which groups the object is in and which permissions it has inherited from those groups.

Modifying Active Directory Permissions

Microsoft provides a tool to modify AD permissions: the Group Policy Management Editor. Go to **Windows > Administrative Tools** and then click Group Policy Management to open the Group Policy Management Editor. Under the Domains, select your domain, right-click Group Policy Objects, and click New to create a new Group Policy Object (GPO). You will then need to right-click the newly created GPO and edit the settings as needed. If you right-click an existing GPO, you can edit the object's settings. Any changes will propagate to all users as their permissions automatically update or as you apply the **GPUpdate** command.

You can also use the Security tab in ADUC. Go to **Windows > Administrative Tools** and then click Active Directory Users and Computers. Right-click the object you wish to edit. Click Properties and then the Security tab. You can edit the permissions via the Allow and Deny options. If you want to see all the permissions, including inherited permissions, for an object, select Advanced in the Security tab and click Edit to view and modify. Figure 4-42 shows the Security tab for a computer in the domain.

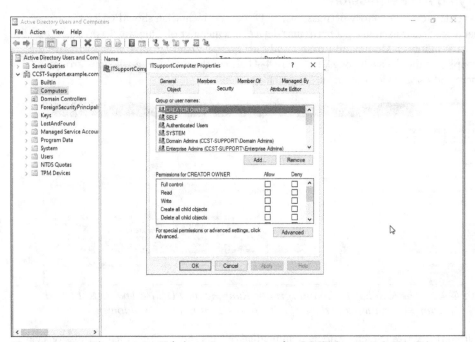

Figure 4-42   *The Security Tab for a Computer in the CCST-Support Active Directory Domain*

When a conflict arises, the **principle of least privilege** takes precedence. This means that if there is a conflict between multiple layers of inherited permissions between allowing an action and denying an action, the action will be to deny the action. Only permissions explicitly applied directly to an object take precedence to override inherited permissions; otherwise, any conflict will be to deny the permission.

Mapping Cloud Drives

Storing data on the network eliminates the need to back up individual computers. While Active Directory makes network storage easier to maintain in File Explorer, it can be cumbersome and does not work for remote workers. In addition, sometimes you will want to use or otherwise access additional information from a cloud storage drive, and for convenience would like to map that drive directly to Windows File Explorer. Luckily, that is easily done.

Most cloud services have their own apps to configure their drive into File Explorer, and they operate in a similar manner. These are not all the cloud services available, but this sample is provided so that you can see the variety of cloud services available and how they might be configured. Other services will be configured in a similar manner.

SMB Drives

SMB stands for Server Message Block; it allows a network-attached drive or shared folder to be shared between Windows, Mac, and Linux systems. The Mac and Linux systems will use the Samba protocol to access the drive.

To connect to an **SMB drive**, simply press Windows and type \\ (two backslashes) and then the IP address of the drive. For instance, to connect to a drive at 192.168.1.88, you would type \\192.168.1.88. Figure 4-43 shows the SMB share drive for 192.168.1.88.

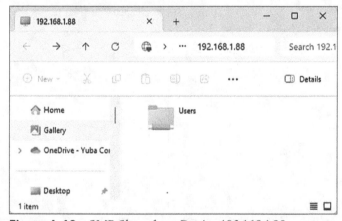

Figure 4-43 *SMB Share from Device 192.168.1.88*

You can also share via the computer's name on the network. In this instance, that would be **\\Lenovo**. Figure 4-44 shows the same SMB share, but this time using the network name to access it.

It is not enough to just connect to a network drive. To mount the network drive as a drive letter, go to File Explorer and then right-click This PC in the left pane. Select Map Network Drive from the options presented. Choose a drive letter and then enter the SMB share address for your SMB drive. See Figure 4-45 for an example of the Map Network Drive dialog box. If you select Browse, you will be able to browse all shared drives on your local network. You can choose the Reconnect at Sign-in option or Connect Using Different Credentials option as well. Figure 4-45 shows the connection configuration window with drive letter Z being mapped to the SMB share at 192.168.1.88, which will reconnect at sign-in.

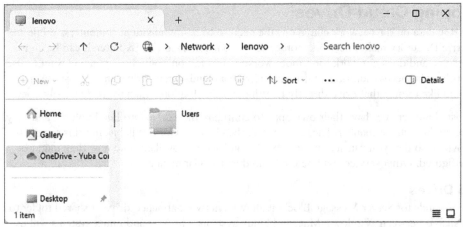

Figure 4-44 *The Same SMB Share from Figure 4-40 but Accessed via the Network Name*

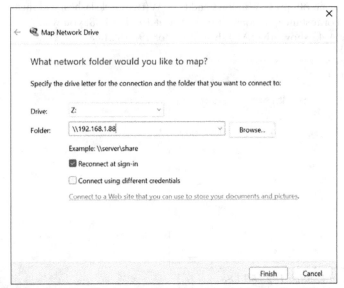

Figure 4-45 *The Map Network Drive Configuration Window, Where Mapping of Network Drives Can Be Done*

Mapping Internet-Based Drives

To map Internet-based drives, go to File Explorer and then right-click **This PC > Map Network Drive**. There, you will see an option to run the Add Network Location wizard, which lets you find a network location online, not just an SMB share. This capability is useful if you have a specific web-based drive you prefer to connect with online. Click the link Connect to a Web Site That You Can Use to Store Your Documents and Pictures to launch the Add Network Location wizard. When you finish working through the wizard, click Finish to finish assigning the network drive to your share.

OneDrive

Microsoft OneDrive is installed by default in Windows and is automatically logged in to your Microsoft account. By default, any of your Microsoft Office 365 documents will be synced and saved to your OneDrive unless changed in Active Directory. As of this writing, the free tier receives 5 GB of cloud storage and free versions of Word, Excel, and PowerPoint.

If you do not see OneDrive in the left-hand pane of your File Manager, you will need to download it from the OneDrive website and follow the installation instructions. It will appear as a share within your File Manager.

Google Drive

Google Drive can be mapped as a drive and can be used as default storage as well. To map the drive, you will need to install the Google Drive for Desktop for Windows application. Download this from the Google Drive website; as of this writing, the file is called GoogleDriveSetup.exe. Once you have downloaded it, simply follow installation instructions. Note that some organizations block use of the Google Drive for Windows application. Figure 4-46 shows the installation option for this application. It will put a link to Google Drive in the File Manager. Other cloud-based drive services have similar applications.

Figure 4-46 *The Installation Screen for Google Drive for Windows*

Dropbox

Dropbox is another cloud-based drive service that provides free storage. As of this writing, Dropbox provides 2 GB storage with a free account. It also provides an installer that will automate the process of installing the drive into File Explorer. Options also can be installed on the toolbar. More than just cloud storage, Dropbox is often used by creatives to store video for secure sharing, and it has secure document storage and tracking services as well. The Dropbox apps integrate with many of the familiar tools such as QuickBooks, Office 365, and Google Suite to further automate workflow.

The Dropbox Desktop app will install Dropbox in File Explorer. Figure 4-47 shows the Dropbox installer's Advanced Settings screen, where advanced settings can be configured.

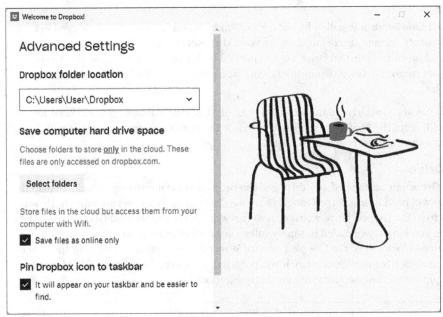

Figure 4-47 *The Dropbox Desktop Application's Advanced Settings Screens*

IDrive's Cloud Drive

IDrive's Cloud Drive is yet another cloud-based storage product. It offers a free tier of 10 GB as of this writing. Like most of the other products, it has an app that will allow you to install the drive link on your desktop and in File Explorer. Figure 4-48 shows the configuration window of the iDrive application. There is a set of security options for your device in this set of screens.

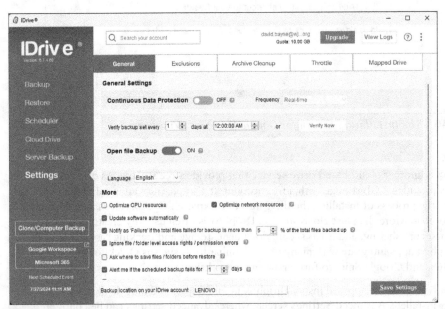

Figure 4-48 *The Cloud Drive Configuration Screen*

Box

More than just storage, **Box** is designed to provide workflow automation. As such, it has more permission levels for uploaded files than the other products and encourages collaboration between users. As of this writing, there is a personal free tier with 10 GB of storage, with additional restrictions imposed. Business tiers have a cost attached.

In addition to the website, Box has the Box Drive app, which integrates into File Explorer.

Amazon S3 Bucket

Amazon allows storage in what it calls *data lakes* and *buckets* using the AWS Simple Storage Service (S3), or **Amazon S3 Bucket**. If you have large amounts of data to store, this method of storing and managing data can be very cost-effective and efficient.

Data lakes represent the amount of data your organization contracts for, and each large container for objects is referred to as a bucket. Data is stored in *objects*. Each object has its own *key* or *key name* to identify it within the bucket. Objects may range in size from 0 bytes to up to 5 TB each.

To add the S3 Bucket as a drive, your organization will need to sign up for AWS and assign an administrator, which could be the IT support technician. That person would then create a user account with administrative access (it can be the same account) that then manages AWS services. Additional user accounts without administrative access are created for those who do not need to manage the AWS services.

Once users are created, the AWS administrator needs to create the S3 bucket. The users or administrators can then go to the AWS console to choose the bucket and upload data directly, either from the web interface or by using a **PUT** command. Data can be processed directly on the AWS S3 servers. Figure 4-49 shows the S3 console with a document uploaded.

Figure 4-49 *The AWS S3 Console Screen*

While AWS S3 can be mounted as a drive using third-party utilities, this approach is discouraged; it is designed to be a storage and processing location rather than an operational file storage location. As such, any changes to files will result in the file being entirely overwritten on the AWS S3 server. Because AWS S3 charges based on usage, and this action causes a delete, an upload, and a write, the costs increase exponentially. Other cloud-based providers such as the ones earlier are more appropriate if the users need to mount the cloud drive as a separate drive. S3 is more appropriate as long-term storage or as a store-and-manage service.

Exam Preparation Tasks

As mentioned in the Introduction, you can customize your strategy for exam preparation. Suggested tasks include the exercises here, Chapter 9, "Final Preparation," and the exam simulation questions on the companion website.

Review All Key Topics

Review the most important topics in this chapter, noted with the Key Topic icon in the outer margin of the page. Table 4-4 lists a reference of these key topics and the page numbers on which each is found.

Table 4-4 Key Topics for Chapter 4

Key Topic Element	Description	Page Number
Section	Display Settings	108
Section	Multiple Displays	111
Section	Brightness	112
Section	BitLocker	113
Section	Windows Update/Microsoft Update	114
Section	Application Updates	115
Section	The Browser Cache	117
Section	Task Manager	117
Section	End Task	119
Section	Sync Files to OneDrive	121
Section	Boot Sequence	122
Section	Boot to Safe Mode	123
Section	Power Management	124
Paragraph	How to use the accessibility tools to allow people with different abilities to use devices more efficiently and effectively	126
Section	Installing Windows Apps from the Microsoft Store	133
Section	Installing Windows Apps Not in the Microsoft Store	134
Section	Email	135
Section	Collaboration Applications	136
Section	Productivity Applications	136
Section	System Information	138
Section	Event Viewer	139
Section	**ipconfig**	139
Section	Active Directory	141
Section	Active Directory Group Policy	141
Section	GPUpdate	142
Section	ADGPUpdate	143
Section	Create New Users	143

Key Topic Element	Description	Page Number
Section	Enabling and Disabling User Accounts	143
Section	Adding Passwords	144
Section	Resetting Passwords	145
Section	Active Directory Groups	145
Section	Verifying AD Permissions	147
Paragraph	How to Use Cloud Drives to Store Data	149
Section	SMB Drives	149
Section	Mapping Internet-Based Drives	150
Section	OneDrive	151
Section	Google Drive	151
Section	Dropbox	151
Section	iDrive's Cloud Drive	152
Section	Box	153
Section	Amazon S3 Bucket	153

Define Key Terms

Define the following key terms from this chapter and check your answers in the glossary:

accessibility, Active Directory/Azure AD, AD Group Policy, ADGPUpdate, Amazon S3 Bucket, BIOS, BitLocker, boot sequence/boot order, Box, brightness, cache, caption, collaboration, collaboration applications, color filter, Contrast Themes, Control Panel, Display/Monitor, Display Settings, distribution group, domain controller, domain local group, Dropbox, dynamic group, Event Viewer, facial recognition, fingerprint recognition, gesture, global group, Google Drive, GPUpdate, iDrive's Cloud Drive, **ipconfig**, language pack, local group, lock/unlock user account, Microsoft OneDrive, Microsoft Store/App Store/Marketplace, mono audio/stereo audio, OneDrive, on-screen keyboard, password, physical security keys, picture passwords, PIN, power scheme, principle of least privilege, productivity applications, Safe Mode, screen magnifier, screen reader, security group, SMB drive, SMTP, special identity group, sync, Task Manager, UEFI, universal group, Windows Recovery Environment (WinRE), Windows Server Update Services (WSUS), Windows Update/Microsoft Update, wireless display

Command Reference to Check Your Memory

This section includes the most important configuration commands covered in this chapter. It might not be necessary to memorize the complete syntax of every command, but you should be able to remember the basic keywords and concepts that are needed.

To test your memory of the commands, cover the right side of Table 4-5 with a piece of paper, read the description on the left side, and then see how much of the command you can remember.

The 100-140 CCST IT Support exam focuses on practical, hands-on skills that are used by a networking professional. Therefore, you should be able to identify the commands needed to configure and complete the task in the left column.

Table 4-5   Command Reference

Task	Command Syntax
Open the Display Control Panel	**Windows > Display**
Connect to a wireless display	Windows+k (lowercase k) **Windows > Display**, then select Connect
Run Windows Update	**Windows > Update**
Check updates in Adobe Acrobat	Open Acrobat; then select **Help > Check for Updates**
Clear the browser cache: Microsoft Edge	In Edge, click the three dots in the upper right-hand corner. Select **Settings > Privacy, search, and services > Clear Browsing Data Now > Choose What to Clear**
Launch the Task Manager	Press Ctrl+Shift+Esc Right-click the toolbar Press Ctrl+Alt+Delete and then select Task Manager **Windows > Control Panel > All Control Panel Items > Windows Tools Menu > Task Manager**
Change boot order one time, on a Dell machine	Press F12
Configure a machine to boot into Start Mode from Windows	**Windows+i (or Windows > Settings) > System > Advanced Startup**
Access accessibility controls	**Windows > Settings > Accessibility**
Access the Microsoft Store	**Windows > Store**
Access Windows System Tools	**Windows > Control Panel > small icons** **Windows > Control Panel > large icons**
Run GPUpdate	**Windows > Command Prompt** and then enter **gpupdate** or **gpupdate/force** at the command prompt Or **Windows > Powershell** and then enter **gpupdate** or **gpupdate/force** at the command prompt
Create new users in Active Directory	On an Active Directory server or a device with AD configuration software and permissions: **Windows > Control Panel > System and Security**, then select **Administrative Tools**, then **Active Directory Users and Computers**. In the left pane, select the folder for the new user. Right-click and select **New > User** and enter the details.
Verify AD groups	**Windows > Command Prompt** and then type **whoami /groups** **Windows > Powershell** and then type **whoami / groups**
Connect to an SMB drive	**Windows > \\[** *ip address*	*device name* **]**

References

Amazon, "What Is Amazon S3? Amazon S3: Object Storage Built to Retrieve Any Amount of Data from Anywhere," https://aws.amazon.com/s3/

Box, https://www.box.com/home

Bridge, K., et al., "Windows Power Management," Microsoft, https://learn.microsoft.com/en-us/windows/win32/power/windows-power-management

Cucino, D., "How to Install Programs Without App Store?" Microsoft, https://answers.microsoft.com/en-us/windows/forum/all/how-to-install-programs-without-app-store/309dad37-8dd1-485f-acff-4bd7adf0b8b0

Dell Technologies, "How to Boot into Safe Mode in Windows 11 or Windows 10," Knowledge Base Article, https://www.dell.com/support/kbdoc/en-us/000124344/how-to-boot-to-safe-mode-in-windows-10

Dropbox, "How to Set Up Dropbox Backup," https://help.dropbox.com/organize/how-to-use-dropbox-backup

Gerend, J., et al., "Step 4: Configure Group Policy Settings for Automatic Updates," Microsoft, https://learn.microsoft.com/en-us/windows-server/administration/windows-server-update-services/deploy/4-configure-group-policy-settings-for-automatic-updates

Google, "Clear Cache & Cookies, Troubleshoot Issues with Google Accounts," https://support.google.com/accounts/answer/32050

Google, "How to Backup Folders with Google Drive for Desktop," https://knowledge.workspace.google.com/kb/how-to-backup-folders-with-google-drive-for-desktop-000009065

Hoffman, C., *Windows Task Manager: The Complete Guide*, HowToGeek, https://www.howtogeek.com/405806/windows-task-manager-the-complete-guide/

IDrive, https://www.idrive.com/idrive/home/

LinkedIn, "What Are the Steps to Troubleshoot Email Issues?" https://www.linkedin.com/advice/1/what-steps-troubleshoot-email-issues-skills-technical-support

Microsoft, "Back Up Your Folders with OneDrive," https://support.microsoft.com/en-us/office/back-up-your-folders-with-onedrive-d61a7930-a6fb-4b95-b28a-6552e77c3057

Microsoft, "Discover Windows Accessibility Features," https://support.microsoft.com/en-us/windows/discover-windows-accessibility-features-8b1068e6-d3b8-4ba8-b027-133dd8911df9#WindowsVersion=Windows_11

Microsoft, "Finding Your BitLocker Recovery Key in Windows," https://support.microsoft.com/en-us/windows/finding-your-bitlocker-recovery-key-in-windows-6b71ad27-0b89-ea08-f143-056f5ab347d6

Microsoft, "Make Windows Easier to Hear," https://support.microsoft.com/en-us/windows/make-windows-easier-to-hear-9c18cfdc-63be-2d47-0f4f-5b00facfd2e1#WindowsVersion=Windows_11

Microsoft, "Make Windows Easier to See," https://support.microsoft.com/en-us/windows/make-windows-easier-to-see-c97c2b0d-cadb-93f0-5fd1-59ccfe19345d#ID0EBF=Windows_11

Microsoft, "Touch Gestures for Windows," https://support.microsoft.com/en-us/windows/touch-gestures-for-windows-a9d28305-4818-a5df-4e2b-e5590f850741#WindowsVersion=Windows_11

4

Microsoft, "Update Windows," https://support.microsoft.com/en-us/windows/update-windows-3c5ae7fc-9fb6-9af1-1984-b5e0412c556a

Microsoft, "Use Live Captions to Better Understand Audio," https://support.microsoft.com/en-us/windows/use-live-captions-to-better-understand-audio-b52da59c-14b8-4031-aeeb-f6a47e6055df

Quest, "What Is Active Directory and How Does It Work?" https://www.quest.com/solutions/active-directory/what-is-active-directory.aspx

Reinders, M. "Using GPUpdate to Manage Group Policy," Petri, https://petri.com/gpupdate-force/

Seagate, "Connect to a Network Drive with SMB," https://www.lacie.com/support/kb/connect-to-a-network-drive-with-smb-006243en/

Slack, "Troubleshoot Connection Issues," https://slack.com/help/articles/205138367-Troubleshoot-connection-issues

SolarWinds, "What Are the Different Types of Groups in Active Directory? What Are Active Directory Groups?" https://www.solarwinds.com/resources/it-glossary/active-directory-groups

Windows Active Directory, "Active Directory Users and Computes (ADUC)—An Introduction and Installation Guide," https://www.windows-active-directory.com/active-directory-users-and-computers-i.html

macOS

This chapter covers the following topics:

■ **macOS System Tools:** This section describes commonly used system tools in macOS.

■ **macOS Security Tools:** The section details important security tools built into macOS.

This chapter covers the basics of macOS from a brief history to commonly used system and security tools built into the operating system. This chapter is not meant to be all encompassing on macOS, because that would require many more chapters, but it does cover important tools to provide an overview of macOS system and security tools while also helping to prepare you for certification.

The chapter covers information related to the following Cisco Certified Support Technician (CCST) IT Support exam objectives:

■ 2.2c Assist end users in using tools to locate information about their device

■ 3.1 Assist users with establishing access to network-based resources

■ 4.2 Assist users in resolving macOS issues

■ 4.5 Assist users in resolving common application issues

"Do I Know This Already?" Quiz

The "Do I Know This Already?" quiz allows you to assess whether you should read this entire chapter thoroughly or jump to the "Exam Preparation Tasks" section. If you are in doubt about your answers to these questions or your own assessment of your knowledge of the topics, read the entire chapter. Table 5-1 lists the major headings in this chapter and their corresponding "Do I Know This Already?" quiz questions. You can find the answers in Appendix A, "Answers to the 'Do I Know This Already?' Quizzes."

Table 5-1 "Do I Know This Already?" Section-to-Question Mapping

Foundation Topics Section	Questions
macOS System Tools	1–5
macOS Security Tools	6–10

CAUTION The goal of self-assessment is to gauge your mastery of the topics in this chapter. If you do not know the answer to a question or are only partially sure of the answer, you should mark that question as wrong for purposes of the self-assessment. Giving yourself credit for an answer you correctly guess skews your self-assessment results and might provide you with a false sense of security.

1. What screen shows a quick overview of the macOS version the device is currently using?
   a. About This Mac
   b. System Settings
   c. Spotlight
   d. Activity Monitor

2. In macOS, if the version is 13.6.5, what does the 6 represent?
   a. The major release number
   b. The minor patch version
   c. The minor release number
   d. The month the release was published

3. What macOS application lets end users quickly find applications, music, documents, and pictures?
   a. About This Mac
   b. System Settings
   c. Apple Search
   d. Spotlight

4. What macOS application is useful for finding a process that is consuming too many CPU cycles?
   a. Activity Monitor
   b. Task Manager
   c. System Monitor
   d. Resource Manager

5. Where would you go in macOS to change Network settings?
   a. Control Panel
   b. Apple Control Center
   c. System Settings
   d. About This Mac

6. What macOS application helps to back up files with snapshot support?
   a. Apple Disk Backup
   b. Time Machine
   c. iStorage
   d. Apple Vault

7. What system utility in macOS securely stores usernames, passwords, and other account information?
   a. Keychain Access
   b. Password Manager
   c. iStorage Access
   d. Apple Vault

8. What system utility in macOS allows the user to encrypt their entire storage device?

   a. Bitlocker

   b. iSecure Drive Encrypt

   c. Apple Vault

   d. FileVault

9. What built-in macOS security tool stops programs from nontrusted developers from being installed?

   a. Security App Guard

   b. Gatekeeper

   c. Firewall

   d. Apple Vault

10. If you need to reinstall macOS, where would you go?

   a. Recovery Mode

   b. System Settings

   c. Terminal Mode

   d. BIOS

Foundation Topics

macOS

The history of macOS is quite interesting but also quite involved. Without trying to be too reductionist, let's look at a brief overview of the history of macOS. Classic Mac OS was the first operating system shipped with the original Apple Macintosh in 1984. It featured a graphical user interface, or **GUI**, which allowed a mouse to navigate the operating system with graphical elements such as icons, buttons, and menus. Prior to this, most computer operating systems were just a command-line interface, or **CLI**, where users had to type in commands to have the computer do anything. While we still use CLI interfaces today, like the Windows command prompt or the Mac Terminal, many users spend most of their time in the GUI of the operating system.

Classic Mac OS developed over the years, with the last version being Mac OS 9 in 1999; it was later renamed Classic Mac OS to differentiate it from the newer and completely different Mac OS that was coming. There are many great books written on Steve Jobs's, the cofounder of Apple, creation of Apple, departure from Apple, and return to Apple. These details are beyond the scope of the certification book. However, it is important to know what when Jobs left Apple in 1985, he started another computer company called NeXT. NeXT computers ran an operating system called NeXTSTEP. NeXTSTEP used a derivative of the BSD operating system. Berkeley Software Distribution (BSD) is an open-source implementation of AT&T's UNIX operating system, which was proprietary and dates to the late 1960s. UNIX (and its open-source counterparts) is incredibly stable and built to be a modular operating system. This means it can be very small and specific or large and full featured.

Apple bought NeXT in 1997, and with that, Steve Jobs returned to Apple. Apple was struggling with sales in the late 1990s, so Jobs decided to completely ditch the Classic Mac OS and make a brand-new operating system for Apple computers based on NeXTSTEP, which is based on BSD. This would be called Mac OS X. This new OS brought incredible stability and performance. After several versions, Mac OS X was renamed macOS with the release of macOS 10.12. This new name helped to avoid consumer confusion when Apple's mobile operating system, iOS, was going to hit its tenth release, iOS 10.

> **NOTE** People often say that macOS is based on UNIX. This is true and not true. It is actually based on BSD, which was an open-source, written mostly from scratch, copy of UNIX. UNIX was copyrighted by AT&T, so computer scientists at University of California, Berkeley, wrote BSD to provide a free alternative while still maintaining the robustness of UNIX. The history is a little more complex than this summary, but that is the crux of it.
>
> You will also hear of the incredibly popular Linux operating system. Linux runs the vast majority of Internet servers and most computer appliances today. The Linux kernel, the heart of the operating system, was written by Linus Torvalds in 1991. He also modeled his operating system on UNIX-like ideals. This is why you will hear people state macOS and Linux are related. They're not, but they're both made on UNIX-like operating systems.

5

macOS System Tools

As an IT support technician, you will likely encounter users on macOS. Therefore, it is important to know some fundamental tools to assist end users on troubleshooting macOS issues and resolving common application issues.

> **NOTE**   While Windows and macOS have a lot of similarities, there are also quite a few differences. One difference that many Windows users aren't accustomed to is the placement of the Close, Minimize, and Full Screen buttons. On Windows, these buttons are on the upper right of the window. On macOS, they are on the upper left and color coded instead of the icon design of Windows.
>
> In macOS, the left red button is Close, yellow is Minimize, and green is Full Screen. However, in macOS, Full Screen is literally the full screen, unlike Windows that still shows the bottom taskbar. To exit full screen in macOS, either hover your mouse toward the top to select the green button again, or press Esc on the keyboard.
>
> Another somewhat important differentiation between the two in this regard is the Close button. In Windows, if you click the Close X button, it exits the program. In macOS, when you select the red Close button, it seemingly exits the program as well, but it actually suspends the program rather than fully exits it. This is similar to iPhones and Android phones that suspend the program instead of exiting when closing the app. The idea is that suspending the app in RAM will allow it to come back faster. When you select the red Close button, and the window disappears, look down at the dock. You will see a small dot under the program icon. This shows the program is suspended rather than closed (see Figure 5-4, later in this chapter). To fully close the application, you can use the keyboard shortcut Command (⌘)+Q or choose **App Name** and **Quit App** in the menu bar (your app window must be selected because the menu bar at the top is context sensitive).

About This Mac

One of the first steps in helping to diagnose an issue with macOS is to gather information about the OS version and its hardware. This task is most easily accomplished by opening the **About This Mac** screen. To do this, click the Apple symbol on macOS in the top-left corner and choose **About This Mac** (see Figure 5-1).

Upon opening this screen, you will see many important attributes of the operating system and the physical hardware. The first item you will see is the operating system version. As of this writing, the current version of macOS is macOS 15, Sequoia. Apple named its macOS releases with big cat names at first—Jaguar, Tiger, Lion—and then moved to names of California locales—Mojave, Catalina, Monterey, and so on. While the names help to quickly identify OS versions, the numbers are more important.

Figure 5-2 shows that the OS running is macOS Monterey, Version 12.7.5. Version 12 is the major release number and corresponds to the name Monterey. The second number, 7, is the minor release number and reflects new features and bug fixes. The last number, 5, is the patch version, which usually represents more minor bug fixes. These are extremely important to see. If an end user is having a certain issue, a first step to troubleshoot might involve seeing if there is a minor or patch version update to their major version of the OS.

Figure 5-1   *How to Open About This Mac Window*

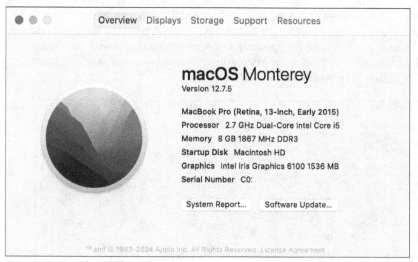

Figure 5-2   *About This Mac*

To update to the newest version of the OS, click **Software Update** on the front page of the About This Mac screen. In addition to the OS version number, this front page also shows important physical information about the machine, including the processor, memory, graphics, and serial number. If the end user still has an active AppleCare subscription, the serial number of the device will be needed. In addition, to see more in-depth hardware information, click **System Report** on the front page of the About This Mac screen.

NOTE   Many macOS users are surprised when they can't upgrade their OS to the newest major version of macOS. They can click Software Update, but it might not show the newest version. This lack of change can be for several reasons. Most often, it is due to hardware limitations. For instance, early Macs used the PowerPC processor. When Macs switched over to Intel processors, they stopped supporting PowerPCs after Mac OS X 10.5. Consequently, users could not upgrade to Mac OS X 10.6 because that version was compiled only for Intel processors. With Apple's move from Intel processors to its own inhouse-made ARM processors, we will most likely see support for Intel processers end soon.

At the top of the About This Mac screen, there are also additional tabs to open: Displays, Storage, Support, and Resources. Displays shows information about the monitor type and current resolution. It also has a button called Display Preferences that will provide a shortcut to the System Preferences-Displays settings. Here you can adjust the screen resolution, turn on Night Shift to help cut harmful blue light from your eyes, and add additional displays. In the Storage tab, information about the internal storage is shown. This information can be helpful for a quick snapshot to see how filled the storage device is. The Support tab is useful for end users who still have active AppleCare subscriptions with the Resources tab being links to Apple help pages.

Spotlight and Finder

There are several different ways to navigate macOS to find programs and documents. One of the simplest ways is to use macOS's Spotlight application. To open Spotlight, click the magnifying glass in the upper-right corner (see Figure 5-3). This will open the Spotlight Search window. From here, you can type any application, document, picture, music, or whatever you are looking for, and it will pull it up. Microsoft Windows has a similar search feature, but macOS's Spotlight is extremely fast and efficient.

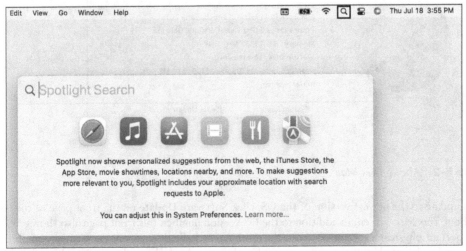

Figure 5-3   *Spotlight Search*

Finder is akin to Microsoft Window's File Explorer. To open Finder, you click the smiling face on the far left of the bottom dock (see Figure 5-4). This will open a window that shows the folders on the left and the contents on the right. This window allows you to access and organize your files. You can create directories, rename files, and get file information here.

Figure 5-4   *Finder*

Activity Monitor

The **Activity Monitor** application in macOS is a crucial utility to help diagnose issues within the OS. It is extremely similar to Microsoft Window's Task Manager. The Activity Monitor allows you to see running processes (see Figure 5-5). To open the Activity Monitor, either utilize Spotlight Search or open the Finder and go to Applications and then the Utilities folder (refer to Figure 5-4). You can sort the process names alphabetically by selecting the Process Name column, or sort by CPU percentage, CPU Time, Threads, GPU Percentage, and more by selecting the corresponding column. This utility makes it easy to spot a rogue app that is consuming too many resources. If a certain app seems to be consuming too many CPU cycles, you can click its name and the select the X button toward the top of the window to stop the app. You can also select a process and click the I button to learn more information about the particular app, which is beneficial in trying to identify more information about it. This utility will even tell you how much memory that process is taking.

NOTE   While it might seem that the terms *app*, short for application, and *process* are being used interchangeably, they are not necessarily. In the macOS Activity Monitor, you will see both applications and processes listed under Process Name. This means that an app is a full-featured program. However, a process might just be a smaller part of something larger. You will often see a lowercase *d* after a name. This means it is a daemon. This term comes from UNIX and is a system process of some sort for the operating system. Its description is beyond the scope of this certification book, but it is an important distinction.

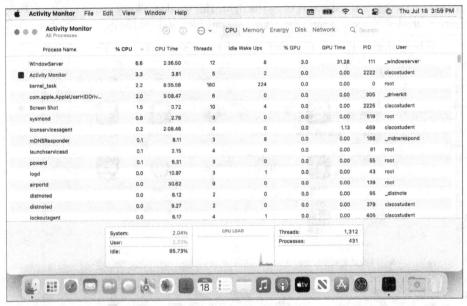

Figure 5-5 *Activity Monitor*

In addition to seeing information about processes and CPU/GPU utilization, you can also select the other tabs Memory, Energy, Disk, and Network toward the top of the Activity Monitor (refer to Figure 5-5). Selecting them will show you the processes and how much RAM they are consuming (and is sortable like CPU), the energy of each process (this is really more for laptops, but the idea is that the more CPU and RAM a process is using, the more energy it will use), disk usage of each process, and finally what processes are using the network. The Network tab is useful when investigating a possible malware app that might be sending off personal information.

System Settings

System Settings, formerly called System Preferences, allows users to modify various system settings. To open it, either click the cogwheel on the Dock, press the Apple button in the top left and select **System Settings**, or use Spotlight to search for it.

System Settings is similar to Microsoft Window's Control Panel/Settings program. It functions as a central hub for customizing and controlling the OS. This allows for customization, system control, hardware configuration, and application general behaviors.

The settings are grouped into categories on the left sidebar, similar to Apple's iPhone Settings, so that when you click the category, the options are presented in the window to the right. This stylistic change looks quite different than the original System Preferences that was grouped into categories in one window (see Figure 5-6). When you clicked the category, it opened the options for that setting. The new System Settings in macOS is an attempt to unify the aesthetics of macOS and the mobile iOS of iPhones.

Figure 5-6 *Original System Preferences Window*

Some important System Settings are Privacy & Security and Users & Groups settings. Privacy & Security settings allow important options like requiring an administrator password for system changes and logging out automatically after inactivity, while the Users & Groups settings allow you to view the list of users, turn on the Guest User account, add users, add groups, and more.

NOTE   To make certain changes in System Settings, you will need to click the small lock icon on the bottom of the Settings window and enter your account password. The reason is to prevent accidental changes in more risky settings. See the padlock icon in Figure 5-9, later in the chapter.

Console

The **Console** app is a helpful utility that acts as a central hub for viewing system logs. The logs are detailed records of what is happening in the operating system and the various apps running. The Console app allows you to view system logs. By analyzing these log messages, you can identify errors, warnings, or unusual activity. The app also allows you to track resource usage, network activity, and application performance.

The Console app allows you to see logs generated in real time (see Figure 5-7). The messages being displayed are not necessarily bad events even if the message itself seems to use language that seems otherwise. Learning how to read these messages is a skill to develop.

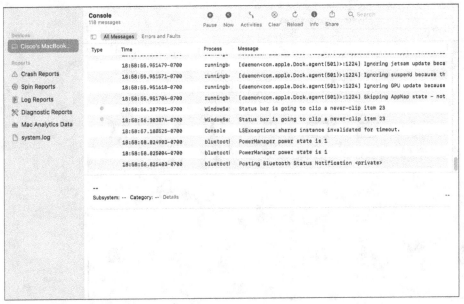

Figure 5-7 *Console Running in Live View*

You can also filter these logs based on severity as well as search within the logs themselves. In addition, you can save and export these logs for further investigation.

Terminal

The Terminal program is the macOS CLI interface. It is the equivalent of the Microsoft Windows command prompt or PowerShell. It allows direct communication with the core of the OS and allows a more powerful and flexible way to manage macOS over the confines of the GUI.

Benefits of using the Terminal's CLI over the GUI include

- **Automation:** You can write scripts (series of commands) to automate repetitive tasks, saving you time and effort.

- **Advanced Control:** Terminal grants access to functionalities not readily available through the GUI, giving you more granular control over your Mac.

- **Troubleshooting:** Many system tools and utilities are accessed through Terminal commands, making it valuable for troubleshooting issues.

ifconfig

Most network settings can be accessed through System Settings. However, the original method of seeing network interfaces is with the Terminal command **ifconfig**. **ifconfig** is a versatile tool for network interface configuration that allows you to view information about network interfaces such as IP addresses, MAC addresses, and more. In addition, it allows you to configure network settings and enable and disable interfaces (see Figure 5-8).

NOTE **ifconfig** has been seen as the UNIX equivalent of **ipconfig**, which is used to do similar activities on Microsoft Windows. However, this is not completely true. While it is true that **ifconfig** has only worked on UNIX-type operating systems and not worked on Microsoft Windows, many modern Linux distributions are including the **ipconfig** program and switching from the use of **ifconfig** to **ipconfig**. This is not currently true with macOS because it only includes the **ifconfig** command and not **ipconfig**. However, using **ifconfig** to actually configure interfaces in macOS is also discouraged now because the system relies on a different system framework for network configuration.

Figure 5-8 ifconfig *in Terminal*

Other Networking CLI Commands

Because of the connection to UNIX, many commands that you learn on Linux will work in Terminal as well. Following are some networking commands that can help you diagnose issues:

- **ping:** This classic tool lets you test network connectivity by sending data packets to a specific host and measuring their response time.

- **traceroute:** This command helps visualize the route that packets take from your Mac to a destination; it is useful for identifying network bottlenecks or connection issues.

- **netstat:** While not as versatile as on Linux, this command can still provide information about network connections, routing tables, and listening ports on your Mac.

Here are other common CLI commands:

- Basic Commands

    - **ls:** List files and directories in the current directory.

    - **cd** *<directory>*: Change the current directory to the specified directory.

    - **pwd:** Print the current directory.

    - **mkdir** *<directory>*: Create a new directory.

    - **rmdir** *<directory>*: Remove an empty directory.

    - **rm** *<file>*: Remove a file.

- File Management

    - **cp** *<source> <destination>*: Copy files or directories.

    - **mv** *<source> <destination>*: Move or rename files or directories.

    - **cat** *<file>*: Display the contents of a file.

- System Information

    - **top:** Display real-time system processes and resource usage.

    - **df:** Display disk usage.

    - **du:** Display directory space usage.

    - **uname -a:** Show system information.

- Permissions and Ownership

    - **chmod** *<permissions> <file>*: Change permissions of a file.

    - **chown** *<user>:<group> <file>*: Change the owner and group of a file.

- Others

    - **man** *<command>*: View the manual page for a specific command.

    - **clear:** Clear the terminal screen.

macOS Security Tools

There is an urban legend that Macs don't get viruses. This is not true. Several malware programs have targeted macOS. One reason there has been more malware on Microsoft Windows rather than macOS is sheer volume of users. Creators of malware go after the biggest fish, which is Microsoft Windows. The end-user base is much larger.

The other reason is design, however. Unlike in Microsoft Windows, on macOS the initial user created is not an administrator. This design is inherently safer. On macOS, you must enter your username and password to elevate to administrator when installing or doing major system changes. While the end user could still input this information for a rogue piece of software, it at least stops them and makes them physically have to enter their credentials. In addition, other important security tools are built into macOS.

Keychain Access

Built into macOS is an app called **Keychain Access**. This program stores your usernames, passwords, and other information in an encrypted file on your OS and can sync, with end-to-end encryption, with Apple's iCloud Keychain to allow access to this information across your Apple devices. This mechanism helps protect against exposed information being stored because it's encrypted. When you log in to your account, you unlock your Keychain Access. This means that your user password needs to be secure because it unlocks the other passwords through Keychain. Originally, Keychain Access only worked on Apple's Safari browser; however, a recent update means you can use it for other web browsers as well.

FileVault Disk Encryption

Like in Microsoft Windows, in macOS, even if the end user has a secure login password setup, a threat actor with physical access to the machine can take out the storage device and browse the files on it. No password required. This is why disk encryption is vital. On Microsoft Windows, this tool is BitLocker. On macOS, it is called **FileVault Disk Encryption**. FileVault encrypts the entire disk with either the end user's iCloud account and password or a Recovery key. The Recovery key is the most secure because it is a randomized string of letters and numbers that the OS generates. However, if you lose the Recovery key and forget your login password to reset it, you will lose all access to your files.

To turn on FileVault, go to System Settings and choose **Privacy & Security**. From there, you will see FileVault and can turn it on.

Firewall

MacOS has a built-in **Firewall** application that helps to control incoming and outgoing network traffic. This is an important security feature that should be turned on. While it can cause issues with some programs not being able to communicate with various servers, this issue can be resolved by letting those ports through in the Firewall Options. To turn it on, go to **System Settings > Privacy & Security**, and choose **Firewall**.

Gatekeeper

Gatekeeper is a built-in security tool in macOS. Most programs that you install in macOS come from the App Store. These applications are vetted by Apple and run in a sandboxed mode to restrict access to other sensitive data. If the program needs access outside of its own code, it must use Apple's APIs to do so. This helps rogue apps from taking over. Gatekeeper only allows programs to be installed directly from the App Store or, if downloaded outside the App Store, from registered developers with Apple. If the program was downloaded from outside the App Store, and it's from a registered developer, you will still have to approve the installation by clicking the **Open** button on the popup.

However, sometimes you might need to install a legitimate program from outside the App Store and from a developer who is not registered with Apple. To do this, you need to turn off Gatekeeper by going to **System Settings > Privacy & Security**, and selecting **Allow Apps Downloaded From: Anywhere**. It is advised that you do this only for programs that you know are free of malware. It is also advised that you to go back and change the setting to App Store or App Store and Identified Developers after installation (see Figure 5-9).

5

NOTE Later versions of macOS removed the Anywhere option for downloaded apps by default. This change was made for security purposes. However, if you need to turn it on, open Terminal and type **sudo spctl -master-disable.**

To remove the Anywhere option again, go back to Terminal and type **sudo spctl -master-enable.**

The **sudo** command temporarily invokes administrator access rights, so you will have to type in your system password to run the command.

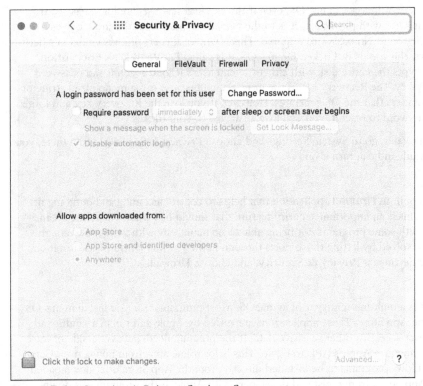

Figure 5-9 *Security & Privacy Settings Screen*

Recovery Mode

Recovery Mode is a powerful utility tool to do many tasks in macOS. To use this tool, you must boot into this mode. To do so, restart your Mac and press Command (⌘)+R. This tool enables you to repair internal storage, reinstall macOS, restore files from Time Machine, reset passwords when not known, and more.

If you are selling or transferring your Mac, it is a good idea to reset the device. First, sign out of iTunes, iMessage, and iCloud. Restart your Mac and enter Recovery Mode. Select **Disk Utility** and then choose **Macintosh HD**, or equivalent name, and select the **Erase** button in the toolbar. This will help to make sure all the data has been erased. Afterward, go back to the Recovery Mode's first screen and select **Reinstall macOS**. When you erased the

Macintosh HD, it did not erase Recovery Mode because it exists in another partition. While Disk Utility exists in the regular mode of macOS, you can't use it to erase the disk as you are currently using it. This is why you enter Recovery Mode for this step.

Resetting Password

If you would like to change your password or reset it, the easiest method is to open Terminal and type **resetpassword**. This will open a Reset Password assistant. If you forgot your password, you can open Terminal from within the Recovery Mode as well. This will assume that you know your Apple ID email and password. If this approach doesn't work, or you don't have access to your Apple ID email and password, or never set it up, you will need to reinstall macOS as outlined in the "Recovery Mode" section.

Time Machine

One incredibly useful tool built into macOS is the **Time Machine** program. This app allows you to connect an external storage device and back up your files. This system can back up your apps, music, photos, and include or exclude any file type you want. Additionally, it allows snapshots. This is an incredibly useful feature that shows changes in files. For instance, traditional backup solutions often just replace the old file with the new file. Snapshots is a form of versioning that keeps track of the changes between the original backup and new ones. This allows you to choose which version of the file you would like to restore. While not foolproof, this is a possible solution to ransomware attacks. See Table 7-3 in Chapter 7, "Security," for more information.

To use Time Machine, plug in an external drive, go to System Settings, and search for Time Machine. There you will Add Backup Disk and choose your settings. To see active snapshots, use the Spotlight and search for Time Machine. This will show you a graphical snapshot of your versions (see Figure 5-10). Additionally, you can restore Time Machine snapshots from within Recovery Mode.

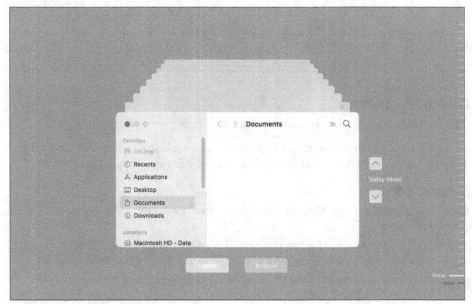

Figure 5-10 *Time Machine*

Exam Preparation Tasks

As mentioned in the Introduction, you can customize your strategy for exam preparation. Suggested tasks include the exercises here, Chapter 9, "Final Preparation," and the exam simulation questions on the companion website.

Review All Key Topics

Review the most important topics in this chapter, noted with the Key Topic icon in the outer margin of the page. Table 5-2 lists a reference of these key topics and the page numbers on which each is found.

Table 5-2   Key Topics for Chapter 5

Key Topic Element	Description	Page Number
Paragraph	About this Mac	164
Paragraph	How to read macOS versions	164
Section	Spotlight and Finder	166
Section	Activity Monitor	167
Section	System Settings	168
Section	Console	169
Section	Terminal	170
Section	**ifconfig**	170
Section	Keychain Access	173
Section	FileVault Disk Encryption	173
Section	Firewall	173
Section	Gatekeeper	173
Section	Recovery Mode	174
Section	Resetting Password	175
Section	Time Machine	175

Define Key Terms

Define the following key terms from this chapter and check your answers in the glossary:

About This Mac, Activity Monitor, CLI, Console, Disk Utility, FileVault Disk Encryption, Firewall, Gatekeeper, GUI, **ifconfig**, Keychain Access, Recovery Mode, Time Machine

References

Apple, "Chapter 3. Learning Mac OS X Basics," https://www.apple.com/voiceover/info/guide/_1122.html

Bohon, C., "20 Mac Terminal Commands Every User Should Know," *Tech Republic*, https://www.techrepublic.com/article/16-terminal-commands-every-user-should-know/

Klara Inc., "History of FreeBSD and Unix and BSD," https://klarasystems.com/articles/history-of-freebsd-unix-and-bsd/

Menchaca, J., "History: The Origins of Mac OS X," *Medium*, https://joachim8675309.medium.com/history-the-origins-of-mac-os-x-d841d34e3aac

CHAPTER 6

Virtualization, Cloud, and Remote Access

This chapter covers the following topics:

- **Introduction:** This section describes the importance of virtualization, cloud computing, and remote access in modern IT environments.

- **Cloud Overview:** This section explores the basic concepts of cloud computing, including its technologies, benefits, and how it is transforming businesses.

- **Cloud Providers:** This section details the key offerings and strengths of major cloud providers—AWS, Microsoft Azure, and Google Cloud Platform.

- **Cloud Services:** This section describes the different cloud service models—SaaS, PaaS, and IaaS—and their use cases.

- **Cloud Models:** This section explores various cloud deployment models—public, private, hybrid, and community clouds—and their advantages and disadvantages.

- **Cloud Computing vs. On-Premises Data Centers:** This section details the differences between cloud computing and on-premises data centers, helping organizations choose the right approach.

- **Virtualization Overview:** This section describes the concept of virtualization, its benefits, and how it enables efficient resource use.

- **Hypervisors and Virtual Machines:** This section details the role of hypervisors in virtualization and explains how virtual machines operate within a virtualized environment.

- **Virtualization and Software-Defined Networking (SDN):** This section explores the relationship between virtualization and SDN, highlighting how they work together to enhance network management.

- **Remote Access:** This section details various remote access tools and their applications in providing secure and efficient IT support across distributed environments.

This chapter covers information related to the following Cisco Certified Support Technician (CCST) IT Support exam objectives:

- 4.4 Describe virtualization and cloud computing

- 6.1 Use remote access software to connect to end user devices and perform remote support tasks

"Do I Know This Already?" Quiz

The "Do I Know This Already?" quiz allows you to assess whether you should read this entire chapter thoroughly or jump to the "Exam Preparation Tasks" section. If you are in doubt about your answers to these questions or your own assessment of your knowledge of the topics, read the entire chapter. Table 6-1 lists the major headings in this chapter and their corresponding "Do I Know This Already?" quiz questions. You can find the answers in Appendix A, "Answers to the 'Do I Know This Already?' Quizzes."

Table 6-1 "Do I Know This Already?" Section-to-Question Mapping

Foundation Topics Section	Questions
Cloud Computing	1
Cloud Providers	2
Cloud Services	3, 4
Cloud Models	5
Cloud Computing vs. On-Premises Data Centers	6
Virtualization	7
Hypervisors and Virtual Machines	8
Virtualization and Software-Defined Networking (SDN)	9
Remote Access	10, 11

CAUTION The goal of self-assessment is to gauge your mastery of the topics in this chapter. If you do not know the answer to a question or are only partially sure of the answer, you should mark that question as wrong for purposes of the self-assessment. Giving yourself credit for an answer you correctly guess skews your self-assessment results and might provide you with a false sense of security.

1. What is a feature of cloud computing?
   a. It requires businesses to purchase hardware up front.
   b. It allows for scalability and flexibility in resource usage.
   c. It ensures full control over physical infrastructure.
   d. It does not require an Internet connection.
2. Which of the following is a key service offered by Amazon Web Services (AWS)?
   a. Google Compute Engine
   b. Azure Virtual Machines
   c. Elastic Compute Cloud (EC2)
   d. Oracle Cloud Infrastructure

3. What does SaaS stand for in the context of cloud services?

   a. Storage as a Service

   b. Software as a Service

   c. Security as a Service

   d. System as a Service

4. What is provided by Platform as a Service (PaaS)?

   a. A fully managed software application for end users

   b. Tools and environment for developers to build, deploy, and manage applications

   c. Virtual machines and storage for running operating systems

   d. Data backup and recovery services for cloud environments

5. Which cloud model combines different cloud environments to allow both shared and dedicated resources?

   a. Public cloud

   b. Private cloud

   c. Community cloud

   d. Hybrid cloud

6. Which of the following is typically true about on-premises data centers compared to cloud computing?

   a. On-premises data centers offer greater scalability.

   b. On-premises data centers are usually less expensive to maintain.

   c. On-premises data centers provide more control over data security.

   d. On-premises data centers require no up-front investment in hardware.

7. What is the primary function of a hypervisor in virtualization?

   a. It physically connects computers in a network.

   b. It runs multiple virtual machines on a single physical machine.

   c. It encrypts data in a cloud environment.

   d. It acts as a firewall between virtual machines.

8. Which type of hypervisor runs directly on the physical hardware without needing a host operating system?

   a. Type 1 hypervisor

   b. Type 2 hypervisor

   c. Hosted hypervisor

   d. Virtual hypervisor

9. In a software-defined networking (SDN) architecture, what is the role of the control plane?

   a. It physically forwards network traffic.

   b. It encrypts data as it passes through the network.

   c. It makes decisions about where to send network traffic.

   d. It installs software on network devices.

10. Which remote access tool is known for enterprise-level communication and collaboration?

    a. Remote Desktop Protocol (RDP)

    b. Cisco Webex

    c. TeamViewer

    d. VNC

11. In which scenario would you most likely use Virtual Network Computing (VNC)?

    a. Managing a cloud-based server with a graphical user interface

    b. Conducting a large-scale video conference

    c. Accessing a Windows desktop remotely

    d. Setting up a new cloud service on AWS

6

Foundation Topics

Introduction

In today's rapidly evolving digital landscape, the ability to adapt and scale IT resources is more crucial than ever. Businesses are increasingly relying on advanced technologies like virtualization, cloud computing, and remote access to maintain their competitive edge and ensure operational efficiency. Virtualization allows organizations to maximize the use of their physical hardware by running multiple virtual environments on a single machine, reducing costs and increasing flexibility. Cloud computing extends this flexibility by offering scalable, on-demand access to computing resources over the Internet, enabling businesses to scale quickly and efficiently without the need for substantial up-front investment. Meanwhile, remote access tools empower employees and IT support teams to connect to systems from anywhere, ensuring business continuity and supporting the growing trend of remote work. This chapter explores the interconnected roles of virtualization, cloud computing, and remote access in an IT environment.

Cloud Computing

Cloud computing is a way to deliver computing services over the Internet. Instead of buying and maintaining physical servers and data centers, an organization can rent computing power, storage, and applications from cloud providers. As a result, organizations can access powerful IT resources on-demand, paying only for what they use, like how they would with utilities such as electricity or water. The cloud providers leverage virtualization technologies to deliver their cloud computing services. Figure 6-1 shows a digital circuit rendering of a cloud.

Figure 6-1 *Digital Cloud*

Virtualization is at the core of cloud computing. Allowing multiple virtual machines (VMs) to run on a single physical server makes cloud computing efficient and cost-effective. Each virtual machine behaves like an independent computer, but they all share the same underlying hardware.

Imagine a hotel with multiple rooms (VMs) that share common facilities like the lobby and elevator (physical hardware). Each guest (user) feels as if they have their own private space, but the hotel (cloud provider) manages all the resources efficiently.

Benefits of Cloud Computing

Cloud computing offers several key advantages for businesses:

- **Cost Savings:** You don't need to invest in expensive hardware up front. Instead, you pay only for what you use, which can be much more cost-effective.

  Think of cloud computing like using a taxi service instead of buying a car. You don't have to worry about maintenance or parking; you just pay for the ride.

- **Scalability:** As your business grows, you can easily increase your computing resources. If you need less, you can scale down just as easily. For example, during a holiday sale, an online retailer might experience a surge in traffic. With cloud computing, the retailer can temporarily increase server capacity to handle the extra demand, then scale back down afterward when sales slow back down.

- **Flexibility:** Cloud computing allows you to access your data and applications from anywhere with an Internet connection. This capability is especially useful for remote work and global collaboration. A good example is that of a project manager working from home who can access the same files and tools as if they were in the office, enabling seamless collaboration with colleagues around the world.

- **Accessibility:** Because cloud services are available over the Internet, employees can work from anywhere, which is increasingly important in today's globalized and remote work environments.

The Pay-As-You-Go Model

One of the most significant benefits of cloud computing is the pay-as-you-go model. Instead of purchasing hardware and software that might go unused, you only pay for the resources you need and use.

A business startup might begin with minimal resources but can scale up cloud usage as the business grows, ensuring the company is never paying for more than it needs.

This model is particularly advantageous for startups and small businesses, because it reduces the financial burden of acquiring IT infrastructure. It also allows larger enterprises to be more agile, responding quickly to changes in demand without the delays associated with physical infrastructure.

6

How Cloud Computing Is Changing Business

Cloud computing is transforming how businesses operate:

- **Agility:** Businesses can quickly launch new products and services without waiting for hardware to be delivered and set up. This speed to market is a competitive advantage. For example, a software company can develop, test, and deploy a new application entirely in the cloud, reducing time-to-market and lowering costs.

- **Innovation:** Cloud computing makes advanced technologies, such as artificial intelligence (AI) and big data analytics, accessible to businesses of all sizes. Companies can innovate without needing specialized hardware or expertise. Imagine a retail company using cloud-based AI tools to analyze customer data and predict trends, allowing the company to stock the right products at the right time.

- **Global Reach:** Companies can easily expand their operations to new markets without the need to establish physical data centers in each location. The cloud enables them to serve customers anywhere in the world with low latency. With global reach, an e-commerce business can use a content delivery network (CDN) hosted in the cloud to ensure that customers worldwide experience fast load times, regardless of their location.

- **Collaboration:** Cloud-based tools enable teams to work together in real time, regardless of their physical location. This capability leads to increased productivity and innovation. Using cloud-based collaboration tools like Google Workspace or Microsoft 365, a multinational team can work on the same project simultaneously, with real-time updates.

Cloud Computing vs. On-Premises Data Centers

When deciding where to host your IT infrastructure, you generally have two options: cloud computing or an on-premises data center. Both approaches have their pros and cons, and the right choice depends on your organization's needs.

Cloud computing is hosted by third-party providers that manage the hardware, software, and networking, allowing businesses to focus on using the services rather than maintaining them. A major advantage of this model is its scalability and flexibility, enabling organizations to quickly adjust resources based on demand. It's also cost-effective, operating on a pay-as-you-go model that avoids large up-front investments and reduces ongoing maintenance costs. However, cloud computing may offer less control over physical infrastructure, which could be a concern for organizations with strict security or compliance requirements.

In contrast, **on-premises** data centers are hosted on-site, meaning they are physically located within your organization's premises. You are responsible for owning and maintaining all the hardware, software, and networking infrastructure, which involves high initial costs. A key feature of this model is fixed capacity; expanding an on-premises data center requires purchasing and installing new hardware, which can be both time-consuming and costly, making it challenging to quickly adapt to changes in demand. However, on-premises data centers offer high levels of control, allowing organizations to manage their physical servers, security protocols, and data storage directly. This level of control is particularly important for businesses that deal with sensitive information or have strict regulatory requirements. Figure 6-2 shows an example of a data center server room.

Figure 6-2 *Data Center Server Room*

Choosing between cloud computing and on-premises data centers depends on your organization's needs, balancing the flexibility and cost savings of the cloud against the control and security of an on-premises solution. Table 6-2 offers a comparison.

Table 6-2 Comparing Cloud Computing to On-Premises Data Centers

Aspect	Cloud Computing	On-Premises Data Centers
Hosting location	Hosted off-site by third-party providers like AWS, Azure, and Google Cloud Platform	Hosted on-site within the organization's premises
Scalability	Highly scalable; resources can be quickly adjusted to meet demand	Limited scalability; requires purchasing and installing new hardware
Cost structure	Pay-as-you-go model; lower up-front costs but ongoing usage fees	High up-front investment in hardware; ongoing maintenance and operational costs
Control	Limited control over physical infrastructure; provider manages hardware and security	Full control over hardware, security, and data management
Maintenance	Provider handles hardware maintenance, updates, and security	Organization responsible for all maintenance, upgrades, and security
Remote access	Accessible from anywhere with an Internet connection; ideal for remote work	Requires secure VPN or other remote access solutions; less convenient for remote work

Aspect	Cloud Computing	On-Premises Data Centers
Security	Security managed by cloud provider; may offer advanced security features, but less control	Full control over security measures; better for sensitive data and compliance
Flexibility	High flexibility; can quickly adapt to changing business needs	Less flexible; hardware changes require time and investment
Use cases	Best for businesses needing scalability, flexibility, and remote access	Best for organizations requiring strict control and compliance, with predictable workloads

The decision between cloud computing and an on-premises data center depends on several factors, including cost, control, scalability, and security needs.

- **Choose Cloud Computing If:**

  - You need to scale resources quickly and efficiently.

  - You prefer a pay-as-you-go model to manage costs.

  - You want to enable remote access and global collaboration.

  - You have limited IT resources and prefer to offload maintenance to a third party.

- **Choose On-Premises Data Centers If:**

  - You require complete control over your IT infrastructure.

  - You handle sensitive data that must be stored on-site for compliance reasons.

  - You have predictable, stable workloads that justify the investment in physical hardware.

  - You have the resources to manage and maintain the infrastructure internally.

Cloud Providers

The cloud computing market is dominated by three major providers: Amazon Web Services (AWS), Microsoft Azure, and Google Cloud Platform (GCP). Each of these providers offers a broad range of services, catering to different needs and industries.

Imagine you are the IT manager at a mid-sized company with a dedicated IT help desk that supports employees across multiple locations. Your company is planning to migrate its internal IT support systems, including ticketing, remote desktop services, and knowledge bases, to the cloud.

You might select AWS for its scalability and extensive range of services, which can handle the varying demands of your help desk operations. AWS's robust infrastructure ensures that your help desk can scale resources up or down based on the number of tickets or remote sessions at any given time.

Azure might be your choice if your help desk heavily relies on Microsoft products like Windows Server and Active Directory. Azure's seamless integration with your existing Windows infrastructure allows for easier migration and management of your help desk tools, such as the integration of Microsoft Teams for internal communications.

You might opt for Google Cloud Platform if your help desk needs advanced data analytics to monitor and improve support processes. GCP's powerful analytics tools can help you analyze ticket trends, identify recurring issues, and optimize your support resources based on real-time data.

Each option supports the unique needs of your IT help desk, from managing day-to-day operations to leveraging data for continuous improvement.

- **Amazon Web Services (AWS):** AWS is the largest cloud provider, offering a vast range of services with unmatched scalability (see Figure 6-3). With flexible virtual servers provided by Elastic Compute Cloud (EC2), reliable storage with Simple Storage Service (S3), and serverless computing (Lambda), AWS can easily scale to meet your needs. Its global infrastructure ensures high performance and availability.

Figure 6-3 *AWS*

- **Microsoft Azure:** Azure is ideal for organizations already using Microsoft products (see Figure 6-4). It integrates seamlessly with tools like Windows Server and Office 365, offering scalable virtual machines and versatile storage. Azure also excels in AI and hybrid cloud solutions, providing flexibility and security for mixed environments.

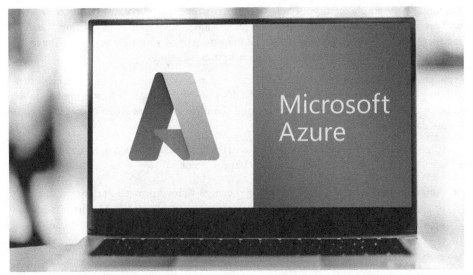

Figure 6-4   *Microsoft Azure*

■ **Google Cloud Platform (GCP):** GCP is known for its strength in data analytics, machine learning, and containerization (see Figure 6-5). It offers powerful virtual machines (Compute Engine), unified storage, and fast data analysis with BigQuery. GCP's leadership in container technology (Kubernetes Engine) and global network make it a top choice for tech-focused businesses.

Figure 6-5   *Google Cloud*

The features of each of the three major cloud providers are compared in Table 6-3.

Table 6-3 Comparing Cloud Service Providers

Feature	AWS	Microsoft Azure	Google Cloud Platform
Strengths	Comprehensive services, scalability	Integration with Microsoft tools	Advanced analytics, Kubernetes
Best for	Large enterprises, broad use cases	Businesses using Microsoft products	Data-driven apps
Key services	ECS, S3, Lambda	Virtual machines, Blob storage, AI	Compute engine, cloud storage, BigQuery
Market share	Largest	No. 2	Growing, strong in specific niches

Cloud Services

Cloud services are typically categorized into three primary models: Software as a Service (SaaS), Platform as a Service (PaaS), and Infrastructure as a Service (IaaS). Each model serves different business needs and levels of control over IT resources.

- **Software as a Service (SaaS):** SaaS provides software applications over the Internet that you can use directly through a web browser without installing anything on your device. Examples include Google Workspace, Salesforce, and Microsoft 365. It's perfect for businesses needing ready-to-use tools for tasks like email, CRM, and collaboration, removing the need for in-house IT management and offering easy and quick setup.

  A good example of SaaS is a small marketing firm that uses Google Workspace for email, document creation, and team collaboration, avoiding the complexities of managing software installations and updates.

- **Platform as a Service (PaaS):** PaaS offers a platform for developers to build, deploy, and manage applications without needing to worry about the underlying infrastructure. The cloud provider handles everything from servers to networking, allowing developers to focus solely on writing code. Examples of PaaS include Microsoft Azure App Services, Google App Engine, and AWS Elastic Beanstalk.

  For an example of PaaS, consider a startup company that is developing a mobile app that can use Google App Engine to host its backend, allowing developers to focus on the app's features rather than server management.

- **Infrastructure as a Service (IaaS):** IaaS offers virtualized network resources over the Internet, giving businesses complete control over the infrastructure. With IaaS, you can rent virtual machines, storage, and networking resources as needed. Examples include Amazon EC2, Microsoft Azure Virtual Machines, and Google Compute Engine. IaaS is best suited for businesses that need full control over their IT environment or want to avoid the capital expense of buying and maintaining physical servers.

  A large enterprise that uses Amazon EC2 to host its websites and run custom applications is an example of IaaS.

6

Selecting the right cloud service model depends on your organization's needs, the level of control you require, and your IT expertise. Figure 6-6 summarizes each of the could service models.

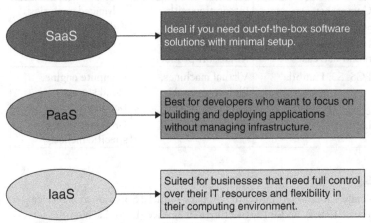

Figure 6-6   *The Three Cloud Service Models*

Choosing the Right Cloud Service Model

Table 6-4 provides a comparison of the features of each of the three major cloud providers. See also Figure 6-6.

Table 6-4   Comparing Cloud Services

Model	Definition	Use Case	Pros	Cons
Software as a Service (SaaS)	SaaS delivers applications over the Internet, managed by a third-party provider.	End-user applications like email, CRM, and collaboration tools (e.g., Gmail, Salesforce)	No need for hardware or software maintenance, accessible from anywhere, scalable	Less control over security and data, dependent on the provider's uptime and policies
Platform as a Service (PaaS)	PaaS provides a platform allowing customers to develop, run, and manage applications without managing underlying infrastructure.	Developing, testing, and deploying applications (e.g., Google App Engine, Microsoft Azure)	Speeds up development process, reduces complexity, developers focus on code rather than infrastructure	Limited control over infrastructure, may be constrained by the platform's capabilities and features
Infrastructure as a Service (IaaS)	IaaS offers virtualized computing resources over the Internet, such as storage, networking, and virtualization.	Hosting websites, backup and recovery, and storage (e.g., Amazon Web Services, Microsoft Azure)	Highly flexible and scalable, full control over the infrastructure, pay-as-you-go pricing	Requires in-house expertise to manage, can be more expensive if not managed properly

Cloud Models

Cloud deployment models define how cloud services are provided and managed. The four primary models are public cloud, private cloud, hybrid cloud, and community cloud. Each offers different levels of control, flexibility, and security.

- **Public Cloud:** A public cloud is a cloud environment offered by third-party providers like AWS, Azure, or Google Cloud. Services are delivered over the Internet, and resources are shared among multiple organizations (tenants). Public clouds are cost-effective and highly scalable, making them ideal for businesses that need to quickly adapt to changing demands without investing in on-premises infrastructure. Public clouds offer the advantage of low up-front costs, easy scalability, and no maintenance required by the user. The disadvantage is they allow less control over data security and compliance.

- **Private Cloud:** A private cloud is a cloud environment dedicated to a single organization, providing more control over security, data, and compliance. It can be hosted on-premises or by a third-party provider. Private clouds are best for organizations with strict regulatory requirements or those handling sensitive data. The advantages of private clouds are their control over data and security and their customizable infrastructure. However, they have higher costs and require management and maintenance.

- **Hybrid Cloud:** A hybrid cloud combines public and private clouds, allowing data and applications to be shared between them. This model offers the flexibility to use the public cloud for general workloads while keeping sensitive operations within the private cloud. Hybrid clouds offer flexibility, optimized workload distribution, and cost-effectiveness for nonsensitive operations, but they·can be complex to manage and integrate, leading to potential security challenges.

- **Community Cloud:** A community cloud is a shared cloud environment for a specific group of organizations with common concerns, such as security, compliance, or mission. It's managed and used by multiple organizations that share similar requirements. Advantages of the community cloud include sharing costs, tailoring to community needs, and fostering collaboration. Disadvantages are their limited scalability compared to the public cloud and their shared governance.

Table 6-5 provides a comparison of the four cloud models.

Table 6-5   Comparing Cloud Models

Aspect	Public Cloud	Private Cloud	Hybrid Cloud	Community Cloud
Definition	Cloud services offered over the Internet by third-party providers, shared among multiple organizations	Dedicated cloud environment for a single organization, either on-premises or hosted by a provider	Combination of public and private clouds, allowing data and applications to be shared between them	Shared cloud environment for a specific community or group of organizations with common concerns

6

Aspect	Public Cloud	Private Cloud	Hybrid Cloud	Community Cloud
Advantages	Cost-effective, easy scalability, minimal maintenance	Greater control over data, security, and compliance	Flexibility, optimized workload distribution, cost-effectiveness for nonsensitive operations	Shared costs, tailored to specific community needs, encourages collaboration
Disadvantages	Less control over data and security, potential compliance issues	Higher costs, requires management and maintenance	Complex management and integration, potential security challenges	Limited scalability, shared governance, potential conflicts of interest among participants
Use cases	Startups, small to mid-sized businesses, rapidly changing workloads	Large enterprises, organizations with strict security and compliance needs	Organizations needing flexibility to balance between public and private resources	Groups of organizations with similar regulatory or operational requirements (e.g., universities, government agencies)

Virtualization

Virtualization is a technology that separates the operating system (OS) from the hardware, allowing multiple virtual machines (VMs) to run on a single physical machine. Instead of each application or service requiring its own dedicated hardware, virtualization allows multiple applications to share the same physical resources. This capability is achieved through software known as a hypervisor, which creates and manages VMs on a single physical server.

By abstracting the hardware, virtualization enables more efficient use of resources, cost savings, and increased flexibility in managing IT environments.

Each virtual machine operates as if it were a standalone physical machine, complete with its own operating system and applications. However, they all share the underlying physical hardware, which leads to better utilization of resources.

There are many benefits driving virtualization:

- **Cost Savings:** Virtualization reduces the need for physical servers, lowering hardware costs and minimizing space, power, and cooling requirements.

- **Scalability and Flexibility:** Organizations can quickly deploy new VMs as needed without purchasing additional hardware, making it easier to scale operations up or down.

- **Improved Disaster Recovery:** VMs can be easily backed up, cloned, or migrated to different physical servers, enhancing business continuity and disaster recovery capabilities.

- **Efficient Resource Utilization:** Virtualization maximizes the use of physical hardware by allowing multiple VMs to run on a single server, reducing waste and improving efficiency.

Virtualization has revolutionized how businesses manage their IT resources. By allowing multiple virtual machines to run on a single physical server, businesses can reduce costs, improve flexibility, and enhance their disaster recovery capabilities. It's a key technology that supports cloud computing, server consolidation, and the efficient operation of modern IT environments.

Hypervisors and Virtual Machines

Hypervisors and virtual machines are the building blocks of virtualization. Together they allow multiple virtual environments to run independently on a single physical machine.

Hypervisors

A **hypervisor** is a software layer that allows multiple virtual machines to run on a single physical machine. It manages the distribution of the physical hardware's resources, such as CPU, memory, and storage, among the various VMs. This way, each VM can operate as if it were an independent physical machine, even though they are all sharing the same underlying hardware. The hypervisor abstracts the physical hardware from the VMs, providing each VM with a virtualized set of hardware resources. This abstraction is what makes virtualization possible.

There are two main types of hypervisors, each suited to different environments and use cases:

- **Type 1 (Bare-Metal) Hypervisors:** These hypervisors run directly on the physical hardware without needing a host operating system (see Figure 6-7). Because they interact directly with the hardware, they offer better performance and are typically used in data centers and enterprise environments.

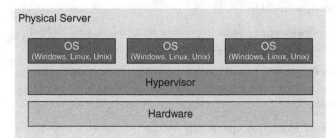

Figure 6-7   *Type 1 Hypervisor*

A use case example of a type 1 hypervisor is a large enterprise using VMware ESXi in its data center to manage hundreds of VMs that run critical business applications, ensuring high performance and resource efficiency.

Examples of type 1 hypervisors include

- **VMware ESXi:** A widely used enterprise-level hypervisor that runs directly on physical hardware, offering robust features for managing large-scale virtualized environments.

- **Microsoft Hyper-V:** A type 1 hypervisor integrated with Windows Server, designed for running and managing virtual machines in both enterprise and small business environments.

- **Citrix Hypervisor (formerly XenServer):** An open-source type 1 hypervisor that runs directly on hardware, known for its scalability and support for various enterprise-grade virtualization features.

- **Type 2 (Hosted) Hypervisors:** These hypervisors run on top of a host operating system (see Figure 6-8). They are often used for desktop virtualization, development, and testing environments. Type 2 hypervisors are easier to set up and use, making them ideal for individual users or smaller-scale projects.

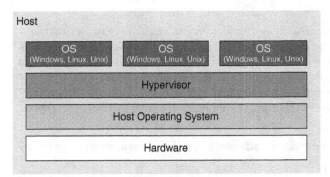

Figure 6-8 *Type 2 Hypervisor*

A use case example of a type 2 hypervisor is a software developer using Oracle VirtualBox on their laptop to run multiple operating systems for testing and development purposes.

Examples of type 2 hypervisors include

- **Oracle VirtualBox:** A popular open-source hypervisor that runs on various host operating systems, including Windows, macOS, Linux, and Solaris.

- **VMware Workstation Pro:** A widely used commercial hypervisor designed for running multiple virtual machines on a Windows or Linux desktop. It is available for free for personal use.

- **VMware Fusion:** A type 2 hypervisor specifically for macOS, allowing users to run Windows, Linux, and other operating systems on a Mac. It is also available for free for personal use.

- **Parallels Desktop:** A hypervisor designed for macOS that enables users to run Windows and other operating systems alongside macOS, often used for seamless integration with Mac applications.

- **QEMU:** An open-source hypervisor that can run on various host systems, often combined with KVM on Linux for enhanced performance, but it can also operate as a standalone type 2 hypervisor on other platforms.

Virtual Machines

A **virtual machine (VM)** is an emulation of a physical computer. Each VM runs its own operating system and applications, just like a physical computer, but it operates within a virtual environment created by the hypervisor. Multiple VMs can run on a single physical machine, sharing the underlying hardware resources.

To install a virtual machine on a hypervisor, you begin by creating a new VM through the hypervisor's management interface, where you allocate resources such as CPU, memory, and storage. Once the VM is set up, you proceed by installing an operating system, just as you would on a physical machine (see Figure 6-9). The OS operates as if it has dedicated hardware. After the OS is installed, you can then install applications on the VM, treating it just like a physical computer.

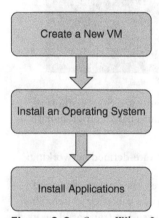

Figure 6-9 *Steps When Installing Virtual Machines*

Virtualization and Software-Defined Networking

Virtualization and **software-defined networking (SDN)** are closely related technologies that together enhance the flexibility, efficiency, and scalability of modern IT environments.

Virtualization abstracts the physical hardware into virtual resources, allowing multiple virtual machines to run on a single physical machine.

SDN takes a similar approach to networking by separating the control plane (the decision-making part of the network) from the data plane (the part that actually moves the data). This separation allows for more dynamic and flexible network management, which is especially beneficial in virtualized environments where network resources need to be allocated and adjusted quickly (see Figure 6-10).

Figure 6-10 *Software-Defined Networking*

While virtualization focuses on optimizing the use of physical hardware, SDN optimizes network management by centralizing control and enabling more automated, programmatic management of network traffic.

Here are the differences between traditional networking and software-defined networking:

- **Traditional Networking:** In traditional network architectures, the control plane and data plane are integrated within each network device, such as a router or switch. This means each device makes its own decisions about where to send traffic, based on its own configuration and protocols. While this approach works, it can be rigid and difficult to manage, especially in large, dynamic environments.

- **Software-Defined Networking:** SDN decouples the control plane from the data plane, centralizing the decision-making process in a software-based SDN controller. The controller communicates with the data plane across the network devices, directing traffic based on a global view of the network. This approach allows for more flexibility, scalability, and ease of management.

For example, in a data center with a traditional network, adding or reconfiguring devices often requires manual changes to each device. With SDN, the network administrator can make changes centrally through the SDN controller, which automatically updates all relevant devices.

Control Plane vs. Data Plane in the SDN

Network devices have a control plane and a data plane. In a traditional environment both planes operate on the devices (routers, switches, access points, and so on) themselves. In an SDN environment these planes are separated as follows:

- **Control Plane:** Typically regarded as the brains of a device, the control plane is responsible for making decisions about how to route traffic through the network. This plane contains Layer 2 and Layer 3 route forwarding mechanisms, such as routing and ARP tables. In traditional networks, each device has its own control plane. In SDN implementations, however, the control plane is centralized in an SDN controller, which has a comprehensive view of the entire network.

- **Data Plane:** The data plane is responsible for forwarding traffic based on the decisions made by the control plane, which is why it is also sometimes called the forwarding plane. Whether in traditional or SDN environments, the data plane operates on the network devices themselves, such as switches and routers.

Think of the control plane as the brains of the network, making decisions about where data should go, while the data plane is like the hands, physically moving the data to its destination.

Advantages of SDN

SDN brings several advantages to virtualized environments:

- **Improved Network Management:** SDN simplifies the management of virtual networks by allowing centralized control and automated configuration, which is especially useful in environments where VMs frequently move between physical hosts.

- **Enhanced Security:** SDN can implement security policies that follow VMs as they move within the network, ensuring consistent protection.

- **Scalability:** SDN makes it easier to scale virtualized environments by simplifying the process of adding or reallocating network resources.

Remote Access

As the digital workplace continues to evolve, IT support technicians are now expected to provide support not just in person, but also remotely. These tools enable technicians to troubleshoot, diagnose, and resolve issues on remote systems as if they were sitting right in front of the computer. With businesses expanding globally and remote work becoming the norm, it is important for technicians to understand available remote access tools and how to use them. Whether they are dealing with a server issue in another country or assisting an employee with a software problem at home, remote access is invaluable for quick and effective support. By using these tools, technicians can keep operations running smoothly, manage IT resources proactively, and prevent small problems from escalating—no matter where they or the users are located (see Figure 6-11).

There is no single remote access tool that fits every situation perfectly; each tool has its own strengths and is best suited for specific scenarios. While some tools excel in secure, enterprise-level remote access, others are more versatile and user-friendly for cross-platform support. The key is to understand the unique capabilities of each tool and choose the one that best aligns with the specific needs of the task at hand.

Figure 6-11 *Remote Access Technology*

Some common remote access tools and example use cases include

■ **Remote Desktop Protocol (RDP):** RDP, developed by Microsoft, lets users remotely control another computer over a network, providing full access to the desktop. It is good for IT teams managing servers or helping remote employees. For example, an IT support technician might use RDP to remotely fix an issue on an employee's computer without needing to be physically present.

■ **Remote Assistance:** Remote Assistance is a built-in Windows feature that lets users share their screen for troubleshooting or support. It's easy to use for quick help sessions. An IT technician could use Remote Assistance to guide an employee through setting up their email in real time.

■ **Cisco Webex:** Cisco Webex is a cloud-based platform for video conferencing, online meetings, and remote device management. It's highly secure and supports large meetings, making it a great choice for enterprises. An IT help desk might use Webex to set up and configure devices for remote employees who are working from home.

■ **TeamViewer:** TeamViewer is a popular tool that supports remote access across different platforms like Windows, macOS, Linux, iOS, and Android. It's user-friendly and secure, making it versatile for various IT support tasks. For instance, an IT support team could use TeamViewer to help employees in different locations, regardless of the operating systems they're using.

- **Virtual Network Computing (VNC):** VNC is an open-source tool that allows users to control another computer remotely by sending keyboard and mouse inputs. It's particularly useful for managing servers or providing support in Linux environments. A system administrator might use VNC to remotely update and maintain a Linux server in a distant data center.

- **PC Anywhere:** PC Anywhere, a discontinued remote access tool, allowed remote control and file transfer between Windows and macOS computers. It was commonly used by IT support teams for managing software updates and troubleshooting issues remotely.

Even though PC Anywhere is discontinued, some organizations may still have older systems in place that were once managed using PC Anywhere, especially in environments that are slow to upgrade. IT support technicians may encounter these legacy systems and need to understand how they operated to transition them to newer, more secure solutions.

Table 6-6 compares remote access tools, highlighting their primary features, strengths, and use cases.

Table 6-6 Comparing Remote Access Tools

Tool	Platform Support	Best Use	Pros	Cons
RDP	Windows	Remote IT support in Windows environments, remote administration	Full desktop access, security features	Requires configuration, firewall issues
Remote Assistance	Windows	Quick, straightforward support tasks in Windows	Easy to use, no extra software needed	Windows-only, limited ongoing use
Cisco Webex	Cross-platform (Windows, macOS, iOS, Android)	Secure, enterprise-level remote access and communication	Secure, integrates with Cisco products	Subscription required, complex setup
TeamViewer	Cross-platform (Windows, macOS, iOS, Android)	IT support to employees across different locations and operating systems	User-friendly, versatile, strong security features	Free version has limitations, may experience connectivity issues

6

Tool	Platform Support	Best Use	Pros	Cons
VNC	Cross-platform	Remote management in Linux or cross-platform environments	Customizable, encrypted connections	Slower performance, manual configuration
PC Anywhere	Windows, macOS	Legacy remote management	Robust management capabilities	Discontinued, outdated

Exam Preparation Tasks

As mentioned in the Introduction, you can customize your strategy for exam preparation. Suggested tasks include the exercises here, Chapter 9, "Final Preparation," and the exam simulation questions on the companion website.

Review All Key Topics

Review the most important topics in this chapter, noted with the Key Topic icon in the outer margin of the page. Table 6-7 lists a reference of these key topics and the page numbers on which each is found.

Table 6-7   Key Topics for Chapter 6

Key Topic Element	Description	Page Number
Section	Benefits of Cloud Computing	183
Table 6-2	Comparing Cloud Computing to On-Premises Data Centers	185
List	Cloud providers	187
Table 6-3	Comparing Cloud Service Providers	189
List	Cloud services	189
Table 6-5	Comparing Cloud Models	191
List	Benefits of Virtualization	192
List	Type 1 and type 2 hypervisors	193
List	Traditional Networking vs. SDN	196
Table 6-6	Comparing Remote Access Tools	199

Define Key Terms

Define the following key terms from this chapter and check your answers in the glossary:

cloud computing, community cloud, hybrid cloud, hypervisor, Infrastructure as a Service, on-premises, Platform as a Service, private cloud, public cloud, Software as a Service, software-defined networking, virtual machine, virtualization

CHAPTER 7

Security

This chapter covers the following topics:

- **Security Threats:** This section describes common security threats and definitions.

- **Security Threat Mitigation:** This section details ways to mitigate security threats.

- **Company Policies and Confidentiality Guidelines:** This section explains how company policies and confidentiality guidelines protect user data.

This chapter covers basic security threats and includes definitions to help identify commonly employed security threats. It also provides methods to mitigate these security threats. While cybersecurity is a large topic, and there is a dedicated exam, CCST Cybersecurity, for this topic, this chapter provides a more general overview that the IT support technician should know.

The chapter covers information related to the following Cisco Certified Support Technician (CCST) IT Support exam objectives:

- 5.1 Describe security threats to the end user, perform basic investigation, and escalate to the appropriate team

- 5.2 Recognize how to avoid becoming a victim of social engineering attacks

- 5.3 Recognize how company policies and confidentiality guidelines protect user data.

"Do I Know This Already?" Quiz

The "Do I Know This Already?" quiz allows you to assess whether you should read this entire chapter thoroughly or jump to the "Exam Preparation Tasks" section. If you are in doubt about your answers to these questions or your own assessment of your knowledge of the topics, read the entire chapter. Table 7-1 lists the major headings in this chapter and their corresponding "Do I Know This Already?" quiz questions. You can find the answers in Appendix A, "Answers to the 'Do I Know This Already?' Quizzes."

Table 7-1 "Do I Know This Already?" Section-to-Question Mapping

Foundation Topics Section	Questions
Security Threats	1–5
Security Threat Mitigation	6–8
Company Policies and Confidentiality Guidelines	9, 10

1. What type of threat actor is motivated by wanting to make a social or political message with their attack?

    a. Hacktivist

    b. Nation state

    c. Thrill seekers

    d. Insider threats

2. What type of person would *not* be considered an insider when looking at insider threats?

    a. Employee

    b. Subcontractor

    c. Customer

    d. IT staff

3. What type of malware is installed in an operating system's bootloader or boot files?

    a. Virus

    b. Ransomware

    c. Trojan horse

    d. Rootkit

4. What type of security threat is it when someone poses as a legitimate agent of a company to elicit information?

    a. Phishing

    b. Insider attack

    c. Unauthorized access

    d. Spoofing

5. What type of security threat is it when a legitimate website or email address is mimicked to impersonate the real one?

    a. Phishing

    b. Insider attack

    c. Unauthorized access

    d. Spoofing

6. How do you recognize if malware is on your system?

    a. Look for red flags in emails that look off.

    b. Use a AAA service.

    c. Look for URLs that are not spelled exactly correct.

    d. Look for slow performance.

7. How do you recognize if you might be the victim of a phishing attack?

    a. Look for red flags in emails that look off.

    b. Use a AAA service.

    c. Look for URLs that are not spelled exactly correct.

    d. Look for slow performance.

8. What security framework can help to identify unauthorized access attempts?

    a. AAA

    b. BBB

    c. CCC

    d. DDD

9. What type of company policy details what employees can and cannot do with company devices and networks?

    a. Employee ethics policy

    b. Acceptable use policy

    c. Network abridgement policy

    d. General contract

10. Who is the number one target of threat actors at a company?

    a. IT staff

    b. CEO

    c. Customers

    d. Clerical staff

Foundation Topics

Security Threats

In the late 1970s and early '80s the first computer viruses were discovered. However, these early viruses were more proof of concept than anything else. It was a demonstration of how code could spread. Fast-forward to the late '90s and the release and massive adoption of the World Wide Web. This changed everything. It was a perfect storm of file-sharing sites like Napster and a network that spanned the globe. In these early days of public Internet access, these malicious pieces of code were called *viruses*. Massive companies such as McAfee and Norton became household names with their antivirus software. However, as we progressed into the 2000s, the types of malicious software became more varied as did the people behind them. Today, we use the blanket term **malware** to describe all types of malicious software.

NOTE People often interchangeably use the terms *Internet* and *World Wide Web*. However, there is a difference. The Internet, the global connection of servers, routers, and switches, was developed from the United States Department of Defense Advanced Research Projects Agency, known as ARPA (now DARPA). This early network was named ARPANET and was the precursor to the Internet as we know it. It wasn't until 1991 when Sir Tim Berners-Lee released his invention of the World Wide Web to the world, free for humanity, that the Internet really took off. The World Wide Web had web pages that people could visit. You can still visit the first website at http://info.cern.ch/. This caused a revolution that we're still feeling today. So, when you visit a web page, you are using the World Wide Web, which utilizes the Internet to send and receive data. If you head straight to a game server on your gaming console, you are only using the Internet without the World Wide Web.

People Behind the Threats

To understand the various security threats out there, you need to look at who is behind these threats. The individual or group with malicious intent to disrupt a computing environment is called a **threat actor** (see Table 7-2). Their motivation tends to dictate what tool they use and how it is used.

Table 7-2 Threat Actors and Their Motivation (Adapted from https://www.cyber.gc.ca/en/guidance/introduction-cyber-threat-environment)

Type of Threat Actor	Motivation
Nation state	Geopolitical; these threat actors are often funded by governments.
Cybercriminals	Profit; these threat actors often came from traditional organized crime and turned their criminal activities online; Russian Mafia is one major such group.
Hacktivists	Ideological; these threat actors carry out cyber attacks to promote a certain social or political cause; Anonymous was one of the more famous hacktivist groups.
Terrorist groups	Ideological violence; these threat actors carry out cyber attacks to disrupt and advance their ideology/propaganda; ISIS/ISIL was a recent group that fit this description.
Thrill seekers	Satisfaction; these threat actors like to disrupt because they can. They are often individuals with very little actual coding experience, called Script Kiddies, who engage in this behavior because of the many prepackaged hacking tools readily available and no sense of ethics.
Insider threats	Discontent; see the next section for more details.

The United States' Cybersecurity and Infrastructure Security Agency, or CISA, describes an "**insider threat** as the threat that an insider will use their authorized access, intentionally or unintentionally, to do harm to the department's mission, resources, personnel, facilities, information, equipment, networks, or systems. Insider threats manifest in various ways: violence, espionage, sabotage, theft, and cyber acts" (https://www.cisa.gov/topics/physical-security/insider-threat-mitigation/defining-insider-threats).

An *insider* is what it sounds like—someone with internal access to an organization. This could be an employee, a subcontractor, or anyone with knowledge of the organization and/or physical access to the organization. While there are insiders who purposely sabotage a company, there are also insiders who do so unintentionally. For example, an employee who falls for a phishing email could be inadvertently exposing the entire company to malware through a malicious link. A friendly company employee who holds the door for a stranger fumbling for their keys might be letting in a criminal who now has physical access to electronic equipment. Unfortunately, this term was developed because it is one of the top ways organizations have been infected with malware.

It is especially important to note that the IT staff of an organization is often a key target for threat actors. From the IT support technician to the chief technical officer, these individuals often have greater access and permissions to key computer devices and services due to their jobs. You need to be extremely cognizant of this fact to not fall victim to any sort of social engineering or malware attacks.

Types of Threats

The following sections describe the types of threats broken into the categories Malware, Social Engineering, Phishing Attacks, Unauthorized Access Attempts, and Spoofing Attacks. This is not an exhaustive list but a general overview of major categories. However, you must note that often a combination of these is what a threat actor will use. For example, a threat actor will often use some sort of social engineering to have an end user or employee unwittingly install malware.

Malware

Table 7-3 describes various types of malware. Unfortunately, this is not an exhaustive list but a highlight of some of the major ones. Threat actors often use a combination of these to carry out their attacks. For instance, an end user might download a free VPN application on the Internet promising to help secure their privacy online—a Trojan horse. This application instead installs spyware or even ransomware on the end user's device.

Table 7-3   Types and Definitions of Malware (Not All Inclusive)

Malware Type	Definition
Virus	An executable program that must be triggered/installed by an end user; it damages the host computer.
Worm	A program that self-replicates and can spread itself over flash drives and networks.
Trojan horse	A malicious program that disguises itself as a legitimate program.
Ransomware	A program that encrypts all the files on an end-user computer or server; the program demands money, often cryptocurrency, to be sent to recover the files; many large organizations and government sectors are targeted with this very serious malware.
Rootkit	A type of malware that is installed in the bootloader or in the early boot process of an operating system; this makes it load and do the damage often before the antimalware program has even loaded; it often runs as administrator, or root, does the damage, or modifies system settings at boot, and then exits.
Spyware	A type of malicious software that tracks user interaction without consent or knowledge and sends that information to a threat actor; this can be keystrokes typed, webcam feed, microphone, and more.

Another type of malware not discussed in Table 7-3 but worthy of mentioning is botnets. A **botnet** is a type of malicious software installed on a machine that lies dormant until a specified time or trigger. The infected machine is called a *zombie*. This malicious software is extremely hard to scan for because most of the time it does nothing. It will often be scripted to check into a central server at a specified time/date. When that time comes, the script reaches out to the server to see if there are directions/commands for it to do. If there are none, it comes back later to check in again. These botnets can be comprised of hundreds of thousands of compromised machines. There are even instances where consumer electronic devices like TV digital video recorder boxes have been infected. The most common attacks with these botnets are distributed denial-of-service (**DDOS**) attacks. In these types of attacks, many devices all send Internet packets toward a specified server or IP address. This effectively overwhelms the targets and causes them to go offline. Threat actors have used this type of attack many times to disrupt companies and organizations, whether to prove a point or cause financial harm.

> **NOTE**   Botnets have garnered a lot of media attention because of high-profile targets they have taken down. This is why many hacktivists use this as one of their primary tools. Many end users' devices are part of a botnet, and they don't even know it. The reason is that it is very hard for malware scanners to detect them because most of the time the program is dormant. Most IT support technicians and cybersecurity researchers find botnets by capturing Internet traffic with a program like Wireshark to look for unusual traffic to random IP addresses at specific time intervals.
>
> For further exploration in this subject, research the Mirai Botnet.

Social Engineering

There is an inside meme among cybersecurity specialists that if you want someone's password, just ask them for it. While this thinking is absurdist in nature, it, unfortunately, is not far from the truth. **Social engineering** is a term used when a person manipulates someone into compromising security. While we use this term in the digital realm to reflect this psychological deception, it is really an evolution of the old con jobs committed by criminals throughout history. There is a reason there is a meme that if you show up to a company in a van with a ladder and a work vest and state you're there to fix something, you will often be let in. This is called **impersonation**. Social engineering is often the first stage of an attack and can be a type of reconnaissance to collect information.

7

Here are some examples of social engineering:

- "Friend" requests on social media from strangers claiming to know you; they gain a lot of personal information about you to later exploit.

- Fumbling for keys at the entrance of an organization's door hoping to have someone "hold the door" for you to gain physical access into a building.

- Posing as a legitimate agent of a company/organization to get sensitive information from you (impersonation); see the next section, "Phishing Attacks."

- An insider who gleans information from fellow coworkers for nefarious purposes; for example, many people use their pets' and children's names as passwords, so if an insider knows that Jane, a fellow employee, has a dog named Spot and her password shows four dots, then her password is probably Spot.

Phishing Attacks

In a **phishing attack**, a threat actor poses as a legitimate company or entity to try and gain sensitive information or access. This security term comes from the term *fishing*. When someone is fishing, they put bait on a hook (or have a lure) and cast it into a body of water to catch a fish. Which fish are they trying to catch? Any that will bite. Often, threat actors are more targeted in their phishing attempts because they have more personal information to tailor their attempt. This is called **spear phishing**.

The most common phishing attack often comes in the form of phishing emails. These emails will claim to be your bank or some other legitimate company and try to create a sense of urgency to get you to click the link. Threat actors know that virtually everyone with an email receives many **spam** emails, or unsolicited email advertisements, every single day. This is why they will try to lure you into clicking the malicious link by stating things like, "Your bank account has had unauthorized access so click here to verify your identity" or scare tactic phrases like that.

Once you click the link, several things could happen. One, a piece of malware is downloaded and possibly installed. Or you are redirected to a site that looks identical to the institution they are claiming to be from, say your bank. You log in to the fake bank page and now they have your username and password. Worse yet, the fake bank page harvests your username and password and redirects you to the legitimate bank site already logged in. You would never know you just got your information stolen.

Unauthorized Access Attempts

In an **unauthorized access attempt**, a threat actor tries to gain access to a system through social engineering, password spraying, or brute-force attacks. You will often hear of passwords being leaked on the Dark Web. Many large organizations have been hacked over the years. Threat actors often target the username and password databases of these organizations. While many organizations have their usernames and passwords encrypted in the databases, which adds another layer of security, some do not. These username/password lists are often sold on the Dark Web for use in password spraying attacks. In a **password spraying** attack, a threat actor uses these lists of known passwords and automated tools to try to gain unauthorized access. This attack is often successful because of how often people reuse passwords. It is much quicker to perform too than traditional brute-force attacks. In **brute-force attacks**, often called dictionary attacks, a threat actor utilizes a program that systematically goes through every combination of characters to crack a password. This is a slow process but can still be successful against low character count and weak passwords.

NOTE   The term *Dark Web* is used quite a bit in mainstream news. These are a collection of websites that can't be found using your traditional search engine; they use the top-level domain .onion usually. The sites exist on servers, like regular websites, but require a specific browser, usually a Tor browser, to access. This anonymity is why so many threat actors utilize these websites. On certain malicious Dark Web sites, there are virtual marketplaces for bad actors to buy and sell hacking software and passwords lists.

When you take a cybersecurity class, you will often use a password list called rockyou. txt to learn how password spraying works so you can take countermeasures. This list was released on the Dark Web and came from a hack against a company called RockYou that stored its users' passwords unencrypted. Ironically, it is now used to learn about the importance of strong passwords and database encryption.

Spoofing Attacks

In a **spoofing attack**, a legitimate website or email address is mimicked to get an end user to believe it is the real one. A phishing email might come from security@bank0famerica.com. While bankofamerica.com is a legitimate banking website, that email address used a zero instead of an *o* in the *of*. It is a small deviation, but one that could cause an end user to not notice. The threat actor would then have a website created that resembles the legitimate one to steal personal information. Unfortunately, if this approach is used in conjunction with something called *DNS poisoning*, which is beyond the scope of this certification book, the website address could be completely indistinguishable from the real one because the real website address is redirected to a malicious IP address through the DNS process. See the "DNS" section in Chapter 3, "Networking and Network Connectivity," for a description of DNS.

> **NOTE**   A new type of spoofing attack that has been making rounds in recent phishing campaigns is called *script spoofing*. It can happen because of the internationalization of domain names. For English speakers, Latin characters are used in domain names. When you go to apple.com, you are going to the Latin character set that spells that name. However, other languages use characters that look like a homoglyph of Latin characters. While completely different in meaning and language, the Greek O, Latin O, and Cyrillic O all look alike. Just like the Cyrillic character *a* looks like the Latin character *a*. See Figure 7-1 for an example of Cyrillic letters. Threat actors have been registering domain names with a mix of character sets to make them almost indistinguishable from the legitimate website names. Luckily, some browsers will show when mixed character sets are being used, but not all do. See this article for a proof of concept of this type of attack: https://www.xudongz.com/blog/2017/idn-phishing/.

Figure 7-1   *An Example of Cyrillic Letters*

Security Threat Mitigation

While there is no magic panacea to negate all security threats, end users and IT support technicians can use some techniques to help mitigate risks, as shown in Table 7-4.

Table 7-4   Security Threat Mitigation Tips

Threat	How to Recognize	Mitigation Techniques
Malware	Look for signs of malware infection that include slow performance, unexpected popups, browser setting changes, and unrecognized programs installed.	Educate end users on how malware infects systems through phishing emails, malicious websites, and downloads; do regular malware scans with a reputable up-to-date malware scanner; keep installed software updated; don't reuse passwords; and have strong, complex passwords (password managers, used correctly with a strong master password, can help with this).
Social engineering/ phishing attacks	Look for red flags in emails that include sender addresses that look off, generic greetings, grammatical errors, requests for personal information; be wary of an individual who is requesting personal information or information about your organization.	Hover over links to see where they are going (this can be problematic with many URL shorteners being used now); verify sender addresses (show the original email message in your email client to see where the email is really being sent from); call the legitimate organization directly from a known good number if being asked to take immediate action (e.g., call the bank directly if an email states you have had a security incident); educate the organization's employees on social engineering techniques so they don't fall victim; don't reuse passwords; and have strong, complex passwords (password managers, used correctly with a strong master password, can help with this).

Threat	How to Recognize	Mitigation Techniques
Unauthorized access attempts	Any system that requires a login should have a **AAA security framework** in place (authentication, authorization, and accounting) to help identify this type of attack.	Encrypt all sensitive data stored in databases or files stored on any network accessible device; check log files on a regular basis; don't reuse passwords; and have strong, complex passwords (password managers, used correctly with a strong master password, can help with this); use multifactor authentication (**MFA**) that requires users to use a password and another form of security like biometric input (face scan or eye scan, for example), text message code sent, or use an authenticator app that randomly generates a code that is timestamped to that server and is unique.
Spoofing attacks	Look for URLs that are not spelled exactly like the legitimate organization's name/domain name; SSL certificates that are nonexistent or not registered to the legitimate organization.	Look for URL typos; check the website SSL certificate to see that it matches the organization's name and is not self-signed; use a trusted DNS provider like OpenDNS that verifies DNS entries; educate users on what spoofing looks like.

Figure 7-2 shows an example of a phishing email. There are several suspect items in this email. First, the email claims to be from Geek Squad; however, the email address is from a Gmail account. Typically, businesses, especially large businesses, don't use Gmail as their From address. Geek Squad is a service from Best Buy, so the email address should be an @bestbuy.com address. Also, look for multiple random colors in the email. This is suspect because it doesn't look professional. You will often see spelling and grammatical errors in phishing emails as well. Most phishing emails will have a link or attachment to open. Don't click the link or open the attachment! It will often contain some sort of malware that can infect your system. The example in Figure 7-2 doesn't have an attachment or link but does have a number to call. The scam in this email is to call the number to complain that you never purchased this subscription. Once you call, the mining for personal information will begin.

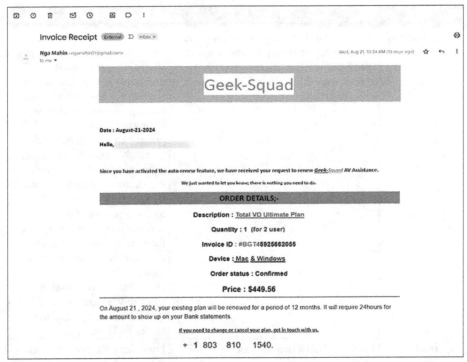

Figure 7-2 *Phishing Email*

Any company server or device that allows logins should be running some sort of AAA security framework service to help against threat actors. AAA stands for authentication, authorization, and accounting. Authentication means that only specified users should be allowed to log in to the system. Authorization means those specific users should have permissions set to only access the sections of the network they need to access. Finally, accounting means that all logins and data accessed should be stored in a log file to examine for suspicious activity or for review if an incident did occur.

Company Policies and Confidentiality Guidelines

To best help stop security incidents from occurring, every organization should have detailed company policies related to data security in place. These company policies should include an **acceptable use policy** that details exactly what employees can and cannot use company devices and networks for, **password policies** that detail complexity and rotation of user passwords, and **confidentiality policies** that outline steps to protect sensitive information (how the company protects employee sensitive information and how employees need to protect customer sensitive information). These types of policies should not only be in place, but every employee should undergo training on exactly what they mean. In fact, there should be ongoing training for all employees about how to recognize and mitigate security threats.

Because threat actors often target IT support technicians in particular, ongoing security awareness training including phishing simulations and training updates should happen at frequent intervals. All employees should be a part of this training, but IT staff in particular need to be frequently trained on security threats. There also needs to be a clear procedure in place for secure handling of user data and escalation steps for suspicious activity including whom to report suspicious activity to in a hierarchical structure.

Exam Preparation Tasks

As mentioned in the Introduction, you can customize your strategy for exam preparation. Suggested tasks include the exercises here, Chapter 9, "Final Preparation," and the exam simulation questions on the companion website.

Review All Key Topics

Review the most important topics in this chapter, noted with the Key Topic icon in the outer margin of the page. Table 7-5 lists a reference of these key topics and the page numbers on which each is found.

Table 7-5 Key Topics for Chapter 7

Key Topic Element	Description	Page Number
Table 7-2	Threat Actors and Their Motivation	205
Paragraph	Insider threats	205
Paragraph	Insider threats and IT staff as key targets	206
Table 7-3	Types and Definitions of Malware	206
Paragraph	Botnets	207
Paragraph	Social engineering	207
List	Examples of social engineering	207
Section	Phishing Attacks	208
Section	Unauthorized Access Attempts	208
Section	Spoofing Attacks	209
Table 7-4	Security Threat Mitigation Tips	210
Paragraph	AAA Security Framework	212
Paragraph	Company policies and confidentiality guidelines	212
Paragraph	Ongoing security awareness training	212

Define Key Terms

Define the following key terms from this chapter and check your answers in the glossary:

AAA security framework, acceptable use policy, botnet, brute force attack, confidentiality policy, DDOS, impersonation, insider threat, malware, MFA, password policy, password spraying, phishing attack, ransomware, rootkit, social engineering, spam, spear phishing, spoofing attack, spyware, threat actor, Trojan horse, unauthorized access attempt, virus, worm

References

Canadian Centre for Cyber Security, "An Introduction to the Cyber Threat Environment," https://www.cyber.gc.ca/en/guidance/introduction-cyber-threat-environment

CERN, "The Birth of the Web," https://home.web.cern.ch/science/computing/birth-web

Cybersecurity and Infrastructure Security Agency, "Defining Insider Threats," https://www.cisa.gov/topics/physical-security/insider-threat-mitigation/defining-insider-threats

Zheng, X., "Phishing with Unicode Domains," https://www.xudongz.com/blog/2017/idn-phishing/

CHAPTER 8

The IT Professional

This chapter covers the following topics:

- **Professionalism:** This section covers how to maintain professionalism while trouble-shooting with users.

- **Company Policies and Confidentiality:** This section helps you understand the nature and importance of confidentiality in the workplace.

- **Remote Access Tools for Troubleshooting:** This section describes tools that an IT support technician will use while troubleshooting issues with a client who is not in the same physical location with them.

- **Research Tools:** This section describes tools that an IT support technician will use while troubleshooting issues with a client.

- **Documentation Tools:** This section covers tools that an IT support technician will use while documenting problems and solutions for problems with a client.

Congratulations! You're almost there! This chapter covers some final topics you need for the exam and reviews some elements that you need to be successful as an IT support technician.

The chapter covers information related to the following Cisco Certified Support Technician (CCST) IT Support exam objectives:

- Interpersonal Skills

- 5.3 Recognize how company policies and confidentiality guidelines protect user data

- 6.1 Use remote access software to connect end user devices

- 6.2 Use appropriate troubleshooting tools to research an issue

"Do I Know This Already?" Quiz

The "Do I Know This Already?" quiz allows you to assess whether you should read this entire chapter thoroughly or jump to the "Exam Preparation Tasks" section. If you are in doubt about your answers to these questions or your own assessment of your knowledge of the topics, read the entire chapter. Table 8-1 lists the major headings in this chapter and their corresponding "Do I Know This Already?" quiz questions. You can find the answers in Appendix A, "Answers to the 'Do I Know This Already?' Quizzes."

Table 8-1 "Do I Know This Already?" Section-to-Question Mapping

Foundation Topics Section	Questions
Professionalism	2–5
Company Policies and Confidentiality	6–8
Remote Access Tools for Troubleshooting	1, 9, 10
Research Tools	11–15
Documentation Tools	16

CAUTION The goal of self-assessment is to gauge your mastery of the topics in this chapter. If you do not know the answer to a question or are only partially sure of the answer, you should mark that question as wrong for purposes of the self-assessment. Giving yourself credit for an answer you correctly guess skews your self-assessment results and might provide you with a false sense of security.

1. What is the purpose of remote management tools for the IT support technician?
   a. Remote management tools allow an IT support technician to see a user's screen.
   b. Remote management tools allow an IT support technician to shut down a remote user's device.
   c. Remote management tools allow an IT support technician to take control of a remote device to make configuration changes.
   d. Remote management tools allow an IT support technician to predict the future.

2. What is a key attitude that IT support technicians should maintain when dealing with frustrated users?
   a. Indifference
   b. Empathy
   c. Authority
   d. Strictness

3. What is the primary reason for being clear and concise in dealing with users?
   a. To save the technician's time
   b. To save the user's time and resolve problems efficiently
   c. To avoid misunderstandings
   d. To avoid humor and camaraderie

4. What should you focus on when practicing active listening?
   a. Your own thoughts and opinions
   b. The speaker's message and body language
   c. Formulating your next question
   d. Finding flaws in the speaker's argument

5. What is a key technique in demonstrating engagement and confirming comprehension in active listening?

   a. Interrupting the speaker to show you are following

   b. Paraphrasing what you have understood in your own words

   c. Taking detailed notes during the conversation

   d. Judging the speaker's message immediately

6. Why is it important to identify confidential data?

   a. To share it with other companies

   b. To safeguard against its unnecessary spread

   c. To make it publicly accessible

   d. To enhance company transparency

7. Proprietary data can be limited by which of the following agreements?

   a. Public service agreements

   b. Social media policies

   c. Employee handbooks

   d. Licensing agreements

8. What can be a consequence of losing personally identifiable information (PII)?

   a. Increased public trust

   b. Greater data transparency

   c. Identity theft or other fraudulent use

   d. Improved data sharing

9. What is the primary benefit of remote management for IT support technicians?

   a. Increased travel requirements

   b. Ability to monitor, control, and maintain systems from any location

   c. Limited ability to support distributed teams

   d. Increased downtime for repairs

10. What is one benefit of remote management for users?

    a. Slower service response times

    b. Faster and more efficient service

    c. Increased downtime

    d. Limited access to support

11. What is a knowledge base in the context of a help desk?

    a. An online library of information about products, services, or topics

    b. A physical library of books and documents

    c. A collection of user manuals

    d. A repository of employee records

12. Why is it important to pay attention to the quality of answers in technical forums?

   a. To collect personal stories

   b. To avoid technical discussions

   c. To ensure accurate information and solutions due to crowdsourcing

   d. To limit responses from industry experts

13. What role does statistical analysis play in predictive AI?

   a. It restricts access to data sets.

   b. It makes forecasts and personalizes experiences.

   c. It uses relationships between data sets to make predictions.

   d. It avoids machine learning.

14. What distinguishes generative AI from other types of AI?

   a. It avoids analyzing entire documents.

   b. It responds to queries in a human-like fashion.

   c. It restricts access to large data sets.

   d. It uses only individual words for analysis.

15. Why is it important for IT support technicians to remember the human aspect of their work?

   a. To avoid hard feelings and dissatisfaction among users

   b. To restrict AI access to organizational systems

   c. To limit AI decision-making capabilities

   d. To prevent AI from making security decisions

16. What is the purpose of writing a summary in the help desk documentation when resolving a problem?

   a. To include repetition and irrelevant information

   b. To prevent understanding of what happened

   c. To quickly inform future technicians of the issue

   d. To review the relevant parts of the software

8

Foundation Topics

Professionalism

Professionalism is defined as conducting oneself with responsibility, integrity, accountability, and excellence. It is critical that the IT support technician always be professional when working with customers and clients, whether that is in person, on the phone, or via email.

Demonstrate Professional Communication Skills When Interacting with Users

Users generally do not contact the help desk unless they have a problem. They are often frustrated that they cannot get their work done. Too often they take that frustration out on the IT support technician, or their frustration prevents them from being able to adequately explain the issues they are having.

IT support technicians must work around the frustrations felt by the end users to help them. Your mindset should be "Help me help you resolve the problem so you (the customer) can get back to work."

Some things to remember when working with people in a professional environment are ideas such as empathizing with your users, showing that you understand what they are facing and that you have a willingness to solve their problem so they can get back to their work.

Show confidence that you can resolve their problem or, if not able to resolve their issue right away, that you will be able to understand the nature of the problem and will be able to research and forward the issue to the correct person to resolve it.

Consider your audience. It is important to never talk down to your customer, but it is also important to prioritize the types of requests to ensure proper use of resources and timely resolution of mission-critical problems that might occur.

In a help desk environment, you will encounter various customer types, each with distinct traits and preferences. Understanding these types and how to interact with them can improve customer satisfaction. Table 8-2 provides some types of customers you might encounter and best practices for engagement. By recognizing these customer types and adapting your communication style accordingly, you can enhance the overall customer experience and resolve issues more effectively.

Table 8-2   Common Help Desk Customer Types

Customer Type	Traits	Best Interaction
The Anxious Customer	Worried about their issue, may have heightened emotions.	Be calm, empathetic, and reassuring. Listen carefully and validate their concerns. Provide clear, step-by-step guidance and ensure they feel supported throughout the process.
The Know-It-All	Confident, may challenge your solutions, often well informed.	Respect their knowledge and engage them in the problem-solving process. Offer detailed explanations and allow them to share their insights. Keep the conversation collaborative rather than confrontational.
The Silent Customer	May not provide much information or feedback. Can be difficult to engage.	Ask open-ended questions to encourage dialogue. Be patient and give them time to respond. Summarize what you understand from their issues to prompt further communication.

Customer Type	Traits	Best Interaction
The Impatient Customer	Wants quick solutions, easily frustrated with delays.	Acknowledge their urgency and prioritize their issues without compromising quality. Keep them informed about the progress and set clear expectations regarding timelines.
The Friendly Customer	Positive attitude, engages easily with the support staff.	Foster a friendly rapport and reciprocate their positivity. Use humor and engage in light conversation when appropriate. Ensure you provide excellent service to maintain their satisfaction.
The Confused Customer	May struggle to articulate their problem or understand technical jargon.	Use simple language and avoid technical jargon. Take time to clarify their issue and provide examples or analogies. Be patient and guide them through the troubleshooting process step-by-step.
The Angry Customer	Frustrated and upset, can escalate easily.	Stay calm and listen actively. Allow them to vent while acknowledging their feelings. Apologize for any inconvenience and work toward a resolution. Keep your tone neutral and avoid escalating the situation further.
The Repetitive Customer	Contacts support frequently about the same issue or topics.	Identify their previous interactions and summarize what's been done. Offer additional solutions or escalations if necessary. Aim to empower them with knowledge to reduce their future reliance on help desk.

It is important to be in control of your own emotions, even if your users choose to express their frustration in a less than professional manner. Continuing to be polite and professional will go a long way toward your being able to resolve issues that your users are experiencing. Their frustration should not become your frustration.

Honesty and kindness go a long way toward building trust with your users, and this trust then becomes the foundation of your being able to help them resolve the issues. This is especially true when the problems must be resolved remotely, since the users do not have the advantage of seeing you in person and working with nonverbal cues to help with the conversation.

Nonverbal cues are important in video and in-person communication. In fact, watching your users, and your users watching you, is sometimes as important, or more important, than the words that are used. You can often tell when someone is leaving out important information from these nonverbal cues. Paying attention to the nonverbal cues is an important step toward building trust with your users and their building trust in you. This relationship will allow for faster and more efficient solutions to the technical problems.

Adapt your communication styles to meet your users' needs. Some users will tend to avoid answering questions directly, instead rambling on and telling stories; in this case, using closed-ended, yes-or-no questions, rather than open-ended questions is best. Some users will tend to leave out important pieces of information because they don't realize it is important. Still other users are no-nonsense and will not allow for any humor or camaraderie. An experienced IT support technician will learn to evaluate each user type and adapt their communication style to match.

Be clear and concise in your dealings with people. Time is valuable, and you need to not waste time getting the relevant information and resolving the problems presented. That isn't to say that that you can't be friendly; it merely means that you need to be aware of the value of your users' time and not use it in a frivolous manner.

Active Listening

According to an old Irish proverb, "God gave us two ears and one mouth, so we ought to listen twice as much as we speak." We should remember it as we go about our IT support technician practice.

Active listening is a form of listening to understand. It is used in many fields but can be summarized as follows:

- Concentrate on the sender. Give your full attention to the speaker and their message.

- Listen for the intended message. Rather than hearing what you want or expect, strive to understand the speaker's intended meaning.

- Refrain from premature judgment. Avoid making swift judgments, especially if your relationship with the sender isn't strong. Observe their body language to gain insights into their attitudes toward the message. Observing is harder in a remote support environment; in that case, listen closely to the auditory cues that the user is giving you.

- Maintain focus. If the user veers off-topic, gently steer the conversation back to the original issue or concern. If a user has trouble staying on topic, use closed-ended questions rather than open-ended questions to help them stay on task.

- Avoid distractions and assumptions. Stay focused on the sender's words rather than letting your thoughts wander or making unfounded assumptions. Remember, they are only contacting the help desk because they are unable to get their work done, and that is frustrating for them.

- Listen fully before responding. Ensure you have heard and understood the entire message before responding. Active listening is a two-way process.

- Reflect and paraphrase. Reiterate what you have understood in your own words. This approach demonstrates your engagement and confirms your comprehension. This rephrasing of the user's issue is critical to ensuring that you have understood the user's issue and have been listening closely to their issues and needs.

- Ask for clarification. Do not hesitate to ask if any part of the message remains unclear. This will ensure accurate understanding and prevent miscommunication.

By practicing active listening, the IT support technician will solve multiple problems at once. First, they will be able to diagnose the actual problem more accurately and quickly because active listening allows the listener to more precisely understand what is being said by the end user. In addition, by practicing active listening, the IT support technician will be able to explain technical concepts to nontechnical users without dumbing things down. Too often, users are hesitant to contact the help desk until a problem becomes a crisis because they worry that they are going to be treated like they are incompetent or otherwise incapable. Users should always be treated as the partners they are, who just happen to need help desk assistance to solve a problem so they can do their work more efficiently and effectively. Take the time to simplify your explanations, explaining in nontechnical language, while not dumbing it down. In so doing, your users will feel that they are partners with you in solving the technical problems. This will make solving their immediate problem not only easier but will also make it more likely that they will contact the help desk earlier in the future before issues become a crisis. One strategy to help simplify language is to try to relate the issue to something the users may see in their everyday lives. Use simplified language without oversimplifying.

This is a good time to adapt and readapt your communication styles to realize the technical abilities of your users; many will know their specific software better than you as the IT support technician. This makes sense because they use the features every day and you are simply providing support, making sure it is up and running. They just may not know the technical language of the back-end processes. Finding nontechnical examples will help you help them understand your technical solutions.

These types of explanations will vary by user. Sometimes users will be technically oriented; other times they will be less technical. By using technical language where appropriate, you will be able to give the best service to your users and resolve issues more quickly and effectively. Since each industry has its own language and vocabulary, work to ensure that you know the specific vocabulary your users use every day so they come to see you as a trusted partner in their work, as an asset helping them do their work more efficiently, rather than seeing the help desk as a liability that just consumes resources without benefiting the bottom line.

As an example, if you are supporting accountants and bookkeepers, you would need to be at least familiar with terms such as *debit*, *credit*, *accounts receivable*, *capital gains*, *general ledger*, and *profit-and-loss*. You should know the difference between fiscal and calendar years. You would not need to know how to calculate any of those nor how the software implements these solutions; that's why you have the accountancy staff. But knowing those terms will allow you to understand what your users are talking about when they call for assistance. By being able to understand their language, you can better assist them and get them up and running more quickly when things go wrong, and they will see you as a valued partner in their success.

Company Policies and Confidentiality

As an IT support technician, you will have access to confidential company data. There are three main types of restricted data that you will generally have access to, each with its own requirements and restrictions, and it is important that you know how to identify this data and keep it private.

Confidential data refers to information that is not intended for the public to see. This includes (but is not limited to) data such as personally identifiable information (discussed further in the following paragraphs); information about suppliers, customers, and vendors; financial records; credit card numbers; management information; employee information; and passwords. Educational institutions would also have personal student information, courses, and grades and be subject to Family Educational Rights and Privacy Act (FERPA) guidelines. Healthcare institutions would be required to follow guidelines under the Health Insurance Portability and Accountability Act (HIPAA) regulations, which include patient privacy. Legal firms attend to attorney-client confidentiality. Most industries and countries have their own regulatory guidelines regarding confidentiality of data.

It is important to be able to identify confidential data so you can safeguard against its unnecessary spread within and outside the company, either accidentally or on purpose, and can mitigate damage should such distribution occur. Organizations should have trust protocols in place to limit access by individuals to data that is relevant to their jobs; IT support technicians often have access to the underlying systems to do their jobs though they do not always need access to the data itself. It is important to not abuse access and instead focus on the business need for any access you are granted.

Proprietary data refers to information for which the rights of ownership are restricted so that the ability to freely distribute the data is limited. This data can be protected by copyright, can be limited by licensing agreements that limit distribution, can be sealed by court order, can be limited by agreements with entities foreign or domestic that limit the distribution rights, can be under contract that limits distribution, or can be relevant to national security. Companies often hold proprietary data under **copyright**, **patent**, and **nondisclosure agreements (NDAs)**, and you might be asked to sign an NDA as part of your onboarding process. Regardless of the data's source, the important thing to remember is that proprietary data is restricted so that only those with permission can access and distribute it. The important point is to focus on the business need for any access you are granted and not abuse such access.

Personally identifiable information (PII) is "any representation of information that permits the identity of an individual to whom the information applies to be reasonably inferred by either direct or indirect means" (https://www.dol.gov/general/ppii). If a person can be identified by the information provided, it is considered PII. Name, address, Social Security number, employee identification number, telephone number, email address, gender, race, birth date, and other descriptors are all considered PII. Essentially, if a piece of data, as a whole or as part of an additional data set, will allow a person to be identified or contacted due to the information, the information should be considered PII.

Loss of PII can result in substantial harm to individuals, including identity theft or other fraudulent use of the information. Because the IT support technician has access to this data as part of their work, it is critical that they keep this information private and not abuse such access. Instead, focus on the business need for which such access is granted.

Remote Access Tools for Troubleshooting

Remote management allows an IT support technician to remotely monitor, control, and maintain systems and networks from any location. Because this capability removes geographical barriers, companies have been able to distribute their teams, moving to a "follow the sun" model of help desk support and enabling work-from-home for many of the technicians. Because the technicians do not have to travel to the user's worksite to update and maintain systems, productivity improves, especially when organizations have multiple locations and/or a distributed workforce.

Travel and downtime are substantially reduced, since the technician can make many repairs remotely rather than traveling to make the repair. Oftentimes the remote management software has proactive monitoring systems that allow the technicians the ability to predict when problems might occur and repair them before they are a problem. This capability reduces the costs associated with downtime and loss of business operations.

Remote management also allows for improved work-life balance for technicians, since they no longer must commute long distances to the distributed offices and other workplaces to make routine repairs or resolve user problems. They also can have flexibility in their schedules, especially when working for large organizations. And users benefit from faster, more efficient service from IT support technicians who can more quickly analyze and repair issues remotely.

Disaster recovery is made easier when management tools are remotely managed. Critical recovery operations can be performed more quickly, reducing recovery time and minimizing the impact on business operations.

By implementing all of these efforts, customers will be more satisfied with the work of the IT support technicians, and the technicians will be more efficient and satisfied with their job. It is truly a win-win.

Some of the leading software used for remote management of systems is detailed in the following paragraphs. This is not an exhaustive and complete list but is intended as an example of what may be on your certification exam and a list of what you may see when in the field.

Windows Remote Desktop allows an IT support technician or even a remote user to connect remotely to a Windows computer from a Windows 10, Windows 11, Android, or iOS device. It allows you to remotely access Windows 10 machines from anywhere, anytime, using almost any device.

Chrome Remote Desktop is similar in concept to Windows Remote Desktop, allowing an IT support technician to remotely access devices to see what users are seeing and provide direct support. Figure 8-1 and Figure 8-2 show the user configuration screens to access the remote machine.

8

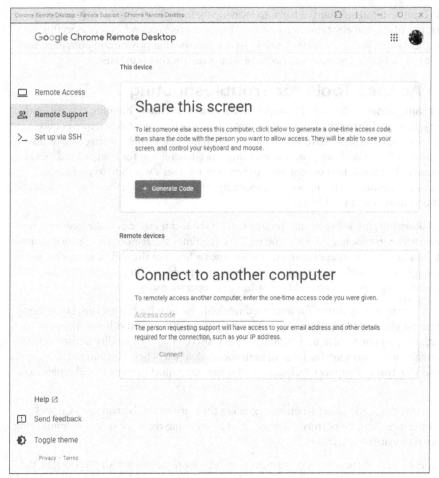

Figure 8-1   *Chrome Remote Desktop Sharing Screen*

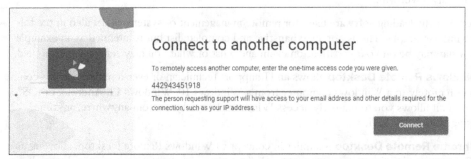

Figure 8-2   *Chrome Remote Desktop Waiting for the Code to Be Entered So It Can Connect to a Remote Device*

Like Chrome Remote Desktop and Windows Remote Desktop, **Windows Remote Assistance/Quick Assist** allow users to get support remotely. Windows Remote Assistance is configured in the Windows Settings Panel, and Quick Assist is available from the Windows Store. Once you have installed Quick Assist, your remote user can ask you to connect remotely with a generated code. They will be able to view your screen(s) and talk you through any repairs. Note that unlike Remote Desktop and Chrome Remote Desktop, with Windows Remote Assistance, the remote user does not have control over the remote computer. They can only view the remote screen.

Figure 8-3 shows the Quick Assist connection options screen where a user or IT support technician can get a code to Get Help or select to enter a code to help someone else. In Figure 8-4, Quick Assist shows a warning to the user that someone is watching their screen remotely. This is an important safety feature; it is important that users know when they are being monitored.

Figure 8-3 *The Quick Assist Options Screen*

Figure 8-4 *Quick Assist Warning the User That Someone Is Watching Their Screen*

Cisco WebEx is a messaging and collaboration tool that began as a teleconference tool and has become one of the premier tools for workplace collaboration and communication. Using WebEx, an IT support technician can use audio and video to communicate with an end user and allow the end user to show their screen in real time, allowing the technician to easily see the problem that the user is facing and to provide solutions. The end user can also give the IT support technician remote control access to their computer screen, allowing the IT support technician to make configuration and other changes quickly and easily in real time while the user waits, not requiring that the user wait for a technician to be dispatched to them.

TeamViewer is designed specifically to allow IT support technicians to provide remote monitoring and support. By monitoring the health of remote devices, patching as system patches become available, and otherwise being proactive in the management of devices, an IT support technician using TeamViewer will be able to fix problems before the end user realizes they exist. In addition, if the end user does contact support, TeamViewer allows the technician to connect with the end user to provide instant support. Unlike some other products, TeamViewer is designed for multiple types of devices, supporting mobile Android and iOS as well as Windows, Mac, and Linux devices, allowing for recognition of problems before they become a big issue. TeamViewer also allows for asset management, an important role when dealing with a distributed workforce, helping ensure that the organization never loses total control of the devices.

Virtual Network Computing (VNC) uses both the graphical user interface (GUI) and command-line interface (CLI) to allow the IT support technician to remotely control another computer. The keyboard and mouse input is shared across the network, and the resulting video is relayed back across the network. VNC is available for most computers and computer types, including most mobile devices. VNC is not specifically packaged as an end-user support tool but is important when managing servers and other devices that do not generally have a GUI installed or needed and that often sit in server cabinets at centralized locations which require travel to reach. By using VNC, an IT support technician can easily maintain these systems without the need for travel.

Symantec's PC Anywhere was a product that allowed an IT support technician to connect to any personal computer running Windows, Linux, MacOS, or PocketPC to take full and complete control. Users praised its ease of use: all an end user needed to do was input a password into the PC Anywhere client device, and they were able to connect remotely to the PC Anywhere–enabled device. As of May 2014, the product has been discontinued.

Many other similar products can be used to manage and support devices and users remotely. Among them are ZenDesk; Dameware Remote Anywhere by SolarWinds; Zoho Assist/Zoho Desk; Go To's LogMeIn, Resolve, GoToMyPC, and Miradore; AnyDesk; and a whole host of other products. For full control of a remote system with fewer other features, an IT support technician may work with Virtual Network Computing (VNC) or Remote Desktop Protocol (RDP), especially when working with Linux systems (VNC) or Windows systems (RDP). If a user only needs remote video conferencing with screen sharing, they may even be able to use products such as Google Meet, Microsoft Teams, or Zoom; like WebEx, these tools are primarily designed for communication and will not have the additional management capabilities of the other listed products. There are many other products in this space as well.

Research Tools

As an IT support technician, you will need to solve user problems, but you won't always know the answer right away. That's OK, especially when you are a new IT support technician. You will, however, need to know where to look to find the answers quickly and efficiently, because knowing where to look to find solutions is critical to getting the job done, and your users are waiting and can't get back to their work until you find the answer and fix their problem.

Knowledge Base

The first place to look is in your firm's own help desk manual, also called a **knowledge base**. A knowledge base is a self-service online library of information about a product, service, department, or topic. In this case, the knowledge base to access would be provided by your company and would include any information about configurations and past problems that have occurred on your company's systems.

You may be given a script to use when working with users; if so, that is a good first place to start. Help desk scripts are often written based on information in the company's knowledge base.

If the script does not resolve the issue, you will need to look further into the knowledge base articles provided by your company. If the issue your user is having has occurred in the past, a solution will hopefully have been recorded in the knowledge base, and you can apply that solution to the problem occurring now. As you resolve problems, your solutions should also be added to this knowledge base for future use by others.

Your industry may have additional specific knowledge bases that you can tap into. For instance, the software you are using may have its own knowledge base with articles about solutions to issues that users face. Access industry knowledge base articles to find and retrieve information on the problem and how to solve it.

Technical Forums

Many **technical forums** available online, not run by any individual company or software or service provider, are designed to help resolve problems. A technical forum, also called a tech support forum or technical discussion forum, is an online discussion website where individuals can discuss technical topics in the form of a post and messages; the post poses the questions, and the messages form the proposed answers. This **crowdsourcing** of solutions brings a wide variety of responses from industry experts and nonexperts, so it is important to pay attention to the quality of the answers provided. However, the wide variety of answers and the large number of responders correcting incorrect information will help weed out incorrect answers for you, and the information gleaned from these sources can help you figure out solutions to troublesome problems. As you become an experienced IT support technician, you will find yourself contributing to the answers in these forums as well, giving back to the very forums that assisted you when you were new. Figure 8-5 shows the home page of a technical support forum website. These forums provide crowdsourced solutions to common problems. Many such websites exist.

Search Engine

Online search engines can be helpful finding resources that will narrow down solutions. They can give you access to a wide variety—and quality—of resources that can help you narrow down the problems. For instance, if a user is getting a particular error code when accessing a piece of software and that error code is not in your help desk knowledge base, typing the name of the software and the error code into a search engine will often bring up an explanation of the error code, along with a possible solution. Where solutions do not exist, at the very least you will have a starting place in resolving the problem. Figure 8-6 shows a search engine search screen.

8

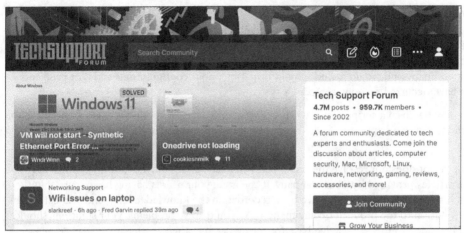

Figure 8-5   *Home Page of a Technical Support Forum Website*

Figure 8-6   *Search Engine Search Screen*

Artificial Intelligence

Artificial intelligence (AI) has become a tool that many people are using to help customers resolve their IT problems and streamline the work of the IT support technician. As with everything, there are benefits to incorporating AI into the workflow of a help desk, and some caveats as well. Figure 8-7 illustrates the relationship between human IT support technicians and the AI that they will work with to do their jobs more effectively.

Figure 8-7 *AI as a Partner with the IT Support Technician*

Predictive AI

Predictive AI uses statistical analysis to identify patterns and make forecasts. Because it harnesses machine learning, this prediction of the future can help an organization prepare for the future and personalize experiences for customers. Predictive AI analyzes huge data sets and uses relationships between this data to make its predictions. Figure 8-8 illustrates how predictive AI operates, using data sets to create relationships between data.

Figure 8-8 *Predictive AI Looks for Relationships Between Data to Predict Behaviors*

Generative AI

Generative AI, on the other hand, uses large data sets and then responds to queries in human-like fashion. These responses to what are effectively arbitrary queries can sound almost human in content and form, but they follow a pattern if you look closely enough. Generative AI analyzes entire documents, not just individual words, when looking for patterns. Because generative AI "sounds" like human speech, it can be incorporated into AI chatbots to better answer customer queries, process large amounts of data, and improve search queries.

However, there are some caveats. Sometimes the generative AI will see patterns that do not actually exist. Generative AI is only as good as the data input into it, and if this data is not accurate, the generative AI will be inaccurate. In addition, confidential data can accidentally leak later if inadvertently used in queries and when teaching the AI. Because generative AI is based on content that already exists, it can in some cases regurgitate and re-create that content, thus causing copyright, plagiarism, or misuse of intellectual property issues. Sometimes the information fed to a generative AI is deliberately false, causing false output. And finally, any bias in the training set will be magnified by the AI. Figure 8-9 shows a sample of what the generative AI can produce.

Figure 8-9 *Generative AI Can Be Used to Generate Documents That "Sound" Human, but Caveats Need to Be Addressed Along the Way*

AI can help improve efficiency and thus cost savings in the help desk and, if implemented successfully, can improve customer satisfaction. Support can be faster, and interactions improve as customer history and preferences are considered right away during the interactions. This allows for greater customization of the user experience than is possible with a human IT support technician.

AI Chatbot

The **AI chatbot** can handle a larger number of client inquiries simultaneously, thus freeing up the IT support technician to work on more complex inquiries and issues. Its use allows for faster and more efficient resolutions of simple and routine inquiries.

The AI help desk chatbot is scalable to larger support volumes. High levels of service can be maintained even as the workload is increased.

There can be cost savings as routine tasks are automated. However, not all tasks can be automated, and the human touch of an IT support technician needs to be retained for many clients.

The AI can analyze trends, seeing issues before they become huge problems and allowing the IT support technician to be proactive in pushing patches and other solutions to users who may not yet have the issue, thus preventing problems before they occur.

The AI can help write knowledge base articles. By analyzing the responses both to the chat and the IT support technician, the AI can draft knowledge base articles for final editing and approval, thus speeding the spread of knowledge throughout the organization.

The AI can summarize the articles in the knowledge base, allowing IT support technicians to quickly and easily find the relevant articles that will help them resolve user problems.

As IT support technicians are responding to their users, the AI can help edit the responses, providing feedback regarding language use and suggesting alternate wording that may be clearer. This capability can provide more accuracy and efficiency to the replies.

When help desk tickets are created, the AI can summarize the content of the tickets, thus allowing for more efficient routing, and once the summary is routed to an IT support technician, the technician can review the summary and be better prepared with a solution. If collaboration with peers is needed, that can be arranged more efficiently due to the information in the summary, without need of reading the entire ticket in advance.

AI can be a great help to the IT support technician. While not replacing the job, it can streamline the workload, allow users to help themselves to solutions, and predict problematic areas before they become huge issues. Going forward, AI will be incorporated in the workplace more and more, and those who feel comfortable working alongside AI will find it to be a useful member of the workplace of the future.

Limitations of AI

AI also has its limitations. While an IT support technician can query AI to research an issue, the commercially available AI such as ChatGPT has a limited actual knowledge base and will make up information that sounds right but is not based on actual knowledge. An IT support technician needs to be careful to not take at face value the word of the AI, instead taking pains to verify the accuracy of any links and information provided.

There also are privacy and security risks when working with AI. If the AI is not controlled by your organization, you do not know where your query data will be stored, and it may not be stored in a way your organization approves. Remember, it is your responsibility to adhere to the guidelines provided under your organization's confidentiality policy. Pay close attention when using AI that it will follow those same policies.

8

With the AI making decisions, pay close attention to whatever code it might create. While the code may run, it may also create unexpected backdoors and other security risks that open your organization's systems to hackers and other unexpected intruders. It is your responsibility as an IT support technician not to open any backdoors inadvertently.

Finally, it is important to not forget that the organization is supporting human beings in their work. Forgetting this will cause a lot of hard feelings and less satisfied users. Always remember the human being on the other end of the help desk call. You are here to help them.

Documentation Tools

It is important to document all user interactions, often in the form of **help desk tickets**. Doing so ensures that the users understand what was done with their equipment, that any solutions pushed to their devices are logged, and that any error messages and resolution are entered into the knowledge base for future help desk inquiries. If a problem cannot be resolved, the problem can easily be elevated to a higher level of IT support technician for resolution. Finally, if a conflict arises about an issue and its resolution, the documentation will help explain the interaction and its resolution.

The documentation should include information about the user raising the issue, ticket classification (which includes the type of issue), status (whether it is assigned, open, project, or complete), description of the issue, priority, and relevant screenshots. Oftentimes steps for re-creating the problem are included as well. Once the issue is fixed, the IT support technician will add comments about the troubleshooting steps and resolution steps that were used to fix the problem.

The completed tickets become the basis for an internal knowledge base of information that future IT support technicians can draw upon to solve future issues. As such, it is critical that you document in such a way that it is useful for future interactions, including any error messages, screenshots of the issue, detailed explanation of the problem faced by the user, any troubleshooting steps attempted including software and hardware changes made, and a detailed explanation of the resolution that finally solved the issue for the user. This writeup of the resolution is critical, since you may need it in the future if the same or similar issues occur.

In other words, your help desk ticket documentation becomes the next set of knowledge base articles that you and other IT support technicians rely on to resolve problems that other users have when they call in. It is critical that you take the time to accurately and completely write your documentation so others can use it in the future when resolving issues.

Be sure to include not just the description of the original problem and the troubleshooting steps you went through with your user but also the results you obtained at each step of the problem-solving process. This will make the documentation useful for future interactions both by you and other IT support technicians, with this and other users.

Summarizing Your Solution

One of the most important parts of the documentation is a clear, concise, factual, and comprehensive description of the problem. Review what happened. Isolate the important points of the interaction, both with the individual user and with the machine they are using. Include everything that is relevant to your understanding of what was really going on. Be sure to include the software that the user was using and any error messages the user received.

As part of your documentation, you should write a short summary. Take the pieces you have documented and draw out the most relevant parts: software in use, error messages, and so on. Be concise, eliminating repetition. This is an overview, not the full detail (that's in your full log). Your summary should be short, no more than one total paragraph, but should include enough information that a later IT support technician can understand what you were working on so they will know quickly if they need to read your entire entry to find a solution to the problem they are resolving.

Don't forget to record how you review your results, ensuring that you have explained in detail how you solved the problem and verified that it remained solved. This will help you and others to replicate those results in the future if needed.

Good luck in your journey to becoming an IT support technician!

Exam Preparation Tasks

As mentioned in the Introduction, you can customize your strategy for exam preparation. Suggested tasks include the exercises here, Chapter 9, "Final Preparation," and the exam simulation questions on the companion website.

Review All Key Topics

Review the most important topics in this chapter, noted with the Key Topic icon in the outer margin of the page. Table 8-3 lists a reference of these key topics and the page numbers on which each is found.

Table 8-3 Key Topics for Chapter 8

Key Topic Element	Description	Page Number
Paragraph	The importance of professionalism in the workplace	217
Section	Demonstrate Professional Communication Skills When Interacting with Users	217
Paragraph	How to use active listening to support your users efficiently and effectively	220
Paragraph	Keeping confidential data private and only within the audience for whom it is intended	222
Paragraph	Identifying proprietary data and keeping it private to those who need access	222
Paragraph	Understanding what personally identifiable information (PII) is and how to keep it private	222
Paragraph	How to use remote access tools to support users	223

Define Key Terms

Define the following key terms from this chapter and check your answers in the glossary:

active listening, AI chatbot, artificial intelligence (AI), Chrome Remote Desktop, Cisco WebEx, confidential data, copyright, crowdsourcing, generative AI, help desk ticket, knowledge base, nondisclosure agreement (NDA), online search engine, patent, personally identifiable information (PII), predictive AI, professionalism, proprietary data, remote management, Symantec's PC Anywhere, TeamViewer, technical forum, Virtual Network Computing (VNC), Windows Remote Assistance/Quick Assist, Windows Remote Desktop

References

Cloudflare, "What is Generative AI?" https://www.cloudflare.com/learning/ai/what-is-generative-ai/

Jha, B., S. Panda, and A. Mahto, "Technical Discussion Forum," *International Research Journal of Engineering and Technology (IRJET)*, May 2016, https://www.irjet.net/archives/V3/i5/IRJET-V3I5135.pdf

Lammertyn, M., "7 Ideas to Use AI in the Service Desk," March 19, 2024, https://blog.invgate.com/ai-service-desk

Pais, N. "What Should an IT Support Ticket Include?" *31 West Global Services*, https://www.31west.net/blog/what-should-an-it-support-ticket-include/

Tennant, K., A. Long, and T. Toney-Butler, *Active Listening* (StatPearls Publishing, 2024). https://www.ncbi.nlm.nih.gov/books/NBK442015/

U.S. Department of Labor, "Professionalism, Skills to Pay the Bills: Mastering Soft Skills for Workplace Success," https://www.dol.gov/sites/dolgov/files/odep/topics/youth/softskills/professionalism.pdf

U.S. Department of Labor, "Guidance on the Protection of Personal Identifiable Information," https://www.dol.gov/general/ppii

U.S. Geological Survey, U.S. Department of the Interior, "Proprietary and Sensitive Data," https://www.usgs.gov/data-management/proprietary-and-sensitive-data

CHAPTER 9

Final Preparation

The preceding chapters introduce the help desk concepts needed to pass the CCST IT Support exam. Among other things, we introduce interpersonal skills, documentation, the problem-solving process, LAN, operating system, application, hardware overview, cybersecurity, and other troubleshooting skills. If you have a photographic memory, you may now be ready to take the exam. However, if not, it's highly recommended that you spend more time studying. Reviewing the exam material will help you identify where you have room for improvement, fill in those gaps, and ultimately pass the exam with flying colors. This chapter provides recommendations for infusing variety and rigor into your exam preparation.

Tools and Resources

One way to concretize your knowledge and deepen your understanding is to get hands-on with the tools and resources this book mentions. While the CCST IT Support exam doesn't have many applied IT Support questions, getting hands-on helps make abstract concepts more concrete. It also lends some variety to the exam preparation journey. Here are some sample activities:

- Review the IP configuration options of your SoHo wireless router.

- Practice interacting with the command-line interfaces of Windows or Mac.

- Familiarize yourself with the Task Manager, System Information, and ipconfig commands.

- Look through system logs such as Event Viewer in Windows.

You can also supplement this book by perusing free online resources. These sources often go into more detail (and can be quite interesting). While the contents of this book cover everything necessary to pass the exam, doing "extra credit" can only help as you pursue future certifications and jobs. Following are some worthwhile resources:

- **The CVE database:** cve.mitre.org

- **The CVSS standard:** first.org/cvss

- **STIX and TAXII standards:** oasis-open.github.io/cti-documentation

- **The ATT&CK matrices:** attack.mitre.org

- **The NIST Computer Security Incident Handling Guide:** doi.org/10.6028/NIST.SP.800-61r2

- **Professionalism, Skills to Pay the Bills, Department of Labor:** www.dol.gov/sites/dolgov/files/odep/topics/youth/softskills/professionalism.pdf

- DHCP Overview, Cisco: www.cisco.com/en/US/docs/ios/12_4t/ip_addr/configuration/guide/htovdhcp.html

- DHCPv6, Networklessons.com: https://networklessons.com/ipv6/cisco-dhcpv6-server-configuration

- CISA's Cybersecurity Best Practices: www.cisa.gov/topics/cybersecurity-best-practices

Study Tips

This book is constructed to streamline studying and review. Consider using the following strategies to gauge your readiness for the CCST IT Support exam. Nothing is required, and you are encouraged to study in whatever way suits you.

1. Review the key topics listed at the end of each chapter. Ensure that you understand each concept and that nothing seems to come out of left field.

2. Check the key terms listed at the end of chapters. Can you explain each term in a sentence or two? Knowing the vocabulary is often half the battle.

3. Quiz yourself with the "Do I Know This Already?" questions. If any knowledge gaps are exposed, emphasize studying them.

4. Where memory tables are available, fill in the blank cells to test your memory of the material.

5. Take practice tests with the Pearson Test Prep software. This experience provides a realistic approximation of the CCST IT Support exam and is excellent preparation for the real thing.

6. Go through the CCST IT Support Blueprint at learningnetwork.cisco.com/s/ccst-it-support-exam-topics. A point-by-point review will ensure you haven't missed a topic and further reinforce concepts in your long-term memory.

One final note: Part of studying is knowing when to stop! Don't cram late into the evening only to start the exam tired and irritable. Get a good night's sleep, arrive at the testing center early (if taking the exam in person), and avoid having to rush and stress out. Beginning the exam with a clear, calm mind will benefit your exam score and the test-taking experience itself.

Summary

The tools and suggestions in this chapter have been designed with one goal in mind: to help you develop the skills required to pass the CCST IT Support exam. This book has been developed from the beginning to both teach you the concepts and how they're applied. No matter your experience level, we hope the many preparation tools, and even the book's structure, will help you breeze through the exam. Help desk support is a dynamic and engaging field, and we want the CCST IT Support certification to be your entry point to a career that never gets old. Good luck with the exam and all your future endeavors!

CHAPTER 10

Cisco Certified Support (CCST) IT Support 100-140 Official Cert Guide Exam Updates

The Purpose of This Chapter

For all the other chapters, the content should remain unchanged throughout this edition of the book. Instead, this chapter will change over time, with an updated online PDF posted so you can see the latest version of the chapter even after you purchase this book.

Why do we need a chapter that updates over time? For two reasons:

1. To add more technical content to the book before it is time to replace the current book edition with the next edition. This chapter will include additional technology content and possibly additional PDFs containing more content.

2. To communicate details about the next version of the exam, to tell you about our publishing plans for that edition, and to help you understand what that means to you.

After the initial publication of this book, Cisco Press will provide supplemental updates as digital downloads for minor exam updates. If an exam has major changes or accumulates enough minor changes, we will then announce a new edition. We will do our best to provide any updates to you free of charge before we release a new edition. However, if the updates are significant enough in between editions, we may release the updates as a low-priced standalone eBook.

If we do produce a free updated version of this chapter, you can access it on the book's companion website. Simply go to the companion website page and go to the "Exam Updates Chapter" section of the page.

If you have not yet accessed the companion website, follow this process by December 31, 2028:

Step 1. Browse to www.ciscopress.com/register.

Step 2. Enter the print book ISBN (even if you are using an eBook): **9780135403921**.

Step 3. After registering the book, go to your account page and select the **Registered Products** tab.

Step 4. Click on the **Access Bonus Content** link to access the companion website. Select the **Exam Updates Chapter** link or scroll down to that section to check for updates.

About Possible Exam Updates

Cisco introduced CCNA and CCNP in 1998. For the first 25 years of those certification tracks, Cisco updated the exams on average every 3–4 years; however, Cisco did not pre-announce the exam changes, so exam changes felt very sudden. Usually, a new exam would be announced, with new exam topics, giving you 3–6 months before your only option was to take the new exam. As a result, you could be studying with no idea about Cisco's plans, and the next day, you had a 3–6-month timeline to either pass the old exam or pivot to prepare for the new exam.

Thankfully, Cisco changed its exam release approach in 2023. Called the Cisco Certification Roadmap (https://cisco.com/go/certroadmap), the new plan includes these features:

1. Cisco considers changes to all exam tracks (CCNA, CCNP Enterprise, CCNP Security, and so on) annually.

2. Cisco uses a predefined annual schedule for each track, so even before any announcements, you know the timing of possible changes to the exam you are studying for.

3. The schedule moves in a quarterly sequence:

    a. Privately review the exam to consider what to change.

    b. Publicly announce whether an exam is changing, and if so, announce details like exam topics and release date.

    c. Release the new exam.

4. Exam changes might not occur each year. If changes occur, Cisco characterizes them as minor (less than 20 percent change) or major (more than 20 percent change).

The specific dates for a given certification track can be confusing because Cisco organizes the work by fiscal year quarters. Figure 10-1 spells out the quarters with an example 2024 fiscal year. Their fiscal year begins in August, so, for example, the first quarter (Q1) of fiscal year (FY) 2024 begins in August 2023.

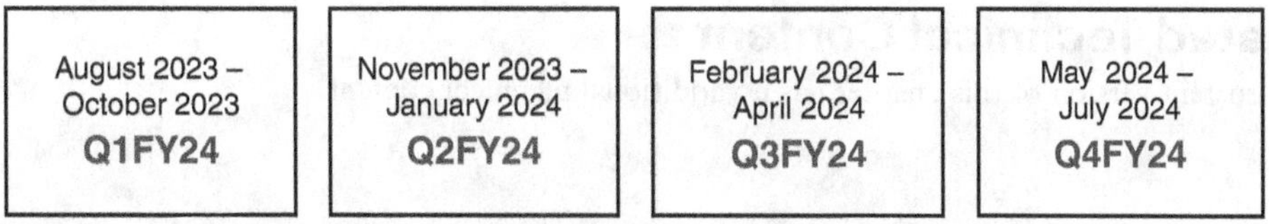

August 2023 – October 2023 **Q1FY24**	November 2023 – January 2024 **Q2FY24**	February 2024 – April 2024 **Q3FY24**	May 2024 – July 2024 **Q4FY24**

Figure 10-1 *Cisco Fiscal Year and Months Example (FY2024)*

Focus more on the sequence of the quarters to understand the plan. Over time, Cisco may make no changes in some years and minor changes in others.

Impact on You and Your Study Plan

Cisco's new policy helps you plan, but it also means that the exam might change before you pass the current exam. That impacts you, affecting how we deliver this book to you. This chapter gives us a way to communicate in detail about those changes as they occur. But you should watch other spaces as well.

For those other information sources to watch, bookmark and check these sites for news. In particular:

- **Cisco:** Check their Certification Roadmap page: https://cisco.com/go/certroadmap. Make sure to sign up for automatic notifications from Cisco on that page.

- **Publisher:** Page about new certification products, offers, discounts, and free downloads related to the more frequent exam updates: https://www.ciscopress.com/newcert

- **Cisco Learning Network:** Subscribe to the CCNA Community at learningnetwork. cisco.com, where you can expect ongoing discussions about exam changes over time. If you have questions, search for "roadmap" in the CCNA community, and if you do not find an answer, ask a new one!

As changes arise, we will update this chapter with more detail about exam and book content. At that point, we will publish an updated version of this chapter, listing our content plans. That detail will likely include the following:

- Content removed, so if you plan to take the new exam version, you can ignore those when studying.

- New content planned per new exam topics, so you know what's coming.

The remainder of the chapter shows the new content that may change over time.

News About the Next Exam Release

This statement was last updated in January 2025, before the publication of the CCST 100-140 Cert Guide.

This version of this chapter has no news to share about the next exam release.

At the most recent version of this chapter, the CCST 100-140 exam version number was Version 1.

Updated Technical Content

The current version of this chapter has no additional technical content.

Answers to the "Do I Know This Already?" Quizzes

Chapter 1

1. c
2. a
3. b
4. b
5. b
6. a, b, d, and f
7. a
8. d
9. b
10. b
11. c
12. a, b, c, and d
13. a

Chapter 2

1. a
2. c
3. d
4. a
5. c
6. b
7. a
8. d
9. b
10. a

Chapter 3

1. b
2. a
3. a
4. d
5. a
6. a
7. b
8. c
9. c
10. a
11. d
12. b

Chapter 4

1. c
2. b
3. c
4. c
5. a
6. d
7. a
8. a
9. c
10. b
11. b
12. a
13. b
14. a
15. a
16. c
17. c
18. a
19. c

Chapter 5

1. a
2. c
3. d
4. a
5. c
6. b
7. a
8. d
9. b
10. a

Chapter 6

1. b
2. c
3. b
4. b
5. d
6. c
7. b
8. a
9. c
10. b
11. a

Chapter 7

1. a
2. c
3. d
4. a
5. d
6. d
7. a
8. a
9. b
10. a

Chapter 8

1. c
2. b
3. b
4. b
5. b
6. b
7. d
8. c
9. b
10. b
11. a
12. c
13. c
14. b
15. a
16. c

Problem-Solving Process

The problem-solving process is a structured approach to tackling issues systematically and effectively. It begins with clearly defining the problem to understand what needs to be addressed. Next, detailed information is gathered to better grasp the situation. Identifying the probable cause of the problem helps in formulating a plan to resolve it. Once a plan is devised, changes are made based on that plan, and their results are observed. If the problem persists, the process is repeated to find a solution. Finally, documenting the changes and outcomes ensures that future issues can be resolved more efficiently. This methodical approach helps in solving problems thoroughly and improving overall problem-solving skills.

Table B-1 Problem-Solving Process

Step	Meaning
1. Define the problem.	Use open- and closed-ended questions to help understand exactly what the user is experiencing.
2. Gather detailed information.	Gather detailed information about the computer and other systems that the user is using, including hardware, software, and error codes.
3. Identify a probable cause of the failure.	Identify likely cause(s) of the issue that the user is experiencing.
4. Devise a plan to resolve the problem.	Decide upon a plan of action for resolving the problem with the user's system.
5. Make necessary changes to implement the plan.	Implement the plan. Make the changes to the user's system that you planned in the prior step.
6. Observe the results of the changes.	Review the results of the changes to ensure that the problem is resolved and does not cause any additional issues.
7. If the problem is not resolved, repeat the process.	Repeat the steps as needed until the user's problem is resolved.
8. Document the changes made to resolve the problem.	Document the changes you made and steps you took to resolve the user's issue. This step is critical to ensure that the next IT support technician who needs to solve the same or similar problem will be able to quickly and easily resolve it.

A

AAA security framework   Authentication, authorization, and accounting; a type of service that makes users who are logging in authenticate to make sure they should log in, gives them appropriate permissions for where they can and cannot go, and logs all interactions with the system.

About This Mac   macOS screen to gather details about Mac software, hardware, network connections, and more.

acceptable use policy   An organization's policy that details what company devices and networks can and cannot be used for.

accessibility   The design of products, devices, services, vehicles, or environments so they can be used by people with disabilities. This includes settings and functionalities that can improve the capacity of those who have different abilities to use the system more effectively and efficiently.

Active Directory/Azure AD   Microsoft's proprietary directory service that runs on Windows Server and enables administrators to manage permissions and access to network resources. AD stores data as objects, which can be users, groups, applications, or devices such as printers. AD is best for organizations that are centralized and have in-person employees. Azure AD is the cloud-based cousin that works for remote users and distributed teams. Both can be used together to manage hybrid organizations.

active listening   A communication skill involving full concentration, understanding, and response to what a customer is saying. It involves listening to understand, asking for clarification, and summarizing as you respond to ensure that you understand. This skill is crucial for accurately diagnosing and resolving issues.

Activity Monitor   macOS utility application used to see running processes and shut them down if necessary.

AD Group Policy   A type of policy that regulates user and computer configurations within Active Directory domains.

adapter   A device that changes plug type when using the same signal, whether digital or analog. It does not convert signal.

Address Resolution Protocol (ARP)   A communication protocol used to show the interconnection between MAC addresses and IP addresses that is cached on a device. This represents Layer 2 and Layer 3 of the OSI model.

AGPUpdate   An AD Group Policy Update tool that is similar to GPUpdate, but for Mac and Linux systems.

AI chatbot   A computer program that simulates human conversation with an end user through natural language processing. When AI chatbots are incorporated into the help desk, simple user queries can be addressed more quickly, leaving the IT support technician to tackle more complex tasks.

Amazon S3 Bucket   Online storage for large data sets. A bucket is a public cloud storage resource in AWS S3 platform. It is good for large blocks of files. Users and organizations can do data processing on files while on the S3 platform without having to download the data set. It also is good for long-term storage of data but not good for routine in-and-out transfer, like many other cloud-based storage providers.

amps   An electrical unit used to measure current. It is the volume of electricity that flows through a circuit.

ARM   RISC processor architecture mainly found in mobile devices.

artificial intelligence (AI)   Machine learning that is obtained from experience, adjusting for new inputs, and performing human-like tasks. The IT support technician may use AI as a tool to help streamline work and manage information more efficiently.

Automatic Private IP Addressing (APIPA)   A mechanism by which a device can set its own IPv4 address if it cannot reach a DHCP server. It will set its own address in the 169.254.x.x/16 range. It uses ARP packets to ensure that the address is not duplicated. These are not publicly routable addresses and are reserved for APIPA.

B

binary   Base 2 numbers, using the symbols 0 and 1, representing OFF and ON or FALSE and TRUE values. Because computers think in terms of OFF and ON, binary can be thought of as the native language of computers.

BIOS   Basic Input/Output System. A minimal operating system that allows a computer to boot and recognize basic devices. It performs a test of this basic hardware known as POST and hands off to the bootloader to boot operating system. It has largely been replaced by UEFI, but many people still refer to UEFI as BIOS.

BitLocker   Windows security feature that encrypts entire volumes. If an error occurs, Bit-Locker can lock the startup process until the user supplies a PIN or inserts a device with a startup key embedded. The PIN will be available from a user's Microsoft account if the user has logged in to the computer in the past.

boot sequence/boot order   A process that controls which device should be searched first when looking for bootfiles for the operating system. It can be modified and rearranged in the BIOS or UEFI of the machine or in Windows if using UEFI.

botnet   Malicious software installed on a device that lies dormant until a specified time/date. It checks in with a central server for directions. An infected machine is called a zombie.

Box   A cloud storage solution where you can store files, documents, and photos and access them from any device. It also can be used for collaboration; it emphasizes secure sharing with other users.

brightness   The maximum amount of light emitted by the screen. Higher brightness means more light and brighter image. This setting also impacts color representation and visibility: lower brightness gets darker; more brightness gets lighter.

brute-force attack   Often called a dictionary attack. An attack that occurs when a threat actor utilizes a program that systematically goes through every combination of characters to crack a password.

C

cache   Memory and/or hard drive space within an operating system, especially web browsers. It is used for high-speed retrieval of data. It is used to speed load times, especially of common elements of web pages such as header images. If web browsing is interrupted or web pages are not loading correctly, emptying the cache often helps.

caption   A transcription of spoken words into text. In Windows, automatic captions capture conversations, whether in person or remote, and provide captions for the conversations onto the screen in near real time.

chipset   A set of components on the motherboard used to communicate between the CPU and other devices such as RAM, graphics card, and USB. They are traditionally separated into Northbridge and Southbridge chipsets.

Chrome Remote Desktop   Software tool similar to Windows Remote Desktop. It allows an IT support technician or other remote user to connect remotely and gain access anywhere, anytime to manage the device.

Cisco WebEx   A messaging and collaboration tool that began as a teleconference/telepresence tool for workplace collaboration. An IT support technician can communicate using audio and video and see the user's end device in real time, and even be given remote control access to make changes to the remote system.

CLI   Command-line interface. A user interface to an operating system that is text-based and requires the user to input commands to interact with the computer.

cloud computing   The delivery of computing services—such as servers, storage, databases, networking, and software—over the Internet (the cloud) to provide faster innovation and flexible resources.

collaboration   The act of working with another person or group of people to accomplish a task. Collaboration is a critical skill in the modern workplace.

collaboration applications   A type of software that allows teams to work together on a project, share information, and communicate with one another in real time, regardless of physical location.

color filter   A Windows tool that changes the color palette on the screen to help you distinguish between things that differ only by color. It can be used by those with color deficits to make the screen more readable.

community cloud   A cloud infrastructure shared by multiple organizations with similar requirements, often managed by one or more of the participating organizations or by a third party.

confidential data   Information not intended for the public to see. It includes personally identifiable information (PII); information about suppliers, customers, and vendors; credit card numbers; financial records; management information; passwords; and employee information. You should keep this data private.

confidentiality policy   An organization's policy that details how sensitive information is stored and used.

conflict resolution   The process of resolving disputes or misunderstandings between customers and technicians, often involving negotiation and problem-solving skills.

Console   A macOS utility app to view system logs.

Contrast Themes   A small palette of colors with high contrast to one another that can help make elements of the user interface easier to see, reduce eye strain, improve text readability, and otherwise make the device more usable.

Control Panel   A unified location in Windows where applets are stored, each of which enables the user to view or change system settings. These include making changes to hardware, software, user accounts, accessibility options, and so on.

converter   A device that changes plug type when using different signals, whether digital to analog or vice versa. It requires power.

copyright   A type of intellectual property that protects original works of authorship. Once an original work is created, it is covered under copyright. It limits who can duplicate, display, and/ or distribute the work.

crowdsourcing   The process of obtaining information or input by enlisting the services of a large number of people, either paid or unpaid, via the Internet.

D

DDOS   Distributed denial-of-service. A type of attack that occurs when many computers send packets to one IP address to overwhelm it and throw it offline. It is often the primary attack type of a botnet. See also *Botnet*.

decimal   Base 10 numbers, using the symbols 0 1 2 3 4 5 6 7 8 9 to represent the values 0 through 9. It is seen in dotted decimal notation with IPv4.

default gateway   The router on a network that a device uses to forward packets to other networks when those packets are not on the local network of the device. A device must have a default gateway configured in order to reach devices outside of its local network.

Device Manager   A Windows setting page that displays information about each device connected to a computer. It is a helpful tool when looking for missing hardware drivers.

DHCP lease   The temporary assignment of an IP address to a device on a network, from a DHCP server's pool of available IP addresses. After the lease time expires, the device either needs to renew the lease, or the IP address returns to the pool for reallocation to a new device.

DHCPv6   A network protocol that allows IPv6 hosts to receive IPv6 addresses, IP prefixes, default routes, local segment MTU, and other configuration data to operate. This is substantially more information than a DHCP server can provide under an IPv4 environment.

Disk utility   A program in macOS to do disk utility operations such manage partitions, erase disks, and more.

display/monitor   A device that displays video output from computers. It can be portable or sit on a desktop or mounted on a wall. Displays are configured in the Windows Display Settings dialog box.

Display Settings   A Windows Control Panel where changes to displays are made. Such changes include scale, color calibration, resolution, and location in relation to other monitors.

DisplayPort   A digital port that can transmit both audio and video.

distribution group   An Active Directory group used to organize users to send common messages or emails.

documentation   The process of recording steps, solutions, and procedures related to help desk support, ensuring that information is available for future reference and knowledge sharing.

domain controller   An Active Directory server that is responsible for managing network and identity security requests.

domain local group   An Active Directory group that can include users from multiple parts of the AD domain. This group is used to allow access to local resources such as printers.

Domain Name Services (DNS)   A service that translates IP addresses to domain names on the Internet. Think of it as the phone book for the Internet.

dotted decimal notation   In IPv4, a way of writing the 32 binary bits as 4 octets (similar to bytes) in decimal numbers, separated by periods. A valid dotted decimal address would be 209.165.200.225.

driver   A software component that translates the raw input from the hardware to the operating system or translates output from the operating system to the hardware.

Dropbox   A cloud storage solution where you can store files, documents, and photos and access them from any device. It also can be used for collaboration.

DVI   A 24-pin video port. DVI-I can carry both analog and digital signals on separate pins; DVI-D is pure digital.

dynamic group   A type of Active Directory group that automatically adds and removes users based on criteria that may change on a fluctuating basis.

Dynamic Host Configuration Protocol (DHCP)   A network management tool for automatically assigning IP addresses, subnet masks, default gateways, and other information to host devices. It works under IPv4 and IPv6 with some differences and options.

E

empathy   The ability to understand and share the feelings of others, helping help desk technicians connect with users and address their concerns more effectively.

ergnonomics   The study of engineering and designing or products and systems to help people—for example, a chair to help promote better posture.

ESD   Electrostatic Discharge. Static electricity that can cause damage to computer components.

Event Viewer   A Windows tool that shows the events of the system. It contains Windows logs of events of note, which can be used to trace issues to their origination.

F

facial recognition   A way of confirming the identity using a user's face.

FIDO (Fast IDentity Online)   Open and free authentication standards provided by FIDO Alliance to reduce reliance on passwords. They are designed to protect security and privacy, and private keys and biometrics never leave a person's device.

FileVault Disk Encryption   Whole disk encryption program for macOS; a password must be entered to see the files even if the drive is physically removed.

fingerprint recognition   The process of verification of a person's identity by comparing their fingerprints with previously recorded samples.

firewall   A network security device that monitors network traffic (incoming and outgoing) based on a defined set of rules, and permits or denies based on those rules.

five nines   A term used to describe 99.999 percent system uptime, representing a high level of reliability often used as a performance goal in IT service agreements.

flashing   Updating firmware of your BIOS.

Fully Qualified Domain Name (FQDN)   An exact and precise location-defined domain name, where all elements of the domain name are listed and defined in DNS. For an individual device, this means that the device and its location are known to DNS.

G

Gatekeeper   Security technology on macOS that allows installation of programs only from the App Store or from registered developers.

generative AI   AI that is capable of generating text, images, videos, and other data that mimics human-created artifacts.

gesture   A translated movement on screen or trackpad. In Windows, the movements are translated into commands for the system. See Table 4-2 and Table 4-3 for a list of common gestures.

global group   High-level group in the AD domain. Subgroups further define the roles of each user or computer in the domain.

Google Drive   A service that can be used to store files online, share, and collaborate. It is integrated with Google Suite, which includes Docs, Sheets, and Slides. Google Drive can be used to back up your computer if set up correctly.

GPU   Graphics processing unit. The processor responsible for outputting video to a monitor; it can be integrated with the CPU or will exist in a separate graphics/video expansion card.

GPUpdate   AD Group Policy Update. It forces an update to the group policies on all connected devices without waiting for the system to do it based on the built-in timers.

GUI   Graphical user interface. A user interface to an operating system with graphical elements such as icons, buttons, and menus; input devices such as a mouse or touch interface are a primary way to interact with a GUI.

H

hard drive   A mechanical, magnetic storage device that is nonvolatile and meant for long-term storage.

HDMI   High-Definition Multimedia Interface. A digital port that can transmit both audio and video.

help desk   A centralized service team that provides technical support and troubleshooting assistance to users within an organization, often handling software, hardware, and network issues.

help desk ticket   An automated request for tracking and logging customer service requests. When a user needs assistance from the IT support technician, a ticket is created; when the IT support technician finishes the task, they log the details of the solution and close the ticket. That closed ticket becomes an item in the organization's knowledge base.

hexadecimal   Base 16 numbers, using the symbols 0 1 2 3 4 5 6 7 8 9 A B C D E F to represent the values 0 through 15. When used in networking, each hexadecimal number represents one nibble (4 bits). Hexadecimal is used when writing IPv6 numbers.

hostname (host name)   A unique label assigned to a device connected to a computer network. This may or may not be used by the DNS servers to identify the device on the Internet.

hybrid cloud   A combination of public and private cloud environments that allows data and applications to be shared between them, offering flexibility and a balance of control and cost-effectiveness.

hypervisor   A software layer that enables virtualization by allowing multiple virtual machines (VMs) to run on a single physical server, managing the allocation of resources to each VM.

I

ICMP echo request/reply   When a ping is sent, an ICMP echo request is sent. The receiving device will reply with an ICMP echo reply.

iDrive's Cloud Drive   A cloud storage solution where you can store files, documents, and photos and access them from any device. It also can be used for collaboration.

ifconfig   A UNIX command-line utility to view and configure network interfaces.

impersonation   The act of pretending to be someone you're not. It is often used in social engineering and phishing attacks. See also *social engineering* and *phishing attack*.

Infrastructure as a Service (IaaS)   A cloud computing model that provides virtualized computing resources over the Internet, such as virtual machines, storage, and networks, offering flexibility and scalability.

input/output device   A device that can both feed information to the computer (an input device) while also sending out information from the computer to a device (an output device). For example, a touchscreen monitor is an input/output device because it outputs graphics but inputs touch responses.

insider threat   A threat coming from someone inside an organization with internal access; it can be intentional or unintentional insider threat.

interface   How a device communicates; it can be hardware or software. See also *input/output device*.

Internet Control Message Protocol (ICMP)   One of the supporting protocols within the IP suite, used by network devices to send error messages and other operational information. It operates at Layer 3 of the OSI model or the Internet layer in the TCP/IP model.

IP address   A unique numerical address that identifies a device on the Internet or a local network.

ipconfig   Internet Protocol Configuration. A command-line utility used to see the Internet protocol and other information about configured network cards on a Windows device.

iproute2   A collection of utilities for controlling TCP/IP networking and connections on Linux systems. It replaces older tools such as **ifconfig** with newer ones such as **ss** and **ip**.

IPv4   Internet Protocol, version 4. The first version of the Internet Protocol (IP) released to the public. It uses 32 binary bits written as four groups of decimal numbers separated by periods, referred to as dotted decimal notation. It is being replaced by IPv6 due to running out of addresses.

IPv6   Internet Protocol, version 6. The newest version of the Internet Protocol (IP) released to the public. It uses 128 binary bits, written as eight groups of four hexadecimal digits separated by colons.

K

key performance indicators (KPIs)   Measurable metrics used to evaluate the efficiency and effectiveness of help desk operations, such as ticket resolution time or customer satisfaction scores.

Keychain access   A program on macOS and iOS that stores usernames, passwords, and account information in a locally encrypted file and supports iCloud Keychain with end-to-end encryption to the cloud.

knowledge base   An online library of solved problems and solutions about a product, service, department, or topic, kept by organizations and software firms to assist IT support technicians who are attempting to resolve user problems. This searchable library includes the problems, error codes, and other information to help find the problems, and also includes the solutions to the problems.

L

language pack   Additional languages available for your operating system. By installing a language pack, you can view menus, dialog boxes, and supported apps and websites in the new language, and dictionaries will be available when you are editing documents. Note that it does not translate documents or words by default.

LGA   Land Grid Array. A CPU socket type where the pins are on the motherboard and not the CPU.

local area network (LAN)   A collection of devices connected together in one physical location such as a building, office, or home, and under control of one organization. A defining characteristic is that they are in a single, limited area.

local group   A group in which you can access resources on the local device only. It is used to store configurations for devices that are not part of AD at all.

localhost   A hostname referencing the current computer. The name is reserved for the loopback address. In general, in DNS the name localhost refers to IPv4 address 127.0.0.1 and IPv6 address ::1.

lock/unlock user account   When a user attempts to log in but is unsuccessful, after a certain number of tries, their account will be locked and must be unlocked by the administrator. Until the account is unlocked, no one can log in to that account.

loopback   A virtual network interface that is used to test network connections and through which data bound for the same machine can be routed. Any traffic sent to the loopback IP address is immediately passed back up the network software stack as if it had been received from another device. Generally, these get the IPv4 address of 127.0.0.1 and/or IPv6 address ::1/128.

M

M.2   A new form factor for storage devices that allows the M.2 drive to be directly mounted to the motherboard with no additional data or power cables needed. It can be SSD or the faster NVMe protocol.

MAC address   Medium Access Control address. A physical address that gives each physical address its own OSI Layer 2 address. The MAC address is not routable. Sometimes it is called a burned-in address.

malware   A general term for any malicious software including viruses, worms, ransomware, root kits, and more.

Microsoft OneDrive   A service which provides personal or business storage that comes with MS Office. It can be used to store documents, photos, and other files in the cloud, share, and collaborate. It is the default location for Office 365 documents unless changed by the user or Active Directory administrator, and can be used to back up your computer if set up correctly.

Microsoft Store/App Store/Marketplace   Originally an app store for Windows, now offers other products such as games, media, and so on, but still focuses on apps for Windows. Apps must be certified for inclusion in the store.

mono audio/stereo audio   Mono audio is limited to one audio channel (which provides the same sound out of all the speakers); stereo sound uses two audio channels (left and right have different sound). If your device has one only speaker, you need to listen to mono audio. Sometimes this adjusts manually; other times you will need to set mono or stereo dynamically.

motherboard   Also called mainboard; a large circuit board that is foundational for other components to connect and communicate through in a computer. The processor is installed on this board.

multifactor authentication (MFA)   A multistep account login technique that requires the user to provide a password and enter information from another form of verification such as a biometric input (face scan, fingerprint scan, and so on), a text message with a unique code sent, or a random time-synced code from an authenticator app. It represents something you know, something you have, and something you are.

N

neighbor advertisement   Messages that are used to respond to neighbor solicitation messages. If sent unsolicited, they provide new information quickly to all known neighbor devices.

Neighbor Discovery Protocol (NDP)   ARP and ICMP Router Discovery and Router Redirect protocols.

neighbor solicitation   Messages that determine the link-layer addresses of neighbor devices. They also verify that neighbor devices are still reachable and for duplicate address detection.

netstat (network statistics)   A command-line utility that displays network protocol statistics and network status. Information about routing tables and interfaces, along with TCP and UDP, is available. This tool allows the user to see all network connections in one place for ease of troubleshooting.

Network Address Translation (NAT)   A service that enables private IP networks to use the public Internet. NAT translates the private IP addresses to public IP addresses before sending them to external networks. This usually happens at the network edge.

next-generation firewall (NGFW)   A device that expands upon the rules-based firewalls, looking for patterns that become suspicious over time. They pair with application awareness, intrusion prevention, threat intelligence, and techniques to address evolving threats to see these new problems and prevent them before they occur.

nondisclosure agreement (NDA)   A legally enforceable contract to not disclose confidential or other proprietary data until after a specific period of time has elapsed. By signing an NDA, both the owner of protected information and recipient of that information agree to protect the confidential information provided to them.

nslookup   A command-line tool that queries the DNS server, responding with the hosts and domains and their particular IPv4 and IPv6 addresses for a particular site.

O

Ohm's law   A basic law of electrical circuits that states V = IR (Volts = Current × Resistance).

OneDrive   See *Microsoft OneDrive*.

online search engine   Search engines such as Google, Yahoo, and Bing that compile an index of multiple websites online. When queried, the index will return relevant results so the user can find information quickly and easily.

on-premises   Hardware and software resources that are hosted and managed within an organization's own physical data center, rather than through cloud services.

on-screen keyboard   A visual on-screen keyboard with all the standard keyboard keys, allowing you to use a mouse or pointing device to type. It also allows for a single key or group of keys to scroll through the keyboard to select the desired input. It can be used in place of or in addition to a traditional keyboard.

Open Systems Interconnect (OSI) model   The basic conceptual framework that divides network communications into seven layers in order to simplify the operation and explanation. Each of the seven layers operates independently to allow networks to communicate.

operating system   System software that manages all of the resources and application programs in a computer.

P

P.A.S.S.   An acronym to help remember how to use a fire extinguisher: Pull, Aim, Squeeze, Sweep.

password   A secret word or phrase that must be used to gain admission to something, such as a computer system.

password policy   An organization's policy that details expected employee password complexity and rotation schedules.

password spraying   Using lists of leaked usernames and passwords with an automated program to try and crack or gain unauthorized access into a system.

patent   A type of intellectual property protecting an inventor to exclude others from making, using, offering for sale, or selling the invention for a limited time.

PCIe   Peripheral Component Interconnect Express. A faster, higher bandwidth port that replaces the older PCI/AGP expansion ports for internal peripheral devices.

peripheral   External peripheral devices such as a mouse or monitor connect to a computer; internal peripheral devices such as graphic cards or wireless cards connect directly to the motherboard. *Peripheral* means *additional*, so it is an additional device connected to a computer.

personally identifiable information (PII)   Any representation of information that permits the identity of an individual to whom the information applies to be reasonably inferred by either direct or indirect means.

PGA   Pin Grid Array. A CPU socket type where the pins are on the CPU.

phishing attack   A type of attack in which a threat actor poses as a legitimate company or entity to try and gain sensitive information or access.

physical security keys   Physical devices used for multifactor authentication. Hardware devices that rely on a computer or laptop to trigger them. See also *FIDO (Fast IDentity Online)*.

picture passwords   An authentication method that enables a user to unlock a device using gestures or patterns on an image.

PIN   Personal identification number. This number is allocated to an individual to help validate electronic transactions or login attempts.

ping/ping6   A network utility that tests the reachability of a host by sending an ICMP Echo Request. The destination host will reply with an ICMP Echo Reply.

pixel   A single dot of color on a computer screen.

Platform as a Service (PaaS)   A cloud computing model that provides a platform allowing developers to build, run, and manage applications without needing to manage the underlying infrastructure.

port   A physical or virtual connection to the computer.

power scheme   A collection of settings that controls the power usage of your computer. It can configure power consumption of individual devices, and can be used to support hibernation, idle time, and sleep states. Generally, it is created within the Power Options application in the Control Panel.

predictive AI   A type of artificial intelligence that uses machine learning algorithms to identify patterns in past events and make predictions about future events. Because it relies on a huge data set, it often can see patterns that humans cannot see.

principle of least privilege   A security concept which maintains that users or entities should have access only to what they need for their specific task, nothing more.

private cloud   A cloud computing environment that is exclusively used by a single organization, providing greater control and security compared to public cloud options.

private IP address   A nonroutable address of a device, assigned either by a DHCP server, APIPA, or some other process. Private IP addresses cannot be routed onto the public Internet; if devices wish to communicate on the public Internet, the packets must go through Network Address Translation (NAT).

private IPv4 address   A nonroutable IPv4 address following RFC 1918 guidelines. These are available to any network administrator to use in their private networks. Note that they are not routable on the public Internet so will require a Network Address Translation (NAT) router before devices will be able to access the Internet. Used due to IPv4 address depletion and security needs.

problem-solving process   A structured approach used by IT support technicians to diagnose and resolve issues, often involving multiple steps such as identifying the problem, analyzing potential solutions, and implementing fixes. By following these steps, IT support technicians can solve the user's problem quickly and without wasting time and resources.

processor   Also called the CPU; the brain of the computer that processes instructions from programs.

productivity applications   Software that allows a user to produce information. Examples include office applications, database management systems, and graphics software.

professionalism   A set of standards by which one conducts oneself with responsibility, integrity, accountability, and excellence. When an IT support technician is working with customers and clients in person, on the phone, or via email, it is critical to exhibit the highest standards of professionalism.

proprietary   In regard to hardware/software, specific and belonging exclusively to one company/product; opposite of universal/open source.

proprietary data   Information for which rights of ownership are restricted and distribution is limited. It can be protected by copyright, patent, licensing, court order, contract, or NDA, for example. Focus on the business need before disclosing any proprietary data.

proxy firewall   A security device that isolates a network by acting as an intermediary, caching each packet before it reaches the network and ensuring that all traffic inbound or outbound passes through the firewall. It is sometimes called a proxy server.

PSU   Power supply unit. A unit that converts AC electricity to DC electricity for computer components.

public cloud   A cloud service offered by third-party providers over the Internet to multiple customers, offering scalable and cost-effective resources but with less control over security.

Q

queue management   The organization and handling of incoming requests in a help desk environment to ensure efficient resolution of issues, often through the use of specialized software.

R

RAM   Random-access memory. Short-term, volatile memory for a computer.

ransomware   A program that encrypts all the files on an end-user computer or server; the program demands money, often cryptocurrency, to be sent to recover the files; many large organizations and government sectors are targeted with this very serious malware.

Recovery mode   A macOS system utility that allows the end user to boot into for repairing internal storage, reinstalling the OS, restoring files, resetting passwords, and more.

remote management   Type of software that allows an IT support technician to remotely monitor, control, and maintain systems and networks from any location.

RJ-45   A connector used for Ethernet cables.

rootkit   A type of malware that is installed in the boot loader or in the early boot process of an operating system; this makes it load and do the damage often before the antimalware program has even loaded. Often it runs as administrator, or root, and does the damage or modifies system settings at boot and then exits.

router advertisement (RA)   A packet that is multicast periodically by each IPv6 router advertising its availability and information about its interfaces. The router also sends this packet when it receives an RS message.

router solicitation (RS)   IPv6 multicast packet where a host sends a request to the network for all routers to respond with router availability and configuration information.

RSI   Repetitive strain injury. An injury stemming from doing the same physical motion over and over; a common type in IT workers is carpal tunnel syndrome.

S

Safe Mode   A diagnostic mode of the Windows operating system. Upon boot in Safe Mode, the system loads just the minimal necessary drivers to operate. Safe Mode with Networking also loads network drivers. It is used to troubleshoot issues and help remove viruses and other malware.

screen magnifier   Software that interfaces with the computer's graphical interface to enlarge the screen content. By enlarging part or all of a screen, people with visual impairments can better see words and images.

screen reader   Software program that allows blind and visually impaired users to read text on-screen with a speech synthesizer. The software interfaces between the operating system, applications, and the user.

security group   An Active Directory group used to simplify user management. It can transfer permissions to groups of users, who then inherit the permissions of the groups.

serial port   An older standard for transferring data that is slow but reliable. Also called RS-232, it is still used in many industrial control systems and routers/switches; however, it has been mostly replaced by USB.

service-level agreements (SLAs)   Contracts between a service provider and customers that define the expected level of service, such as response times and resolution deadlines for help desk tickets.

service set identifier (SSID)   The name of a WLAN (Wi-Fi) network. It may have up to 32 characters.

Short Message Service (SMS) The text message service available from most cell phone providers. It is insecure and easily hacked but convenient and easy to use. SMS allows up to 160 characters.

SMB drive Server Message Block drive. This protocol allows devices to share folders and files. It can be used by Windows, Macs, and Linux devices.

SMTP Simple Mail Transfer Protocol. The standard for transmitting electronic mail over the network or Internet. For retrieving email, users would use POP or IMAP protocols; SMTP is for sending only, usually between servers.

social engineering Manipulating someone into compromising security. It is often the type of attack used in phishing emails. See also *phishing attack*.

Software as a Service (SaaS) A cloud computing service model where applications are delivered over the Internet on a subscription basis, removing the need for local installation or maintenance.

software-defined networking (SDN) A network management approach that allows administrators to programmatically control network behavior through software, making it easier to manage and optimize network resources.

spam Unsolicited email advertisements.

spear phishing A more targeted phishing attack in which the threat actor has more personalized information to get target to "bite." See also *phishing attack*.

special identity group Like an Active Directory security group but automatically managed. If a user needs a resource, that resource is made available to them. When they are done, the resource is removed from them. If the user never accesses the resource, they never know about the resource at all.

spoofing attack A type of attack in which a legitimate website or email address is mimicked to get an end user to believe it is the real one.

spyware A type of malicious software that tracks user interaction without consent or knowledge and sends that information to a threat actor; this can be keystrokes typed, webcam feed, microphone, and more.

ss Socket statistics. Tool similar to **netstat** but for Linux machines. Part of the **iproute2** collection of utilities.

SSD Solid-state drive; a nonmechanical, nonmagnetic storage device that is nonvolatile and meant for long-term storage.

stateful inspection firewall Technology that controls the packets passing through the firewall by ensuring they have an established session (a state). If a connection does not have an established connection, incoming connections will not be permitted.

Stateless Address Autoconfiguration (SLAAC) A mechanism that an IPv6 device uses to automatically configure a unique IPv6 address without any other device (such as a DHCPv6 server) keeping track of or issuing an IPv6 address to it. The device will get the network prefix from the network and then generate the rest of the IPv6 address itself, using a process of conflict resolution to ensure no overlap between IPv6 addresses across the network. These are generally refreshed weekly to ensure privacy.

STP   Shielded-twisted pair. Ethernet cabling that does have shielding from electromagnetic interference.

subnet mask   In IPv4, a 32-bit address that separates an IP address into network bits and host bits to determine which network a particular host is a member of.

support tier   A hierarchical structure in help desk operations, with different levels (tiers) of support providing increasingly specialized expertise to handle more complex issues.

Symantec's PC Anywhere   A suite of programs that allowed for simple access and management of Windows, Linux, MacOS, and PocketPC devices. It was discontinued in May 2014.

sync   To synchronize between multiple devices. In computing, this term is often used to refer to synchronizing multiple files across systems. When you synchronize files, they will update across all devices where they are stored. No more leaving a flash drive around; synced files are the same and available in every device, any time.

T

Task Manager   Windows utility that allows a user to view the performance of the system. You can look at overall performance, performance per package or per process, and users currently logged in.

TeamViewer   Dedicated help desk software that allows remote monitoring and support. Software patches can be sent remotely, allowing for proactive management of devices. It allows for Windows, Mac, Linux, iOS, and Android support. It also includes asset management.

technical forum   Also called a tech support forum or technical discussion forum; an online discussion website where users can discuss technical topics in the form of a post and messages; the post poses the questions and the messages form the proposed answers. Similar to a company knowledge base, but open to the public.

Threat actor   An individual or group with malicious intent to disrupt a computing environment.

threat-focused NGFW   Like traditional NGFW but with more advanced threat detection. These firewalls can quickly react to attacks, detect evasive or suspicious activity with network and endpoint event correlation, decrease time from detection to cleanup, and ease administration with unified policies.

Thunderbolt   A proprietary implementation of USB C capable of bandwidth exceeding 20 Gbps.

Time Machine   A macOS system utility to create backups of files and apps; it includes support for versioning/snapshots.

time management   The ability to efficiently allocate time and prioritize tasks, ensuring that IT support technicians meet deadlines and handle multiple requests effectively.

traceroute/tracert A command-line tool that provides a map of how data on the network travels from the source to the destination. It does this by sending ICMP echo requests with various time-to-live values; the responding host will reply when a packet reaches its end-of-life.

Transmission Control Protocol/Internet Protocol (TCP/IP) model A basic conceptual framework dividing network communication into four layers in order to simplify the operation and explanation. Each of the four layers operates independently to allow networks to communicate.

triaging The process of determining the priority of incoming help desk requests based on the urgency and impact of the issue, ensuring that the most critical problems are addressed first.

Trojan horse A malicious program that disguises itself as a legitimate program.

trouble ticket A record used by IT support teams to track and manage the resolution of a technical issue reported by a user, detailing the problem, status, and steps taken.

U

UEFI Unified Extensible Firmware Interface; defines the architecture of the firmware used to boot the hardware and interface for interaction with the operating system. It replaces BIOS; many users still incorrectly refer to *UEFI* as *BIOS*. It is highly extensible, with security baked right in, and it can automatically detect boot loaders. It has the capability to invoke Secure Boot, which restricts boot loaders not digitally signed. It also can communicate directly with a UEFI-aware operating system to pass parameters such as boot devices.

unauthorized access attempt A type of attack that occurs when a threat actor tries to gain access to a system through social engineering, password spraying, or brute-force attacks.

Unified Threat Management (UTM) firewall A single device that provides multiple security functions. In the case of UTM appliances, the device may also administer other security tools at the same time.

universal group In Active Directory (AD), a type of group that enables both users and other groups from different domains within the same AD forest to access resources across the forest, regardless of the domain hierarchy. Universal groups are typically used when there is a need for seamless access to resources across multiple domains, such as when users frequently collaborate across regions or travel between different locations.

USB Universal Serial Bus; a common port for transferring data and power.

USB form factors The various forms USB ports have; the most common are Type A, B, Micro, and USB-C.

USB-C A 24-pin port capable of power, data, video, and audio; various technologies utilize this form factor.

UTP Unshielded-twisted pair. Ethernet cabling that does not have shielding from electromagnetic interference.

V

VGA A 15-pin analog video port.

virtual firewall A virtual appliance in the cloud. These firewalls protect cloud environments and virtualized infrastructure. They can adapt quickly to the changing network environment and help your cloud-based virtual servers and software-defined networking (SDN) be more efficient and effective.

virtual machine (VM) A software emulation of a physical computer that runs an operating system and applications, allowing multiple VMs to run on a single piece of hardware.

Virtual Network Computing (VNC) GUI and CLI tools that allow for management of headless servers across the network. While not designed for end-user support, VNC can be used for that if needed.

virtualization The process of creating a virtual version of a physical computing resource, such as a server or network, allowing for more efficient utilization of hardware.

virus An executable program that must be triggered/installed by the end user that damages the host computer.

volts The electrical unit of measurement for voltage; volts indicate the speed or pressure of electricity that flows through a circuit.

W

Windows Recovery Environment (WinRE) A recovery environment that can repair common causes of unbootable operating systems. Based on the Windows Preinstallation Environment (Windows PE), it can have drivers and other troubleshooting tools preinstalled. It is available and preinstalled with Windows 10 and 11 systems along with some other Windows distributions.

Windows Remote Assistance/Quick Assist An application for Windows 11 and later systems that allows an IT support technician or other remote user to connect remotely and access anywhere, anytime to manage the device. Remote Assistance is installed by default, but Quick Assist must be downloaded before a user can seek support for their issues.

Windows Remote Desktop Software tool for Windows 10 systems that allows an IT support technician or other remote user to connect remotely and access anywhere, anytime to manage the device.

Windows Server Update Services (WSUS) A service that enables IT administrators to control and deploy the latest product updates, especially from Microsoft. It can be used to control which and to which users/devices the updates are sent.

Windows Update/Microsoft Update Microsoft service that is used to provide updates to Windows systems; it was called Microsoft Update in some earlier versions of Windows. Most of these updates are for Windows itself, but others are for other Microsoft software and services; yet others are for third parties who contract with Microsoft to send updates such as driver and BIOS updates to machines.

wireless display   An external monitor that connects without wires. It can be used to mirror the screen of another PC or to a large screen for presentations.

wireless local area network (WLAN)   A LAN connected via wireless connections rather than wired connections. If you are using Wi-Fi to connect, you are connected via a WLAN.

worm   A program that self-replicates and can spread itself over flash drives and networks.

X

x86/x64   CISC processor architectures mainly found in desktop/laptops.

Index

J-K

Register your product at **ciscopress.com/register**
to unlock additional benefits:

- Save 35%* on your next purchase with an exclusive discount code

- Find companion files, errata, and product updates if available

- Sign up to receive special offers on new editions and related titles

Get more when you shop at **ciscopress.com**:

- Everyday discounts on books, eBooks, video courses, and more

- Free U.S. shipping on all orders

- Multi-format eBooks to read on your preferred device

- Print and eBook Best Value Packs

Cisco Press